Faulkner: Myth and Motion

Faulkner: Myth and Motion

RICHARD P. ADAMS

Princeton, New Jersey
Princeton University Press
1968

FOR JEAN

Preface

This is a critical study of William Faulkner's fiction, in which I try to develop a general theory to explain what Faulkner intended to do, how he went about doing it, and how well he succeeded. My focus is mainly on his better novels, but I give considerable space to a discussion of the poetry and prose written before 1925, because it seems to me that this apprentice work shows more clearly what Faulkner wanted to do, and how he learned to do it, than the more finished and therefore less transparent works of his later years. I do not say very much about the later short stories, not because they are inferior, but because I believe that Faulkner's purpose, method, and achievement can be sufficiently seen in the early work and the novels; and I want to avoid redundancy.

My discussion is limited to materials which have been printed, the reasoning being that the word "Faulkner" means, at any given moment, that body of Faulkner's work, and the commentary thereon, which is more or less freely available, in some form, to the public. I have dealt, therefore, with *Sartoris*, and not with *Flags in the Dust*, which, although it is presumably closer to what Faulkner intended, was not in print when I was writing. Similarly, I would like very much to know more than I do about Faulkner's life; but I am not a biographer, so I glean what I can from the admittedly inadequate accounts that have thus far been published. Any conscientious critic must be tempted to wait until all the returns are in—and then he must put the temptation firmly aside and say what he has to say. The returns are never all in.

My arrangement of materials may be somewhat overingenious; I try to proceed both chronologically and thematically. The first chapter, "Apprenticeship," is about Faulkner's literary intentions and his beginning experiments. Here I discuss his early works, up through his third published novel, *Sartoris*. In the second chapter, "Tools: Structure," I analyze his use of the "mythical method" as defined by T.S. Eliot, and I try to identify some of the myths that serve as externally provided structural devices in *Sanctuary*, *As I Lay Dying*, *Light in August*, and *Pylon*. Chapter 3, "Tools: Texture," is devoted to such matters as style, rhetoric, and imagery in relation to Faulkner's intentions and structural techniques, chiefly in *The Wild Palms* and *The Hamlet*. The fourth chapter, "Moral," includes a fairly long discussion of *Go Down, Moses* and shorter treatments of *Intruder in the Dust*, *Requiem for a Nun*, *The Town*, *The Mansion*, *A Fable*, and *The Reivers*, in the course of which I explore the moral themes and meanings of Faulkner's fiction. In my last two chapters, "Work: *Absalom, Absalom!*" and "Work: *The Sound and the Fury*," I apply what has been developed in the preceding discussions to a full-dress analysis of two of Faulkner's novels in their quality as individual works of art. The six chapters are not watertight; I try to relate the various works and the various topics as I go along, so that in my final paragraph I can say everything about all the works at once. That last paragraph has not done all that I hoped it would, but the labor of getting there has been its own reward.

I am greatly indebted to the host of critics who have preceded me into the jungles of Faulkner's works, and I have tried, with fair success, to read everything they report. I am grateful to all of them, especially Carvel Collins, Olga W. Vickery, Hyatt H. Waggoner, Michael Millgate, and R.W.B. Lewis. My study has also benefited from the biographical researches of Joseph L. Blotner, from the bibliographical pioneering of James B. Meriwether, and from occasional conversations over a period of some years with Phil Stone. James W. Webb, head of the English department, and Dorothy Oldham, curator of the Mississippi Room and the Faulkner house at the University of Mississippi, have been unfailingly kind and helpful during my visits to Oxford. The Tulane University Council on Research has given me a year's leave of absence and several summer grants, and the Tulane English department secretaries, Sarah Kost and Maybelle M. Hyde, have typed a good many more pages of manuscript than have found their way into the final draft. My colleagues John D. Husband and Joseph P. Roppolo have read the text and made helpful suggestions—one of which prompted me to rewrite a chapter that I had hoped, after a couple of previous rewritings, was substantially in final form. Students in my classes and seminars, and those who have written theses and dissertations under my direction, have contributed far more to my thinking than I can specifically acknowledge.

Although it seems not to be customary in prefaces, I would like to mention a few debts of a more general nature. First to my parents, who housed me with many books. Second, to Paul N. Landis, Professor of English at the University of Illinois, who put me through two years of tough undergraduate tutorial reading. Third, to Grant C. Knight and Francis Gallaway, Professors of English at the University of Kentucky, who inducted me into the systematic study of American and modern literature. Fourth, to Lionel Trilling and Mark Van Doren, who took turns directing my dissertation at Columbia University. Fifth, to Richard Fogle, whose critical style and intelligence have been an example to me for many years. Sixth, to Morse Peckham, who has been giving me pre- and post-doctoral tutelage since the fall of 1947, when we both became instructors at Rutgers University. I have disagreed with all of these people, and with many more to whom I am grateful for help along the way; they are not to blame for making me what I am; but they have made it possible for me to do what I am responsible for having done.

R.P.A.

Tulane University
August 1968

Contents

Faulkner works quoted in text:

Absalom, Absalom!, New York, Modern Library, 1951 (a photographic reproduction of the first edition, New York: Random House, 1936).

A Fable, New York: Random House, 1954.

As I Lay Dying, New York: Random House, 1964.   *AILD*

Go Down, Moses, New York: Random House, 1942.   *GDM*

The Hamlet, New York: Random House, 1940.   *Ham*

Intruder in the Dust, New York: Random House, 1948.

Light in August, New York: Harrison Smith and   *LIA*
Robert Haas, 1932.

The Mansion, New York: Random House, 1959.   *Man*

Mosquitoes, New York: Horace Liveright, 1927.   *Mos*

Pylon, New York: Harrison Smith and Robert Haas, 1935.

The Reivers, New York: Random House, 1962.

Requiem for a Nun, New York: Random House, 1951.

Sanctuary, New York: Random House [1962].

Sartoris, New York: Random House [1962] (a photographic reproduction of the first edition, New York: Harcourt, Brace, 1929).

The Sound and the Fury, New York: Random   *S&F*
House [1965] (a photographic reproduction of the first edition, New York: Jonathan Cape and Harrison Smith, 1929).

Soldiers' Pay, New York: Liveright Publishing   *SP*
Corp., 1954 (a reprint of the first edition, New York: Boni & Liveright, 1926).

The Marble Faun and A Green Bough, New York: *TMF*
Random House [1967] (photographic reproductions of the first editions of *The Marble Faun*,

Boston: Four Seas, 1924, and *A Green Bough*, New York: Harrison Smith and Robert Haas, 1933).

The Town, New York: Random House, 1957.   *Town*

The Unvanquished, New York: Random House, 1938.

The Wild Palms, New York: Random House, 1939.

William Faulkner: Early Prose and Poetry, Boston: *EPP*
Little, Brown, 1962.

William Faulkner: New Orleans Sketches, New   *NOS*
Brunswick, N.J.: Rutgers University Press, 1958.

Faulkner: Myth and Motion

Introduction

William Faulkner had an exceedingly large and complex mind, and a creative genius that assimilated the most astonishing amount and variety of cultural materials into itself and the work it produced. In spite of the vigorous growth of Faulkner scholarship and criticism in recent years, we have not come to any firm conclusions about his work, except perhaps to agree that it is intensely interesting. There seems good reason to hope that we will never fully explain it, and that its interest will never be exhausted by our efforts to understand it.

My purpose here is to offer a new synthesis, which I hope will go a step beyond those now in print, and perhaps, with luck, point toward other steps to be taken as our understanding and appreciation of Faulkner continue to develop. This study does not pretend to explain all aspects of Faulkner's writing. Its focus is narrow and its approach is only one of many that may be profitable. But I believe that it strikes somewhere near the center of what Faulkner tried to do and did do.

The basic hypothesis of my investigation is expressed in two statements made by Faulkner in 1954, in an interview with Jean Stein for the *Paris Review*. He said that "Life is motion" and that "The aim of every artist is to arrest motion, which is life, by artificial means and hold it fixed so that a hundred years later, when a stranger looks at it, it moves again since it is life."[1] These two apparently simple remarks imply a profound and complex attitude toward the world and man's destiny, which requires for its expression a difficult esthetic doctrine and an elaborate exercise of artistic and technical discipline.

My belief is—and my hypothesis therefore holds—that Faulkner had this attitude from the beginning of his career, that he learned what it meant and what it demanded esthetically, and that in time he developed adequate strategies and techniques to embody it in his fiction. During his early period, before *The Sound and the Fury*, he was probably not as clear about it as he was in 1954. In his later period, after *Go Down, Moses*, he was less successful in practice than he had been from 1929 to 1942. But I think his intention was always pretty much the same. During the thirteen years when his powers matched his purposes, although he sometimes failed to bring off the effects he must have aimed at—for example, in *Pylon* or *The Wild Palms*—he wrote seven novels which I believe will stand with the best that has been thought and said: *The Sound and the Fury, Sanctuary, As I Lay Dying, Light in August, Absalom, Absalom!, The Hamlet*, and *Go Down, Moses*.

The proposition that "Life is motion" committed Faulkner to the imagination of a world in which the concrete experience of humanity is continual change. Such a world is extremely hard to conceive, and quite impossible to formulate, because all formulas are static. If life is motion, always changing, never the same in any two views or moments, it cannot be directly represented in a work of art or logically explained in a philosophical or critical essay. Every statement about its concrete manifestations is false because, by the time the statement has been made and heard, the object has become something else,

[1] *Writers at Work*, ed. Malcolm Cowley (New York: Viking Press, 1959), pp. 138, 139.

the relationships between the object and the observers have shifted, and the maker and the hearer of the statement have themselves whirled onward, not to return.

Faulkner therefore is not trying to formulate experience in any direct or logical way. He is trying to organize impressions of speed and energy in order to build the most intense possible concentrations of force, and then to confine them in the most tightly blocked possible situations. The phrase "to arrest motion" is a rather tricky paradox, if motion is what is to be represented; but it is a paradox imposed by the nature of the problem. Because motion cannot be directly described, it must be demonstrated indirectly by the static "artificial means" the artist has to work with. If we conceive of motion as a stream (an image often used by Faulkner) we find that its power cannot be felt by someone moving with it, or in it, as living people normally do. If, however, some object, or better if some person, can be made to stand still against its flow, the result will be a dramatic and possibly disastrous manifestation of its energy.

Faulkner commands a wide variety of techniques, and some of them are more positively dynamic than his statement of the artist's aim would strictly seem to allow. His use of violence, for example, involves both a negative and a positive aspect. Its purpose is not merely to shock the reader, much less to cater to a sadistic fascination with the horrible for its own sake, as some early detractors assumed, but rather to dramatize the unquenchable vigor of life by showing it in the act of overwhelming and crushing static obstacles in its path. The accompanying imagery generally tends in one way or another, or in several ways at once, to build up a feeling of tremendous force and speed. Flood, fire, wind, stampeding animals, moving crowds of people, burgeoning vegetation, hot sunshine, odors of growth and decay, flocks of birds, and swarms of buzzing insects carry the sense of universal motion in hundreds of scenes where potential or actual violence is, as Faulkner once remarked, "the by-product of the speed and the motion . . . ."[2] The violence is inevitable and necessary, as the obstacles are, to show the power in concerted action. The strategy is especially successful when it involves great suffering on the part of a character who has the reader's sympathy.

It is in aid of this strategy that some of Faulkner's most static and intrinsically least attractive characters, such as Popeye in *Sanctuary*, Joe Christmas in *Light in August*, and Jason Compson in *The Sound and the Fury*, are given attributes which make them parallel to Christ. Conversely, some of the most attractive characters, many of whom are also Christlike, such as Ike McCaslin in *Go Down, Moses*, Horace Benbow in *Sanctuary*, and Jason's brother Quentin in *The Sound and the Fury*, are also among the most static; they are more effective as instruments of Faulkner's purpose only because we care more what happens to them. Quentin is the most effective of all, for most readers, because he is so sensitive, so naïvely innocent, so intelligent, and so completely and inevitably doomed. He is driven to suicide by his inability to accept the illegitimate pregnancy of his sister Caddy, and more generally by his revulsion from any kind of mature sexual activity. Mr. Compson, his father, points out that pregnancy is a particularly vital manifestation of the motion of life through time, remarking quite rightly that "It's nature is hurting you not Caddy" (p. 143);[3] and Quentin is driven all the harder toward his death by his realization of this truth. Time, as Mr. Compson also remarks, is Quentin's "misfortune" (p. 129) because he is hysterically determined not to accept the complications of mature behavior. The only way he can preserve his youth-

---

[2] *Essays Speeches & Public Letters by William Faulkner*, ed. James B. Meriwether (New York: Random House, 1965), p. 49.

[3] A list of Faulkner editions quoted herein is given above on pp. xiii-xiv. Where the text names the work, the citation will be parenthetically by page number only. Where the work is not clearly identified, an abbreviated title will be included in the parentheses. Abbreviations are also given on pp. xiii-xiv.

ful innocence is to die. Horace Benbow, Joe Christmas, and
Ike McCaslin are faced with similar dilemmas, but their fate is
less clear and somewhat less deeply moving because they compromise. They accept maturity and then find that they cannot cope with the problems and responsibilities that it brings.

Another technique that Faulkner uses to concentrate the
motion of life is his management of time. Conventionally, we
think of narrative as being more or less chronological, and in
the actual world we think of motion as taking place in four
dimensions, of which the dimension of time is perhaps the
most important, as well as the most difficult to get hold of in
terms of either concrete sensual impressions or abstract logical
thinking. Intuitively, we are aware of time going on, and of
temporal relations among events as they happen. But Faulkner
often departs from a straight chronological presentation in his
fiction, and, by a calculated scrambling of the time dimension,
short-circuits our intuition so as to concentrate the energy of a
large amount of motion on a single, artificially fixed and
isolated moment. When it succeeds, this technique may have
the effect of compressing a lifetime into a single event. The
scrambling prevents our feeling time as a thin, straight string
with events marked off at measured intervals; instead, we feel
it as a heavy cluster, knot, or tangle, with all the ends lost in
the middle. Motion is lost, or stopped, and time is held still
for esthetic contemplation.

A closely related technique is Faulkner's use of "counterpoint," that is, the juxtaposition or alternation of superficially
unrelated matters in such a way that esthetic tensions build
up between or among them. When Faulkner defined the term
most clearly, he was talking about *The Wild Palms*, in which
two completely separate series of events take place, in alter-
nate chapters, throughout the novel, which he nevertheless insisted was "one story—the story of Charlotte Rittenmeyer and
Harry Wilbourne, who sacrificed everything for love, and
then lost that." But this story had a fatal tendency to run

down, and whenever it did, Faulkner said, "I wrote on the 'Old Man' story until 'The Wild Palms' story rose back to pitch."[4] The two stories are completely separated in time and space, they have no characters in common, and their thematic relations are not obvious. However, after much discussion and argument, most critics now seem to feel that the book as Faulkner published it, and claimed he composed it, is better than either of its parts alone, although it is still not regarded as one of Faulkner's best.

Counterpoint works in more complex ways toward more impressive results in some of Faulkner's other novels. The three main stories that make up *Light in August* are hardly more closely tied than the two in *The Wild Palms*; and the four narrators of *The Sound and the Fury* are so different in attitude, temperament, and point of view that they give quite different accounts of the situation. Similar effects are achieved by the several narrators of *As I Lay Dying* and *Absalom, Absalom!*, by the various points of view in *The Hamlet*, and by the assembly of loosely related stories in *Go Down, Moses*. All these devices serve the same purpose. Their presentation of sharply separate views, which become simultaneous in the reader's mind, makes it possible for Faulkner to arrange his static impressions of moving life in clusters and patterns that heighten both the motion and the stasis, an effect that would be spoiled if the parts were more smoothly articulated.

Another effect that Faulkner often gets from the contrapuntal juxtaposition of incongruous materials is a lusty, wild, and frequently violent humor, very like that of the South-western yarnspinners popular before and after the Civil War, two of whom, Mark Twain and George Washington Harris, writer of the Sut Lovingood stories, were among his favorite authors. Daniel Hoffman has suggested that the better works in this vein describe "a cultural tug-of-war" between American

[4] *Writers at Work*, p. 133.

folk-heroes and those of the older European tradition.[5] This tension is continually present in Faulkner's work, but seldom in a simple form or for its own sake alone. It operates most effectively in stories such as *Sanctuary* and *As I Lay Dying*, where the "European" tradition thins out to a brittle rustic or small-town conventionalism, scandalized and outraged by the bizarre and sometimes horrible things that living people do in a world of motion. The result is not tragedy, or even merely pathos, but, as Hoffman also remarks, "a uniquely comic view of life and an optimistic conviction of human destiny."[6] The frequent savagery of Faulkner's humor, instead of preventing, actually enhances the optimistic outcome. The appalling hardships which are overcome by his comic heroes, such as the Bundrens (except Darl), the tall convict in *The Wild Palms*, and Mink Snopes, together with the inordinate amounts of energy they spend against the obstacles in their way are proof, in the end, that man will prevail in spite of everything. The more pathetic and absurd their predicaments become, the more triumphantly the power of life asserts itself in their survivals and their often ridiculous victories.

Much of the material that Faulkner used to construct his works was borrowed or, as he preferred to say, stolen from other authors, whose monuments he looted as ruthlessly as the popes did those of ancient Rome, and for purposes as foreign to their original intent. From his richest mine, the King James Bible, his favorite story was that of Christ's Passion; but he also referred often to the story of Eden, and occasionally to those of Abraham and Isaac, David and Absalom, Joseph and his brothers, and many more. Another great store was classical mythology, which Faulkner found not only in Homer, the Greek playwrights, and the Latin poets, but also in the works of classical anthropologists such as Sir James Frazer, Jane Harrison, and Gilbert Murray. He often used the Persephone

[5] Daniel Hoffman, *Form and Fable in American Fiction* (New York: Oxford University Press, 1965), p. 9.
[6] *Ibid.*, p. 8.

myth, and his fiction is permeated with imagery drawn from fertility legend and ritual. He used medieval lore and literature in much the same way, especially the legend of the Holy Grail, which he got from a number of sources, including T.S. Eliot's *The Waste Land* and probably Jessie L. Weston's *From Ritual to Romance*. He was well read in Shakespeare and English poetry, notably Keats, Swinburne, and Housman. He knew a good deal of French poetry, especially of the Symbolists, and he was able to read it in French. He had a wide knowledge of fiction, and a particular interest in Balzac, Flaubert, Dickens, Mark Twain, Conrad, and Joyce (although he repelled suggestions of an influence by Joyce on his work). His interest in American literature may have developed more slowly, but by the 1930s he evidently knew Cooper, Poe, Hawthorne, and Melville, and had read some Emerson, Thoreau, Whitman, and James. He absorbed vast quantities of contemporary writing—so much that it is fairly safe to assume some knowledge on his part of just about anything that was current in 1910 to 1930, including popular works of science, philosophy, and history.[7] In addition, he was saturated with talk, which is still an artistic medium in north Mississippi, and from which, as he said in an interview or two, he got much of his awareness of the traditions, legends, and what we may call the mythology of the South. He used this material in the same way as he used the Bible and the classical mythology, as a thief by sovereign right, and often with scant respect for the pieties in which it might be invested by conventional people.

The contrapuntal method works in a somewhat special way, in Faulkner's fiction as in that of Joyce and in the poetry of Eliot, when it is used on materials taken from traditional, legendary, mythological, and literary sources. These materials bring some of their own connotations with them, and repre-

---

[7] For more detailed discussion, see my "Apprenticeship of William Faulkner," *Tulane Studies in English*, XII (1962), 113-56, and Michael Millgate's more authoritative treatment in *The Achievement of William Faulkner* (London: Constable, 1966), *passim*.

sent their own times. When we find them in a modern work, and especially when several of them appear side by side, a startling sense of temporal dislocation may arise. When a character is made to look like Christ, or when, in *The Hamlet*, Eula Varner is characterized as the Helen of Frenchman's Bend and the idiot Ike Snopes falls gallantly in love with Houston's cow, Houston himself being something of a cross between a knight and a centaur, or when Quentin Compson in *Absalom, Absalom!* is haunted to the point of being possessed by the aristocratic ghosts of Civil War soldiers, the resulting intrusion of the Biblical, the classical, the feudal, or the American legendary past into the modern situation contradicts the flow of time and provides an artificially static moment into which Faulkner can compress great quantities of life.

His more specifically literary allusions have the same effect, particularly when they point to more than one source at a time. A complex example is the phrase "in another country," which is used in *A Fable* and paraphrased in *Light in August*. The chances are that Faulkner had seen the phrase and various paraphrases of it in several places besides its original source in Marlowe's *The Jew of Malta*, the most likely being Hemingway's short story "In Another Country" and his novel *The Sun Also Rises*, and T.S. Eliot's epigraph to "Portrait of a Lady."[8] The phrase may have had a special appeal for its borrowers because it suggested the technique they were using: the more or less criminal appropriation of material from works written, very often, in other countries by authors a long time dead. It is an effective device for producing the kind of temporal dislocation, arrest, and compression that Faulkner wanted.

The arrest of motion is accomplished most often and most

[8] See Phyllis Bartlett, "Other Countries, Other Wenches," *Modern Fiction Studies*, III (Winter 1957-58), 345-49, for uses of the quotation by Eliot, Hemingway, Faulkner, John Bayley, and Frederic Brown.

directly in Faulkner's work by imagery in which the dynamic quality of life is immediately and sharply opposed to artificial stasis. This device creates the "frozen moment" that has been defined and studied by several critics.[9] Examples are far too numerous to list, but we may note a few, by way of random illustration. They occur in Faulkner's early work in such images as that of the statue in the garden in *The Marble Faun*, and in the description of an equestrian statue of Andrew Jackson in "Out of Nazareth," one of the sketches written in New Orleans in 1925, where horse and rider are seen "in terrific arrested motion" (*NOS* 101). In *As I Lay Dying* the same effect is achieved more vividly by a description of living figures when Jewel Bundren catches his horse and holds it "rigid, motionless, terrific" (p. 12) before mounting to ride. The same kind of imagery occurs in connection with the death of Joe Christmas in *Light in August*. It is used in the passingly noticed vision of a man, a mule, and a plow in *Intruder in the Dust*, and in the account of Boon Hogganbeck's tremendous efforts to get an automobile out of a mudhole in *The Reivers*. The point in each of these passages, and in many others where such imagery occurs, is the contrast it contains between an aspect of speed or intense effort, representing motion, and an opposing aspect of impediment or countering force that stops the motion or slows it so much that it seems to stop. The same contrast was doubtless what attracted Faulkner to Keats's "Ode on a Grecian Urn," which he quotes in *Sartoris* and *Go Down, Moses* and to which he refers, directly or indirectly, in a number of other places where he mentions urns, vases, statues, or sculptured friezes to suggest the impression of stopped motion.

The moral implications of Faulkner's world of motion have not been well understood by most critics. Many have assumed

[9] Notably Karl E. Zink in "Flux and the Frozen Moment: The Imagery of Stasis in Faulkner's Prose," *PMLA*, LXXI (June 1956), 285-301; and Walter J. Slatoff in *Quest for Failure: A Study of William Faulkner* (Ithaca, N.Y.: Cornell University Press), 1960.

that he is describing a static world, in which life would be impossible, and these have logically concluded that the only moral outcome is despair. Even after the Nobel Prize speech, many have been content to adopt the term "endure" as the key to Faulkner's meaning. But in the speech, in many interviews, and in all his artistic works, if we read them rightly, Faulkner has said that "man will not merely endure: he will prevail." What Faulkner liked to call not virtues but "verities . . . of the heart" were such as "love and honor and pity and pride and compassion and sacrifice,"[10] all of which he conceived in active terms. His most completely defeated characters, such as Quentin Compson, Horace Benbow, or Joe Christmas, go down because they are fundamentally opposed to life. They try to find something unchanging to stand on, motionless in the midst of change. But motion sweeps them on so relentlessly that their only escape is one or another kind of suicide. They are not vital spirits crushed by the inert weight of matter. On the contrary, they are desperate because a living world keeps forcing them into action in spite of their desire for security, peace, and stasis. They are crushed because they are trying not to move, and because, by Faulkner's logic, the only way to be motionless is to be dead.

They and others like them are Faulkner's most useful characters because they provide the most dramatic contrasts between the motion of life and the static obstacles that, by opposing, demonstrate its power. They serve their purpose best, as we have seen, when they most engage the reader's sympathy. But they are not morally admirable. On the other hand, characters such as Caddy Compson, Ruby Lamar, and especially Lena Grove are so much in harmony with the motion that they, by themselves, could hardly show it at all. Their moral and esthetic value can be dramatized only by contrast with static characters such as Quentin, Horace (or Popeye), and Christmas.

10 *Essays*, p. 120.

In an effort to represent morally admirable qualities of human nature more directly, Faulkner invented another kind of character, so conceived that he has to learn the value of life, more or less against his inclinations, and, by hard struggle, ally himself with it actively in the effort to overcome whatever obstacles may be. Byron Bunch in *Light in August*, Chick Mallison in *Intruder in the Dust*, the battalion Runner in *A Fable*, and Lucius Priest in *The Reivers* are perhaps the handiest examples, in that they most clearly represent the learning process, which is an excellent image of dynamic energy working against the drag of ignorance and sloth. V.K. Ratliff, the sewing machine agent, is morally active and admirable in *The Hamlet*, *The Town*, and *The Mansion*; but he is not as effective as the others in a dramatic way because he seems more fully armed from the start, and has less painful development to undergo. In general, the better Faulkner's characters are in their moral alliance with life or in their natural adjustment to its pace and rhythm, the less they are able to do for the esthetic success of his work. Those who serve him best are the discontented, the maladjusted, the desperate, and the morally bad.

Faulkner's greatness as the creator of a world and as the chronicler of its legendary history has tended, in the minds of some critics, to obscure his greatness as an artist, that is, primarily as a novelist. But Yoknapatawpha County would never have been more than potentially interesting or important if it had not been embodied in successful works of art. Its whole existence, now that Faulkner is dead, is in the works; and we may reasonably assume that it might never have existed except as a way to make them possible. It is not untrue to say, as Malcolm Cowley does in his introduction to *The Portable Faulkner*, that the works were carved out of an amazingly large and complete conception in Faulkner's mind, and that they are somewhat arbitrarily separated fragments of a whole that must have been greater than their sum. But I prefer to emphasize the opposing view, which Faulkner often suggested, that the world of Yoknapatawpha grew as the works were created, and because they were created. This view permits us to regard the individual novels as organically complete works of art in themselves, without denying that their ensemble is an even larger work, which in some ways may transcend them all.

However we choose to look at it, Faulkner's work is a magnificent achievement. In each of his better novels, in many short stories, and in the total body of his fiction, we receive a profound and comprehensive impression of life. The first characteristic that distinguishes this fiction from most other literature is that, in the whole and in the parts, down to the smallest details of matter and of method, it moves. The second is that the motion is rendered visible and artistically usable by a marvelous variety of technical devices that arrest it for esthetic and moral contemplation. It comes to us as highly compressed vital energy, which we can release, if we take it rightly, to make our own lives move more widely and deeply than they otherwise might. Faulkner's greatness is that he has added life to life and a world of richly imagined motion to the moving world in which we live.

One / Apprenticeship

Faulkner had ceased to be an apprentice by the time *The Sound and the Fury* was published, October 7, 1929. We do not know when he began. Much of what he wrote when young has been lost; much of what remains has not been published; and much research needs to be done on the dating of manuscripts before any firm biographical or critical conclusions can be drawn. But if, as I have suggested, Faulkner's career as a writer was founded on the artistic aim of stopping motion, he was headed the right way by the time he first broke into print.

The occasion was the appearance in the *New Republic* for August 6, 1919, of his poem called, after Mallarmé, "L'Apres-Midi d'un Faune." The speaker of the poem, presumably the faun of the title, pursues a girl or nymph, whom he associates with water, air, fire, and earth, with life in the form of insects and trees, and with the movement of time in the season and the day. Some kind of union between the speaker and all of these is coyly predicted when he says, "The dusk will take her by some stream / In silent meadows, dim and deep—" suggesting not merely a sexual consummation but a comprehensive joining of human love with all the natural powers.

In the second and final section of the poem, the faun expresses "a nameless wish to go" farther still, "To some far silent midnight noon" where "blond limbed dancers" under a "senile . . . moon" will seem like "petals drifting on the breeze," with an effect of fusing humanity and nature still more closely. But the temporal paradox hinted by "midnight noon" and by the juxtaposition of "dancers" with "senile . . . moon" turns in the last lines to contradict the wish:

> Then suddenly on all of these,
> A sound like some great deep bell stroke
> Falls, and they dance, unclad and cold—
> It was the earth's great heart that broke
> For springs before the world grew old.
>
> (*EPP* 39-40)

The implied deficiency is apparently not with "the earth's great heart" but with some human failure that prevents such harmony with nature as we like to suppose there may have been in the lost Arcadian past.

The whole poem is an effort to organize sound, imagery, and thematic suggestion so as to isolate and fix a timeless moment in which the union between man and nature will be vividly imagined by the love-inspired faun, and simultaneously denied by the impossibility of actual reconciliation between old age and youth, between time past and time now passing or about to pass. The structure, however, is neither clear enough nor strong enough to assimilate the imagery so as to produce a satisfactory effect. Instead of the intense straining and frustration of life that is apparently aimed at, we get a feeling that does not even succeed in being wearily sophisticated, but falls into sophomoric sentimentalism.

The Marble Faun, Faulkner's first published book, which appeared in 1924 but which was written, according to the dates printed at the end, in "April, May, June, 1919," is a more am-

bitious and somewhat more successful attempt. The speaker
this time is a different kind of faun, not a modern young man
cut off by time and culture from the classical harmony with
nature, but a marble statue endowed, as a literary device, with
consciousness but not with the power of motion. Standing in
the midst of a fertile garden, he is tantalizingly surrounded by
vegetable, animal, and human life into which he projects himself by using a vivid imagination but in which he cannot really
participate. "That quick green snake," he complains,

> Is free to come and go, while I
> Am prisoner to dream and sigh
> For things I know, yet cannot know,
> 'Twixt sky above and earth below. . . .
> The whole world breathes and calls to me
> Who marble-bound must ever be.
>
> (p. 12)

The imagery is like that of "L'Apres-Midi," except that there
is more of it. Again we have the four elements, and again, with
additions and somewhat more variety, dynamic aspects of life
are elaborated in the changing scene. Poplars "Like slender
girls," flowers "Like poised dancers," a fountain "Gracefully
slim as are the trees" (p. 11), showering its water down on the
"fair / Flecked face" (p. 12) of its pool—everything is permeated with moving beauty, and everything, even the marble
speaker, responds in some way to the musical call of Pan's
pipe: "Come, ye living, stir and wake!" (p. 14).

The body of the poem is given a potentially effective structure by a progressive description of the seasons—in the same
order as in Thoreau's *Walden*—spring, summer, autumn, winter, and spring again. The speaker follows their varying
courses, roused by the spring, permeated by summer's growth-
producing heat, lulled by the ripeness of autumn, and con-
soled by winter's frozen peace. As the sun warms him in the
second spring, he persuades himself that he is being released:

I leave my pedestal and flow
Quietly along each row,
Breathing in their fragrant breath
And that of the earth beneath.
Time may now unheeded pass:
I am the life that warms the grass—

Or does the earth warm me? I know
Not, nor do I care to know.
I am with the flowers one,
Now that is my bondage done;
And in the earth I shall sleep
To never wake, to never weep
For things I know, yet cannot know,
'Twixt sky above and earth below,
For Pan's understanding eyes
Quietly bless me from the skies,
Giving me, who knew his sorrow,
The gift of sleep to be my morrow.

(p. 49)

But the faun's dilemma is not so easily resolved. In the end he can neither escape from time nor dissolve himself into its flow. Again, as he wakes with the buzzing life of May, he cries his frustration:

Ah, how all this calls to me
Who marble-bound must ever be
While turn unchangingly the years.
My heart is full, yet sheds no tears
To cool my burning carven eyes
Bent to the unchanging skies:
I would be sad with changing year,
Instead, a sad, bound prisoner,
For though about me seasons go
My heart knows only winter snow.

(pp. 50-51)

What he really wants is not sleep but life, with its pains as well as its pleasures. The faun, the legendary wildwood creature, half man, half beast, pursuer of nymphs and follower of Pan, is fixed in the motionless marble, a thing of beauty, of immortality, and of despair.

The idea, as Keats proved, is good. The imagery is appropriate. The structure, as an abstract pattern, is sound. But the poem is not successful, and there are several good reasons for its failure. Most obvious, perhaps, is the pervasive and often disastrous awkwardness of style. "And in the earth I shall sleep" cannot possibly be read as an octosyllabic line. The contorted syntax of "I am with the flowers one, / Now that is my bondage done" sounds as if it had been insufficiently translated from Latin. "To never wake, to never weep" splits infinitives as if they were stove wood, and the phrase " 'Twixt sky" is not only obsolete but unpronounceable.

The imagery of the poem is so repetitious, and in such a flatly redundant way, that its effect is lost in monotony; and this flatness blurs what ought to have been a clear and firm differentiation of the seasons, without which even the friendliest reader can hardly keep track of them. To lose that track is to miss the only solid structure the poem has.

The pastoral mode is used with comparable lack of skill or grace, and with an adulterous mixture of Arcadian, English, and Mississippi scenery: nightingales and dogwood, sheep and mocking birds. Literary borrowings are undigested. Chekhov is allowed to obtrude in both "L'Apres-Midi" and *The Marble Faun*. The "great deep bell stroke" representing the breaking of earth's heart in the one is matched by the more casual and literal use of a "twanging . . . string" (*TMF* 14) in the other, where, farther on, to compound the crime, "Cherry orchards" transplanted from Russia are grafted with "wet black boughs" (p. 18) seen previously in the Metro by Ezra Pound.

The same or similar faults appear in Faulkner's other verse, which continued to be published for some years, sporadically, but which he apparently stopped writing after about 1926. The principal collection, *A Green Bough,* was published in 1933. Carvel Collins notes that this volume was "greatly revised from its original manuscript form" (*NOS,* Intro., p. 34), but the revision did not change its essential quality. Phil Stone was probably right when he remarked about Faulkner in 1931, "I doubt if it was his early ambition to be a poet as much as it was my ambition for him to be one";[1] and Faulkner described himself in later interviews as "a failed poet." He added, on one of these occasions, "Maybe every novelist wants to write poetry first, finds he can't, and then tries the short story, which is the most demanding form after poetry. And, failing at that, only then does he take up novel writing."[2]

A more accurate statement would be that Faulkner failed as a writer of verse, and continued to be a poet writing in prose, for the rhythms of which his ear was excellent. As his technical ability grew in the freer medium, he retained what he had learned, particularly in the way of imagery, and he vigorously continued experimenting with artificial ways of demonstrating motion by stopping it.

Some of this development was begun in early poems and extended into the fiction of later periods. For example, a frustrated speaker comparable to those of "L'Apres-Midi" and *The Marble Faun* is given more realistic and dramatic treatment in the poem "The Lilacs: to A......and H......, Royal Air Force: August 1925," which was used as the first poem in *A Green Bough* but which had been published in *The Double Dealer* for June 1925 and which Collins says was "written much earlier" (*NOS* 29; see also *EPP* 11). The anonymous speaker is sitting with two friends, among a larger company, drinking tea. His hostess, passing by, stops to ask if he wants anything, ignoring his two companions and saying, "You are a bit lonely,

---

[1] Letter from Phil Stone to Louis Cochran, Dec. 28, 1931, printed in James B. Meriwether, "Early Notices of Faulkner by Phil Stone and Louis Cochran," *Mississippi Quarterly,* XVII (Summer 1964), 139.

[2] *Writers at Work,* p. 123.

I fear." She and other women present seem like "figures on a masque" as we overhear snatches of their talk:

> ... Who? ... shot down
> Last spring... poor chap, his mind...
> The doctors say... hoping rest will bring....

In an interior monologue, the speaker tells how, at dawn on a May morning, he had been stalking "A white woman, a white wanton" at the edge of a cloud "In my little pointed-eared machine," and got "a bullet through my heart. . . ." He was sure of catching her, he says, "But now I wonder if I found her, after all." He remarks several times that "One should not die like this." Finally his two companions

> bend their heads toward me as one head.
> ...Old man... they say... How did you die?...
> I—I am not dead.
> I hear their voices as from a great distance... Not dead
> He's not dead, poor chap; he didn't die....[3]

Here we have the same theme of pursuit as in "L'Apres-Midi" (except that the faun image is shifted, whimsically, from the man to his airplane), and there is much of the same imagery of life in the earth and sky. This time the speaker's effort to unite with the world's life has failed because, unlike his two sympathetic friends, "he didn't die." Traumatized by his wound, he can neither participate as a living man in the human life around him nor, as a dead man, merge into the life of things which is apparently, though vaguely, represented by the "white woman" in the air. He is a forerunner of Donald Mahon in *Soldiers' Pay* and, less obviously, of Benjy Compson in *The Sound and the Fury* and Ike Snopes in *The Hamlet*. They all have faunlike qualities, but they are all immobilized by mindlessness.

A more complex foreshadowing, again involving the faun

---

[3] *Double Dealer*, VII (June 1925), 185-87.

image, can be seen in "Twilight," which was used as the tenth poem in *A Green Bough* but which was first published in *Contempo* for February 1, 1932, and which was probably written some years earlier. The poem describes a young man going home from a day's work, at sunset, momentarily relieved by physical weariness from some of the intensity of life: "The dream that hurt him, the blood that whipped him / Dustward, slowed and gave him ease." He experiences, in this interval between days, a static moment into which Faulkner tries to compress as much time, and as much mythical and literary allusion, as possible:

> Nymph and faun in this dusk might riot
> Beyond Time's cold greenish bar
> To shrilling pipes, to cymbals' hissing
> Beneath a single icy star
>
> Where he, to his own compulsion
> —A terrific figure on an urn—
> Is caught between his two horizons,
> Forgetting that he must return.[4]

The meaning of this is not very clear, partly because the images are too abstract and partly because the context is thin. Faulkner may not have been quite clear as to what he wanted to mean; in *A Green Bough* the last line reads "Forgetting that he cant return" (p. 30). The moderately dramatic quality of "The Lilacs" is missing, and the lyric intensity that seems to have been intended is not very strong. For these reasons, and because of the technical awkwardness of the verse, "Twilight" is not a successful poem.

It is, however, a useful document in our study of Faulkner's literary development because a prose version of it is also available in print. This piece, an impressionistic sketch entitled "The Hill," looks as if it had been written at about the same

---

[4] *Contempo*, I (Feb. 1, 1932), 1.

time, but it was printed ten years earlier in the University of Mississippi campus newspaper, *The Mississippian*, for March 10, 1922. It may have been composed either as a preliminary study for the poem or as an alternative effort to express the same feeling in prose. In either event, it avoids many of the faults from which the poem suffers and it has virtues which the poem lacks.

It begins with a striking image of arrested motion which has no parallel in the poem. The young man, as he climbs the hill, walks against "a sibilant invisibility of wind like a sheet of water," which makes his clothing flap and his hair stir. At the same time, because the sun is low on the horizon behind him, "His long shadow legs rose perpendicularly and fell, ludicrously, as though without power of progression, as though his body had been mesmerized by a whimsical God to a futile puppet-like activity upon one spot, while time and life terrifically passed him and left him behind."

This image is followed and reinforced, as the young man reaches the crest, by a double-visioned description of the valley and town below. The only perceptible movement is in a trio of poplars, but, in the next paragraph, the impression of stasis is opposed by some rather brutal evidences of life, which are only vaguely hinted at in the abstract terms of the poem. "From the hilltop the valley was a motionless mosaic of tree and house; from the hilltop were to be seen no cluttered barren lots sodden with spring rain and churned and torn by hoof of horse and cattle, no piles of winter ashes and rusting tin cans, no dingy hoardings covered with the tattered insanities of posted salacities and advertisements. There was no suggestion of striving, of whipped vanities, of ambition and lusts, of the drying spittle of religious controversy; he could not see that the sonorous simplicity of the court house columns were discolored and stained with casual tobacco." For a moment, unaware of what he is doing, the young man tries to think: "The slow featureless mediocrity of his face twisted to an inner impulse: the terrific groping of his mind." However, as the sun sets, "his mind that troubled him for the first time, became quieted." The sketch ends with the same image as the poem: "Here, in the dusk, nymphs and fauns might riot to a shrilling of thin pipes, to a shivering and hissing of cymbals in a sharp volcanic abasement beneath a tall icy star. *** Behind him was the motionless conflagration of sunset, before him was the opposite valley rim upon the changing sky. For a while he stood on one horizon and stared across at the other, far above a world of endless toil and troubled slumber; untouched, untouchable; forgetting, for a space, that he must return. *** He slowly descended the hill."[5]

"The Hill," although at first glance it seems merely casual, and although it is marred by infelicities of style and tone, is nevertheless the most important and best organized of Faulkner's early experimental pieces; and it is the one which has the most echoes in his later work. In each of its main divisions, beginning, middle, and end, there is a fairly concentrated image of arrested motion. In the beginning, the dynamic wind, symbolic of lively movement in the poems and in the great novels alike, is counterpoised by the ludicrously puppet-like shadow, which Faulkner consistently used as a symbol of death and stasis. In the middle, the distant impression of beautiful motionlessness in the valley is contradicted by both beautiful and messy evidences of human, animal, and vegetable life. At the end, when the young man's tentative movement of thought has lapsed, the twilight interval is a moment in which time contracts to a point at which the woodland spirits of the distant past "might" dance again their ancient harmony of universal life, and in which the young man, if only momentarily, is "far above" the world where imperious forces of change will drive him into another day.

The effect is not entirely successful, because there is no in-

[5] "The Hill" is reprinted in *Early Prose and Poetry*, pp. 90-92; however, I have used the text as it appeared in *The Mississippian*, March 10, 1922, p. 2.

clusive pattern of symbolic relations capable of organizing the three main images into a unified whole. But the elements of a great artistic career are present in this obscure youthful sketch, waiting only for some added touch of catalytic strength or skill to make them cohere and crystallize.

Michael Millgate, in a perceptive observation, has called attention to the importance of the twilight moment in Faulkner's work, particularly *The Sound and the Fury*, the manuscript of which has the title "Twilight" on its first page.[6] The main evidence cited by Millgate is Quentin's identification of "twilight" as "that quality of light as if time really had stopped for a while" and his feeling that "all stable things had become shadowy paradoxical all I had done shadows all I had felt suffered taking visible form antic and perverse mocking without relevance inherent themselves with the denial of the significance they should have affirmed . . ." (*S&F* 209-10, 211). Millgate points out the parallel between this passage and the poem "Twilight"; but it seems to me that the closer and more extended parallel with "The Hill" is even more significant, especially in connection with Quentin's phrase "as if time really had stopped" and its relation to Faulkner's artistic aim and method. The symbolic stopping of time not only implies the momentary illusion of beauty for the young man on the hilltop, or the impossible goal of Quentin's day-long effort to escape the process of growth; it also provides the "artificial means" to enable Faulkner "to arrest motion," which can only occur in time, "and hold it fixed" for esthetic purposes.

In *The Sound and the Fury* this arrest is effected so brilliantly and so subtly that the result tends to blind us to the procedure and foil our analysis of its technique. Examination of "Twilight" and "The Hill," along with other apprentice work, is useful in showing us that Faulkner was pursuing the same artistic aim near the beginning of his career that he defined later on; and it is even more useful in helping us to es-

[6] Millgate, p. 86.

tablish and maintain a correct understanding of the relations between means and ends in his fiction. The aim of *The Sound and the Fury*, for example, is not, as so many critics have supposed, to describe the decay of a typical Southern family. Its aim is to evoke a feeling of the motion of life. The Compson family is there to help supply what is lacking in "Twilight" and to a less extent in "The Hill": a dense context of concrete circumstance and a strong dramatic situation in terms of which to construct a pattern of symbolic relations capable of assimilating the imagery into a powerfully cogent work of art. The aim, the imagery, and the basic method are almost exactly the same in the apprentice poems and sketches as they are in the masterpieces; but in the apprentice pieces they are a good deal easier to see.

A minor but significant symptom of this continuity is the use of the word "terrific" in both "Twilight" and "The Hill." In "Twilight" the young man is "A terrific figure on an urn"; in "The Hill" his shadow gives the impression of "a futile puppet-like activity upon one spot, while time and life terrifically passed him and left him behind," and his moment of static contemplation is preceded by "an inner impulse: the terrific groping of his mind." The adjective "terrific" and the adverb "terrifically" appear again and again throughout Faulkner's work, almost always in a context that associates them with imagery of arrested motion.[7] Whenever we see them, we should be alerted to the probability that Faulkner is attempting one of his more direct sallies at what he believed to be the artist's aim.

Another aspect of Faulkner's apprenticeship, very necessary to the clarification of his purpose as an artist and to the development of suitable techniques for achieving it, was a certain amount of theoretical speculation. The published record

[7] Hyatt H. Waggoner, *William Faulkner: From Jefferson to the World* (Lexington: University of Kentucky Press, 1959), pp. 71-76, discusses the word "terrific" in connection with *As I Lay Dying*.

of this activity is thus far very sparse, consisting mainly of Faulkner's reviews and critical essays on W. A. Percy, Conrad Aiken, Edna St. Vincent Millay, Eugene O'Neill, "American Drama: Inhibitions," Joseph Hergesheimer, "Criticism," and "Verse Old and Nascent: A Pilgrimage." The first six of these pieces appeared in *The Mississippian* during 1920, 1921, and 1922; the last two in *The Double Dealer* in 1925.[8] Critics of Faulkner have paid relatively little attention to them, probably because, as criticism, they are not worth much.[9] They should be more carefully studied, however, for the evidence they offer concerning what Faulkner was thinking, not about other people's writing, but about his own. A few of his statements, although they tend to be awkward and often cryptic, suggest that his thoughts already had some of the depth and complexity we find in his later fiction.

For example, in his review of Conrad Aiken's *Turns and Movies*, Faulkner remarked, "The most interesting phase of Mr. Aiken's work is his experiments with an abstract three dimensional verse patterned on polyphonic music form: The Jig of Forslin and The House of Dust. This is interesting because of the utterly unlimited possibilities of it, he has the whole world before him; for as yet no one has made a successful attempt to synthesize musical reactions with abstract documentary reactions" (*EPP* 76). For our purposes (luckily) it is not necessary to know exactly what Faulkner thought Aiken was doing, or whether Aiken really was doing it. Rightly or wrongly, Faulkner believed that what Aiken was doing opened up new and significant literary directions; and he set out to pursue them. His own early poems and experimental sketches tended heavily to musical effects, and his later use of what he called "counterpoint" was, as I have suggested, one of his most effective techniques.

[8] They are all reprinted in *Early Prose and Poetry*.

[9] An honorable exception is George P. Garrett, "Faulkner's Early Literary Criticism," *Texas Studies in Literature and Language*, I (Spring 1959), 3-10.

A similar observation arises out of his comparison of "stage language" in O'Neill's plays to that used by J.M. Synge in *The Playboy of the Western World.* "The Emperor Jones' 'who dat dare whistle in de Emperor's palace?'" Faulkner said, "goes back to the 'Playboy's' 'the likes of which would make the mitred bishops themselves strain at the bars of paradise for to see the lady Helen walking in her golden shawl.'" Faulkner went on to suggest that O'Neill might be assisting at the birth of "A national literature," not out of "folk lore," which Faulkner thought was too various in America, or out of "our slang," but out of "the strength of imaginative idiom which is understandable by all who read English." He concluded the review by claiming that "Nowhere today, saving in parts of Ireland, is the English language spoken with the same earthy strength as it is in the United States; though we are, as a nation, still inarticulate" (*EPP* 88, 89). Perhaps what he meant was that he himself was inarticulate because he had not yet learned to use the language of north Mississippi—or its folklore either—for literary purposes. In *The Hamlet,* and later in *The Mansion,* he not only made brilliant use of colloquial style, he also paraphrased the quotation from Synge: "Helen and the bishops, the kings and the graceless seraphim" (*Ham* 213; cf. p. 207); "Helen and the bishops, the kings and the unhomed angels, the scornful and graceless seraphim" (*Man* 436).[10]

Two quotations from the review of Joseph Hergesheimer's fiction will show the degree to which Faulkner was conscious, in 1922, of "arrested motion" as an artistic literary effect. Hergesheimer, he said, "has never written a novel . . . Linda Condon, in which he reached his apex, is not a novel. It is

[10] Cf. *A Green Bough,* III l. 21: "Kings and mitred bishops tired of sin . . . ." Millgate, pp. 112 and 315, notes 17 and 18, points to these paraphrases, remarks that "it seems fair to speak of Faulkner as having achieved something comparable to the Irish folk-dramas of Synge," and suggests that *As I Lay Dying,* in particular, carries out the program recommended in Synge's preface to *The Playboy of the Western World* for the use of "rich and copious" language "in countries where the imagination of the people, and the language they use, is rich and living . . . ."

more like a lovely Byzantine frieze: a few unforgettable figures in silent arrested motion, forever beyond the reach of
time and troubling the heart like music." He added, in his
final paragraph, that Hergesheimer "is like an emasculate
priest surrounded by the puppets he has carved and clothed
and painted—a terrific world without motion or meaning"
(*EPP* 101, 103). Faulkner did not altogether approve of
Hergesheimer's attitude or results, but he was very much interested in the technique, which he compared with that of
Conrad (p. 102).

Whoever would understand Faulkner must accept the fact
that he was not only immensely intelligent but well read,
highly educated, and widely traveled. He was also extremely
ambitious. Phil Stone reports in his preface, dated September
23, 1924, to *The Marble Faun* that "On one of our long walks
through the hills, I remarked that I thought the main trouble
with Amy Lowell and her gang of drum-beaters was . . . that
they always had one eye on the ball and the other eye on the
grandstand.[11] To which the author of these poems replied that
his personal trouble as a poet seemed to be that he had one eye
on the ball and the other on Babe Ruth" (*TMF* 8). A literal
identity for the figurative Babe Ruth is suggested in a parallel
anecdote related by James K. Feibleman, who became acquainted with Faulkner in New Orleans. He recalls an occasion at the office of *The Double Dealer* when Faulkner, after
listening in silence for some time to talk about Shakespeare,
and specifically about *Hamlet*, finally said, " 'I could write a
play like *Hamlet* if I wanted to . . . .' "[12]

Undoubtedly he wanted to write something as good as

[11] Faulkner used the same metaphor, in almost exactly the same words, in
his review of Edna St. Vincent Millay's *Aria da Capo*, to characterize "the
aesthetic messiahs of our emotional Valhalla"; but he did not specify who
they were (*EPP* 84).

[12] James K. Feibleman, "Literary New Orleans Between the Wars,"
Southern Review, n.s. I (Summer 1965), 706. Feibleman dates this conversation in 1921.

Hamlet, but he was not always so confident that he could. "The Artist," one of his prose sketches published in *The Double Dealer* in 1925, although it is a dramatic monologue and not a personal statement, probably expresses something of his feeling. Artistic inspiration, the speaker says, is "A dream and a fire which I cannot control"; he muses on the weakness of mortal flesh and predicts "that I can never give to the world that which is crying in me to be freed." However, he is not discouraged. "But to create!" he says in the final paragraph. "Which among ye who have not this fire, can know this joy, let it be ever so fleet?" (*NOS* 47, 48). It was inevitable that Faulkner should sometimes feel the frustration, as well as the pride and the burning desire for greatness; he still had much to learn. But he was on his way, and his progress, after 1925, was tremendously fast. In less than four years he learned enough to write *The Sound and the Fury.*

The few months Faulkner spent during the spring of 1925 in New Orleans, where he was more or less closely associated with Sherwood Anderson, mark the most important phase of his apprenticeship, because at this time, aided by Anderson's example and encouragement, he stopped trying to be primarily a poet and became primarily a novelist.

He had, as we have seen, written prose before. In fact, one of his earliest published pieces had been a conventional (and very poorly done) short story, "Landing in Luck," printed in *The Mississippian* for November 19, 1919; "The Hill" appeared in 1922; and there are several unpublished short stories apparently dating from the early 1920s.[13] In 1925 he published two groups of prose sketches: one consisted of eleven short dramatic monologues (of which "The Artist" is a fair sample) in *The Double Dealer* for January-February, and the other was a series of sixteen pieces of description, character study, and embryonic narration in the *Times-Picayune Sun-*

---

[13] See Millgate, pp. 10-12.

day Magazine, the first on February 8, and the last on September 27.[14]

In these experimental pieces we see Faulkner working to convert himself from poetry to the writing of fiction. His problem in so doing was not to adorn a tale but to invent one that would achieve the effect he had been trying for in his poems. The results, at first, were fumbling. The monologues in *The Double Dealer* are character sketches in which the language is archaically stiff and the characters remain abstract. There is little in the way of setting or event, and the effect is missed because there is not enough potential energy of motion to make a stop impressive. What the speakers contemplate seems almost as static as the artificial moment of contemplation itself.

The *Times-Picayune* sketches are longer, more various, and more narrative. All are at least anecdotes, and ten of the sixteen are cast in more or less recognizable short-story forms. Two are expansions of themes which had been less fully developed in the *Double Dealer* group. The *Times-Picayune* version of "The Cobbler," like the version in *The Double Dealer*, is a dramatic monologue, but it tells considerably more of the Cobbler's story. "The Kid Learns" is based on the situation of the *Double Dealer* monologue entitled "Frankie and Johnny"; and here the conversion is more radical. The point of view is shifted from the first person to an omniscient author, a series of events is added, and the situation itself is somewhat modified. These changes point in a hopeful direction, but none of the sketches is developed into a successful story. Faulkner had not yet created a fictional protagonist who could adequately experience an arrest of motion, nor had he discovered the kind of situation that would properly dramatize such an arrest. He was, however, rapidly extending his competence in the medium of prose, and, as Carvel Collins points out (*NOS* 23, 26, 27-30), the sketches in many ways foreshadow later work.

[14] All twenty-seven of these are reprinted in *New Orleans Sketches*.

Probably the most important one, from this point of view, is "Out of Nazareth," published in the *Times-Picayune* for Easter Sunday, April 12, 1925. The opening scene is described with the help of imagery typical of the early poems, including the Jackson statue, flowers "like poised dancers," "sparrows delirious in a mimosa, and a vague Diana in tortuous escape from marble draperies . . . ." The speaker (presumably Faulkner) and his friend Spratling[15] encounter a young man in Jackson Square looking up at "the spire of the Cathedral, or perhaps it was something in the sky he was watching." Collins notices parallels between the young man and Christ (*NOS* 28); the speaker imagines "young David looking like that," and "Jonathan getting that look from David, and, serving that highest function of which sorry man is capable, being the two of them beautiful in similar peace and simplicity—beautiful as gods, as no woman can ever be," and adds, "He was eternal, of the earth itself." Although he is uneducated, he has "a battered 'Shropshire Lad' " in his pocket, and he leaves a manuscript of his own composition with the speaker. He is very much like the young man who feels the classical world around him in "Twilight." His relation to the classical fertility cults is suggested by his liking for trees, corn, hot sunshine, and agricultural labor. In "The Hill" this typical young man is almost made to think; now, like Faulkner, he has begun to write.

His manuscript, which the speaker quotes entire, describes "a day spent in constant motion in the open air." Its moral is, first, "true communion with nature," which its author feels in the early morning, and then "the fraternity of the open road," in which he participates at a camp where he stops for the night. The speaker characterizes the manuscript, justly

[15] William Spratling, an instructor in architecture at Tulane University, collaborated with Faulkner in producing the humorous booklet *Sherwood Anderson & Other Famous Creoles*, published in December 1926, and accompanied him on his trip to Europe in 1925. "Out of Nazareth" was illustrated with an impressionistic sketch of Jackson Square by Spratling.

enough, as "blundering and childish and 'arty,' " but he senses "something back of it, some impulse which caused him to want to write it out on paper." The young man, he says, reminding us again that the sentiments of the interviews and the Nobel speech were not new to Faulkner in the 1950s, "with his clean young face and his beautiful faith that life, the world, the race, is somewhere good and sound and beautiful, is good to see" (*NOS* 101-10).

The style of this also reminds us, unhappily, that Faulkner was almost as "blundering and childish and 'arty' " at times as the author his speaker is criticizing, and particularly so in the *Times-Picayune* and *Double Dealer* sketches. "Out of Nazareth" is less successful than "The Hill" in evoking the feeling of life. The imagery is there, but the writing is technically soft, and the protagonist moves too easily in harmony with nature and other people; the essential element of opposition is lacking.

Nevertheless the practice Faulkner got in writing these sketches, and seeing them in print, was undoubtedly good for his art as well as his morale. One reason for their shallowness was probably the fact that he was hard at work on another project, much larger, more ambitious, and in its completion more successful than they.

Soldiers' Pay

Donald Mahon, the wounded protagonist of *Soldiers' Pay*, embodies the same image of stasis as the flyer who unluckily "didn't die" in "The Lilacs." He is twice compared explicitly to a faun (pp. 69, 83), and he is remembered by his father, his fiancée, and his lover as a wild, free, beautiful boy. His lover, Emmy, says that " 'his face was like—it was like he ought to live in the woods' " (p. 125). The faun image is complemented by the description of Januarius Jones as "a fat satyr" (p. 286) whose "face was a round mirror before which fauns and nymphs might have wantoned when the world was

young" (p. 58) and of Donald's father, the rector, as "a
laureled Jove" (p. 60) whose gardening makes him, symbolically, a kind of fertility god. The action takes place in spring
and early summer, and the book is crammed with images of
life in earth, air, fire, and water, in trees, grass, birds, insects,
and frogs, in rain, wind, sunlight, and moonlight, in the day,
and in the night. Against this background, and in the midst
of a great deal of lively comic activity by other characters,
the formerly and perhaps still potentially faun-like Donald,
wounded in the head and the hand, sits detached, isolated, going blind, and finally dying. The opposition of his stasis to
the dynamism of life that surrounds him in nature and other
people establishes the technical strategy and the moral meaning of the book.

The moral content is carried mainly by Joe Gilligan and
Margaret Powers, who appoint themselves Donald's guardians
and try to bring him back to life. They fail, and they make at
least one mistake when Margaret marries him instead of urg-
ing Emmy to do so. But they agree that they have, as Gilligan
puts it, " 'done the best we could' " (p. 107), or, as he says
later, " 'tried to help nature make a good job out of a poor one
without having no luck at it' " (p. 303). Their efforts and their
characterization provide further evidence of Faulkner's early
interest in the prevalence of man, and look forward to the
creation of characters such as Byron Bunch and others who
actively take the part of life. Joe and Margaret are not adequately conceived, however, and the end of the story is weak-
ened by their failure to depart together as Byron and Lena do
in *Light in August*.

The younger girls, Emmy and Cecily, are presented largely
in terms of imagery that tends to identify them with nature
goddesses. Emmy is most often associated with water, in her
role as housekeeper, floor mopper, and dishwasher, and in her
memory of the night she and Donald swam together in the
creek and made love in the dew-soaked grass. The tone is

often comic, as when Jones falls over her pail in the dark hall-way and is lifted up, "a sodden Venus," by the rector (p. 65), or when he is soaked again by her tears on the day of Donald's funeral (p. 297). But she is Donald's most skillful as well as his most devoted nurse, and she plays, not altogether absurdly, a kind of homely Egeria to Donald's faun and Jones's satyr.

Cecily Saunders is also associated with water, especially by her puerile lover, George Farr, who thinks of her naked body in the moonlight "as a narrow pool sweetly dividing: two sil-ver streams from a single source . . ." (p. 196; cf. pp. 212, 238, 242, 261, and 268). But she is also figured as a wood nymph; Jones for example calls her a "Hamadryad, a slim jeweled one" (p. 77). She is one of Faulkner's typical "epicene" girls (pp. 143, 224, 249, 290), like Patricia Robyn in *Mosquitoes* or Temple Drake in *Sanctuary*, whose sex is as dubious as their morality. She is, however, invested with a perverse attractive-ness, consisting mainly in the impression she gives of intense and vibrant life. Jones later thinks of "Her long legs, not for locomotion, but for the studied completion of a rhythm carried to its *nth*: compulsion of progress, movement; her body cre-ated for all men to dream after. A poplar, vain and pliant . . . . Not for maternity, not even for love: a thing for the eye and the mind" (p. 224). She is often compared to a flower or a bird, and once even to a bat, almost always with some explicit reference to quick and graceful motion. This quality in her offers a striking contrast to the dull inertness of Donald as he sits "motionless, hopeless as Time" (p. 170), being read to by Gilligan, who " 'never can tell when he's asleep and when he ain't . . .' " (p. 172).

Cecily's arboreal quality is reinforced by one tree in particu-lar, a poplar, which is the most emphatic natural image of beautiful arrested motion in the book. "At the corner of the house was a tree covered with tiny white-bellied leaves like a mist, like a swirl of arrested silver water" (p. 109), which is further characterized, with a redundancy that becomes tedious, as "a swirling silver veil stood on end, a fountain arrested forever: carven water" (p. 247), "the tree that, unseen but suggested, swirled upward in an ecstasy of never-escaping silver-bellied leaves" (p. 254), "hushed its never-still never-escaping ecstasy" (p. 272), "yet swirled its white-bellied leaves in never-escaping skyward ecstasies" (p. 281), "vain as a girl darkly in an arrested passionate ecstasy" (p. 286), "twilight-musicked ecstasy" (p. 291), "a leafed and passionate Atalanta, poising her golden apple" (p. 292), "the hushed slumbrous passion of the silver tree" (p. 316). It is the rector's lover, as all the life in his garden is; "a tree at the corner of the house turning upward its white-bellied leaves in a passionate arrested rush: it and the rector faced each other in ecstasy," and when he speaks, "The tree to his voice took a more unbearable ecstasy, its twinkling leaves swirled in a never escaping silver skyward rush" (p. 252).

Faulkner was obviously not yet ready to handle a leitmotif with a master's tact; but, a few years later, in *The Sound and the Fury*, he used the same one, distilled, in Benjy's phrase "Caddy smelled like trees," so as to prove that the apprentice was the master's father. He had used it in its crude form earlier by telling how the three poplars in "The Hill" "bent narrowly to the quiet resistless compulsion of April in their branches, then were still and straight again except for the silver mist of their never ceasing, never escaping leaves" (*EPP* 91). The poplar in *Soldiers' Pay*, overhandled though it is, helps to relate the rector to Cecily, who shows more love for him than for anyone else, and both of them to Donald and Emmy and the others—even the egregious George—in a pattern of nature imagery that weaves threads of life throughout the fabric of the book.

The liveliest character is, paradoxically, the ridiculous and often repulsive Januarius Jones. In spite of a labored insistence on his intellectual cleverness and his ability to seem "calm, circumspect, lazy and remote as an idol" (p. 230), the dominant impression is of his frantic physical activity, of one of the girls escaping, and "Jones . . . leaping after her, hopelessly distanced" (p. 286). Like the lover on Keats's urn, he seems most happy when the pursuit is nearing but not reaching the goal. When Cecily stops running, he repulses her; and after he has succeeded with Emmy, and Gilligan has chased him away from her window, he gives "a sigh of pure ennui" (p. 315). Gilligan says that Jones is " 'lucky. . . . he gets what he wants . . . . he don't get all the women he wants. He has failed twice to my knowledge. But failure don't seem to worry him. That's what I mean by lucky' " (p. 304). This explanation corresponds to an attitude often taken by Faulkner toward his own works, which pleased him in proportion to the gallantry of their failure to attain the level of his most ambitious conceptions. The happiness is proportioned to the discontent. For Jones, its highest point is reached when his chase of Emmy is most desperately frustrated. "It had got to where, had she acceded suddenly he would have been completely reft of one of his motivating impulses, of his elemental impulse to live: he might have died. Yet he knew that if he didn't get her soon he would become crazy, an imbecile" (p. 283). Like Cecily, Jones provides an image of intense motion as counterpoint to the intense stasis represented by Donald.

Many details of *Soldiers' Pay* remind us of Faulkner's poems and experimental prose sketches, and at the same time look forward to his later work. Margaret Powers feels that her room in a hotel is "like an appointed tomb . . . high above a world of joy and sorrow and lust for living, high above imperious trees occupied solely with maternity and spring" (p. 44), putting a new twist on the image used to describe the young man's feeling in "The Hill" (*EPP* 92). The same sketch is recalled by the "fauns and nymphs" associated with Jones's satyr face, and by a passing reference to the courthouse in Donald's home town, the "beautiful Ionic columns" of which are "stained with generations of casual tobacco" (p. 112; cf. *EPP* 91, and also *LIA* 393, where the wording of the final phrase is exactly the same). One of Donald's relics is "a cheap paper-covered 'Shropshire Lad'" (p. 68) like that carried by the young man in "Out of Nazareth" (*NOS* 104).

We even find some of the same quotations being used in the same unassimilated way. Margaret, for example, thinking of her dead first husband, paraphrases one of two lines from Swinburne's "In the Orchard" which appear in the monologue of "The Priest" in the *Double Dealer* series (*SP* 181, 182; *NOS* 39). Another, still more awkward, is the misprinted quotation from Eliot's "Rhapsody on a Windy Night," rendered in *Soldiers' Pay* as "'La lune en grade aucune rancune'" (p. 134). Faulkner had borrowed this line, with dashing incongruity, for the ending of his translation (otherwise reasonably faithful) of Verlaine's "Fantoches," which appeared in *The Mississippian* for February 25, 1920, misprinted in the same way. One wonders whether he knew that Eliot was referring in turn to Laforgue's "*Complainte de cette bonne lune*": "*—Là, voyons, mam'zelle la Lune, / Ne gardons pas ainsi rancune . . . .*"

Among the images carried over into later work are several that are used with far greater skill and effectiveness in *The Sound and the Fury*: Jones and the rector "trod their shadows across the lawn" (p. 65; cf. *S&F* 118, 124, 138, 149); Jones calls Gilligan "'Mr. Galahad'" and "'the squire of dames'" (pp. 289, 313; cf. *S&F* 136, 207); and the rector says, "'The saddest thing about love, Joe, is that not only the love cannot last forever, but even the heartbreak is soon forgotten'" (p. 318; cf. *S&F* 221-22). Throughout *Soldiers' Pay* we find the young author trying various ways of using materials, many of which he had used before, and many of which he would soon learn to use much better.

In the ending of *Soldiers' Pay*, as in *The Sound and the Fury*, a Negro church service is used as part of Faulkner's effort to resolve the feeling of the book. Gilligan and the rector, standing in darkness outside, receive intimations of life, "the imminence of sex after harsh labor along the mooned land," and they hear "the crooning submerged passion of the dark race. It was nothing, it was everything; then it swelled to an ecstasy . . . . All the longing of mankind for a Oneness with Something, somewhere." This is balanced by an opposing intimation: "Then the singing died, fading away along the mooned land inevitable with to-morrow and sweat, with sex and death and damnation; and they turned townward under the moon, feeling dust in their shoes" (p. 319). The intended effect is of some timeless realization, in a twilight moment like that of "The Hill" and the poem "Twilight," of the quality of life. It is not altogether unsuccessful, but it is rather badly spoiled by clumsiness and a tendency to abstraction that makes the rhetoric both heavy and hollow. We would hardly be moved to predict, on the basis of this qualified success, that Faulkner would be able to make a Negro church service work as it does in *The Sound and the Fury*.

In *Soldiers' Pay* Faulkner had not yet found his true voice, because he had not acquired the ability, which is largely technical, to dramatize the feelings he wanted to express. But *Soldiers' Pay* is not bad, and its ending is considerably better than its beginning. It is more successful as prose than most of Faulkner's poems are as verse; and it carries forward much of the experimentation that Faulkner began in his prose sketches. It is a very promising work.

Mosquitoes

Faulkner's next completed novel, *Mosquitoes*, published by Liveright on April 30, 1927, is a more negative but perhaps almost equally valuable effort. In itself, it is a failure, dealing mostly with materials, settings, and people that Faulkner could not handle then and never succeeded in handling later. However, it also deals with ideas and problems that the apprentice had to work his way through before he could work effectively as an artist in fiction.

The theme is the relation of art to society and to nature, society being figured in the mixed lot of people who make up Mrs. Maurier's yachting party, and nature in Lake Pontchartrain, the swampy jungle on its northern shore, and the insects of the title, which not only swarm in the swamps but which invade the city of New Orleans as well.

On the social side, the general rule is that the characters who talk the most are the least creative. The sculptor Gordon, who is all artist, hardly says a word, whereas Mr. Talliaferro, all dilettante, out of Januarius Jones by J. Alfred Prufrock,[16] endlessly plans campaigns for the seduction of women, and succeeds only in talking himself into an engagement to marry the apparently sterile Mrs. Maurier. After a particularly clever exchange of abstract statements by some of the other characters, Gordon silently anathematizes them: "Talk, talk, talk: the utter and heartbreaking stupidity of words. . . . Ideas, thoughts, became mere sounds to be bandied about until they were dead" (p. 186). Gordon's esthetic statements are made in the nonverbal media of wood, stone, and clay; one of them in particular (as described in the omniscient narrator's words) is an eloquent embodiment of the artist's aim as Faulkner defined it. "As you entered the room the thing drew your eyes: you turned sharply as to a sound, expecting movement. But it was marble, it could not move. And when you tore your eyes away and turned your back on it at last, you got again untarnished and high and clean that sense of swiftness, of space encompassed; but on looking again it was as before: motionless and passionately eternal—the virginal breastless torso of a girl, headless, armless, legless, in marble temporarily

---

[16] For parallels between *Mosquitoes* and T. S. Eliot's early work, see F.L. Gwynn, "Faulkner's Prufrock—and Other Observations," *Journal of English and Germanic Philology*, LII (January 1953), 63-70.

caught and hushed yet passionate still for escape, passionate and simple and eternal in the equivocal derisive darkness of the world" (p. 11). An ideal solution—for a sculptor.

But Faulkner was a writer, and he had probably been describing his own situation and feeling when he made his speaker in "Out of Nazareth" remark that his friend Spratling's "hand has been shaped to a brush as mine has (alas!) not" and that "words are my meat and bread and drink . . ." (*NOS* 102, 110). He had to look for a solution lying within the fact, which he must have found paradoxical, that the medium of literary art is nothing but words. In *Mosquitoes*, much of the talk that Gordon so scornfully rejects is addressed to the problem of how to make something concretely and esthetically moving out of the abstract material of language.

Dawson Fairchild, the novelist who resembles Sherwood Anderson, advises Mr. Talliaferro (as Jones is advised by Margaret Powers in *Soldiers' Pay*) that women cannot be seduced with words. Another character, whose first name is Julius but who is most often referred to, awkwardly, as "the Semitic man," objects: " 'Well, why not with words? . . . you are a funny sort to disparage words . . . . It's the word that overturns thrones and political parties and instigates vice crusades, not things: the Thing is merely the symbol for the Word' " (p. 130). Fairchild, not satisfied with this formulation, tries several times to better it. Without abandoning his opinion that words are " 'a kind of sterility,' " he comes round to saying that " 'words brought into a happy conjunction produce something that lives, just as soil and climate and an acorn in proper conjunction will produce a tree' " (p. 210). That is, a pattern of organic relationship in a literary work may lend a quality of life to words, even though words are sterile in themselves. Later Fairchild adds the suggestion that great poetry catches " 'A kind of singing rhythm in the world that you get into without knowing it, like a swimmer gets into a current' " (p. 248). This dynamic formula is evoked by Fairchild's dipping into a volume of verse attributed to Julius's sister, Mrs. Eva Wiseman, but actually written by Faulkner himself. In *Mosquitoes* it is called *Satyricon in Starlight*; the poems from which Fairchild quotes were published six years later in *A Green Bough*.

One problem which Faulkner had a particular interest in solving was that of a writer's relation to his region. In his review of O'Neill (1922), he had acknowledged that art may be "preeminently provincial,"[17] but had expressed strong doubts about the artistic value of the American environment (*EPP* 86-89). In *Mosquitoes*, Julius and his sister discuss the same problem, with Fairchild as their subject. The crux, as they see it, is that Fairchild's " 'writing seems fumbling, not because life is unclear to him, but because of his innate humorless belief that, though it bewilder him at times, life at bottom is sound and admirable and fine; and because . . . the ghosts of the Emersons and Lowells and other exemplifiers of Education with a capital E' " are too intimidating to him. Julius concludes that Fairchild needs two apparently contradictory determinations: " 'a conviction that his talent need not be restricted to delineating things which his conscious mind assures him are American reactions' " and a belief that, " 'by getting himself and his own bewilderment and inhibitions out of the way by describing, in a manner that even translation cannot injure (as Balzac did) American life as American life is, it will become eternal and timeless despite him' " (pp. 242-43). The statement is not clear, but it seems to mean that a writer should base himself solidly in his own experience, and therefore in his own local culture, in order to make his work universal. Faulkner, who was not yet ready to take this advice, was still fumbling.

Another problem that emerges with more force than clarity

[17] Faulkner guessed that this had been said by "a Frenchman, probably; they have said everything," but Stone, in his introduction to *The Marble Faun*, attributed the idea to George Moore.

in *Mosquitoes* is the relation between art and sex, which seems roughly parallel to the relation between art and nature, but which is involved with some puzzling inconsistencies. Gordon seems to be sexually as well as artistically the most potent of the major male characters, and Mr. Talliaferro is again at the other end of the scale. But it is Mr. Talliaferro who is attracted to Jenny Steinbauer, a personification of fertility, and Gordon who unwillingly becomes obsessed with the boylike, "sexless" Patricia Robyn. Moreover, the marble statue Gordon has carved is an image, as Fairchild observes, of timeless and inviolable virginity (p. 318).

Fairchild says that art is a means of helping people to " 'forget time' " (" 'like one who spends his time forgetting death or digestion,' " Julius objects), and also that it is a way of " 'getting into life, getting into it and wrapping it around you, becoming a part of it,' " as women do naturally by conceiving and bearing children. " 'But in art,' " he says, " 'a man can create without any assistance at all: what he does is his. A perversion, I grant you, but a perversion that builds Chartres and invents Lear is a pretty good thing' " (pp. 319, 320). These efforts to define the relations and differences between the creative power of men, which results in art, and the creative power of nature, which is fertility, do not in themselves arrive at any clear result.

Natural fertility is powerfully but not pleasantly represented in *Mosquitoes* by the swampy lakeshore along which Patricia goes with the steward, David West, on her way, she hopes, to Europe. But the swamp, the heat, the lack of drinkable water, and the mosquitoes rapidly prove too much for Pat, who is a fugitive only from the restrictions of society, not its comforts; and David is not strong enough either to dominate her or support her. When they both give up, she wants " 'to do something for you. . . . Anything, just anything' " (p. 213); but he takes no advantage of the offer. Their humiliation is completed by the ugly, foul-mouthed swamper who takes them back to

the yacht in his boat. " 'Git a real man, next time,' " he advises
(p. 214). This material is far removed, in theory, from the
abstract concepts and definitions of art pursued by Gordon
and Fairchild and the others. But the swamp and its primitive
forms of life are rendered in a more artistically convincing
and satisfactory way than anything else in the book.

Again in *Mosquitoes*, as in *Soldiers' Pay*, we see Faulkner
using techniques and materials which he had experimented
with in the earlier prose sketches and poems, and some of
which he would use in more successful works later. Since the
setting of *Mosquitoes* is partly in New Orleans, we are not
surprised to find echoes of the New Orleans sketches. The
image of the city as "an aging yet still beautiful courtesan"
(*Mos* 10) is borrowed from "The Tourist": "A courtesan,
not old and yet no longer young . . ." (*NOS* 49). The cry of
the artist, "But to create!" (*NOS* 48), is repeated incongru-
ously in Mrs. Maurier's exclamation, " 'To create, to create' "
(*Mos* 18); and Mrs. Maurier has another inspiration which
comes perhaps as much from the poems and sketches as it does
from her character or background as given in *Mosquitoes*
when she looks at Gordon in moonlight and thinks, "It's like
a silver faun's face . . ." (p. 152). There are at least two echoes
in *Mosquitoes* from "Out of Nazareth": Andrew Jackson is
again seen "in childish effigy bestriding the terrific arrested
plunge of his curly balanced horse" (*Mos* 14; cf. *NOS* 101),
and David West is evidently the same young man who was
encountered in Jackson Square by the speaker of the sketch
(*Mos* 123; cf. *NOS* 102-105). He is a further development of
the young man in "Twilight" and "The Hill," and another
forerunner of naïve characters such as Benjy, Ike Snopes, and
Ike McCaslin, whose points of view cut across the conventions
of society in later works.

The shadow image, which appears in "The Hill" and in
Soldiers' Pay, is developed in *Mosquitoes* when David, carrying Patricia on his back, watches their shadow in a trance of

suffering: "two steps more and he would tread upon it and through it as he did the sparse shadows of pines, but it moved on just ahead of him . . . keeping its distance effortlessly in the uneven dust" (p. 204). The symbolism is vague, but its relation to that of Quentin's section of *The Sound and the Fury* is reinforced by Fairchild's later suggestion, echoing Macbeth's speech, " 'that there are shadowy people in the world, people to whom life is a kind of antic shadow' " (*Mos* 231; cf. *S&F* 211). There may also be a dim forecast of Quentin's incestuous relation to Caddy in the odd goings-on between Patricia and her brother Theodore, and of Benjy's feeling for Caddy in Mr. Talliaferro's observation of Pat, "the clean young odor of her, like that of young trees . . ." (*Mos* 21). These images are not effectively organized in *Mosquitoes*, but they are there, awaiting Faulkner's discovery of a dramatic structure that would invest them with esthetic weight and value.

The two young girls in *Mosquitoes* are contrasted in much the same way as Cecily and Emmy in *Soldiers' Pay*, but more sharply. Emmy seems unfocused, but in Jenny we have a full-blown, if not overblown, version of the earth-mother image represented later by Lena Grove in *Light in August* and Eula Varner in *The Hamlet*. Although the symbolic structure of *Mosquitoes* is not strong enough to make the contrast work as well as it should, the clarity with which it appears may help us to understand the functions of such characters as Narcissa Benbow in *Sartoris* and *Sanctuary*, Temple Drake in *Sanctuary*, Dewey Dell Bundren in *As I Lay Dying*, and Linda Snopes in *The Town* and *The Mansion*. All of these, and perhaps also Houston's cow in *The Hamlet*, operate more or less in terms of the contrast between the fertility embodied in Jenny and the perverse energy of Patricia.

Near the end of *Mosquitoes*, in a climactic passage of highly impressionistic revery, Faulkner tries to concentrate all of this material, particularly the imagery, into a single definition of art that will be both unified and comprehensive. Fairchild, who has got very drunk on Gordon's whiskey, is walking through the dark streets of the Vieux Carré with Gordon and Julius. Death is present in the form of a beggar's corpse lying under a gateway, religion in six priests, love in a swarm of prostitutes, and " 'Beauty,' " Julius insists; " 'a thing unseen, suggested: natural and fecund and foul—you don't stop for it; you pass on' " (p. 335).

The text, however, does stop for an attempt to grasp an impression of it, the awkwardness of which is partly indicated by a heavy incidence of pretentious literary allusions. Julius silently quotes a passage from Théophile Gautier's *Mademoiselle de Maupin* which is also quoted by the "Wealthy Jew" in the first monologue of the *Double Dealer* series: "I love three things: gold, marble and purple . . . form solidity color" (pp. 335, 336, 338, 339, 340; cf. *NOS* 37, 38).[18] He also silently remarks that "Dante invented Beatrice, creating himself a maid that life had not had time to create, and laid upon her frail and unbowed shoulders the whole burden of man's history of his impossible heart's desire" (p. 339). Eliot is echoed in the image of three rats *"dragging their hot bellies over"* the beggar's corpse (p. 336; cf. *The Waste Land*, ll. 187-88); the Tristan legend is invoked by Fairchild (pp. 339-40); and Flaubert's *Salammbô* is recalled by the author's image of *"a maiden in an ungirdled robe and with a thin bright chain between her ankles . . ."* (p. 337).[19]

---

[18] The source is pointed out by Millgate, p. 300, n. 95. The quotation in "Wealthy Jew," "I love three things: gold; marble and purple; splendor, solidity, color" (*NOS* 37), is, aside from punctuation, a somewhat more accurate translation of Gautier's text. A possible source of some of Faulkner's other imagery is a passage in the same work where Madelaine de Maupin, writing to her friend Graciosa, recalls a night scene when they walked together in a moonlit garden, *"dans cette allée triste et peu fréquentée, terminée d'un coté par une statue de Faune jouant de la flûte . . ."* (Paris, 1878, p. 210). There may be something also in the fact that Madelaine, disguised as a man, falls in love with a man named Theodore, who returns her love (much to his own dismay) before he discovers her true sex.

[19] Another image possibly derived from Flaubert is the "sound of inflated rubber on asphalt, like a tearing of endless silk" (p. 15). Flaubert uses this image to describe the distant sound of a volley fired by soldiers into a crowd

The purpose of these references is to provide a context for Fairchild's effort to define genius in terms of the Crucifixion story—an attempt which, as critics have noted, foreshadows Faulkner's use of that story in his later novels. " 'People confuse it so, you see,' " Fairchild says. " 'They have got it now to where it signifies only an active state of the mind in which a picture is painted or a poem is written. When it is not that at all. It is that Passion Week of the heart, that instant of timeless beatitude which some never know, which some, I suppose, gain at will, which others gain through an outside agency like alcohol, like to-night—that passive state of the heart with which the mind, the brain, has nothing to do at all, in which the hackneyed accidents which make up this world—love and life and death and sex and sorrow—brought together by chance in perfect proportions, take on a kind of splendid and timeless beauty' " (p. 339). Fairchild is trying to describe the moment of timeless contemplation that Faulkner had been trying to pin down "by artificial means" in his early experiments.

Mosquitoes fails to arrive at the full effect because the structure does not develop a sufficiently powerful and concentrated confrontation between the motion of life and the stasis of the artificially timeless moment. There are occasional effective images of dynamic stasis in the text, as we have seen; but they dribble away in a chaos of insufficiently related details, instead of converging to support an effective symbolic structure.

Faulkner had two more steps to take before he could emerge on the high ground of his genius. First, he had to plant himself solidly in his native region. Second, he had to make " 'that Passion Week of the heart' " something more than a matter of

---

of rebellious Parisians in February of 1848: *"un bruit, pareil au cracquement d'une immense pièce de soie que l'on déchire"* (*L'éducation sentimentale* [Paris: Bibliothèque-Charpentier, 1911], p. 346). The same image appears twice in *The Wild Palms* (pp. 65, 67), three times in *Intruder in the Dust* (pp. 186, 190, 218), and once in "That Evening Sun" (*These 13* [New York, Jonathan Cape & Harrison Smith, 1931], p. 55).

chance; he had to learn to achieve it by the consistent use of dependable organizing patterns.

Sartoris

The first of these steps was taken in *Sartoris*. As Faulkner explained in the *Paris Review* interview, "Beginning with *Sartoris* I discovered that my own little postage stamp of native soil was worth writing about and that I would never live long enough to exhaust it, and that by sublimating the actual into the apocryphal I would have complete liberty to use whatever talent I might have to its absolute top."[20] *Sartoris* is the first of Faulkner's novels to make full use of north Mississippi scenes and characters. It creates, in one astounding stroke, the world of Yoknapatawpha County, in itself a major achievement, the importance of which as a cornerstone of Faulkner's subsequent career can hardly be exaggerated. And yet, in most ways, and especially in its technical aspects, *Sartoris* must be regarded as the last of his apprentice works—the last of his immature and relatively unsuccessful experiments in learning how to deal artistically with his feeling for life as motion—rather than as the first of his mature masterpieces. It is at least as closely related to the poems and the prose sketches as it is to the successful novels.

The strategy in *Sartoris* is to confront the motion of life with the emotional block in the protagonist, young Bayard Sartoris. Like the speaker in "Lilacs" and Donald Mahon in *Soldiers' Pay*, young Bayard is immobilized as a result of his experience as a combat pilot in the first World War. His wound is psychic rather than physical. He has seen his brother John shot down and killed in spite of his own efforts to intervene. He is haunted and crippled by his waking and his nightmare memories of that moment, and by his obsessive desire somehow still to keep it from happening, or from having happened. He is trying to loop back in time, to enter the mov-

[20] *Writers at Work*, p. 141.

49

ing stream of life and change its course at a point in the past. Of course he cannot, and his efforts to do so keep him from moving with the stream in the present. He exists in a kind of living death, from which the only release possible for him is death itself.

Because of his error, he never succeeds in growing up. He consistently behaves like a selfish, irresponsible child, as he realizes when he runs away after having caused the death of his grandfather, old Bayard, by driving his car at reckless speed with old Bayard as passenger. Even then, he tries to repudiate the responsibility; "he saw the recent months of his life coldly in all their headlong and heedless wastefulness . . . culminating in that which he had been warned against and that any fool might have foreseen. Well, damn it, suppose it had: was he to blame? Had he insisted that his grandfather ride with him? Had he given the old fellow a bum heart? and then, coldly: *You were afraid to go home. You made a nigger sneak your horse out to you. You, who deliberately do things your judgment tells you may not be successful, even possible, are afraid to face the consequences of your own acts.* Then again something bitter and deep and sleepless in him blazed out in vindication and justification and accusation; what, he knew not, blazing out at what, Whom, he did not know: *You did it! You caused it all; you killed Johnny!*" (p. 311). His protest is really against life, which kills us all sooner or later. He goes on to evade his responsibilities to his wife and unborn child by staying away from home, and in the end evades all responsibility by testing an extremely unsafe airplane, with which he finally succeeds in killing himself.

Young Bayard is also haunted by memories of his proud, reckless, irresponsible Sartoris forebears. His great-grandfather, Colonel John, is referred to as "that arrogant shade which dominated the house and the life that went on there and the whole scene itself . . ." (p. 113). Colonel John was a brave but violent man, who ended his string of killings by letting himself be shot to death by a rival whom he had provoked. Another haunting shade is the Colonel's brother, "Carolina Bayard" Sartoris, who died, according to the story more and more elaborately told by Miss Jenny Du Pre, in a one-man raid on a Union army headquarters to get a can of anchovies. When Miss Jenny sits in the seldom used parlor, listening to piano music, "in all the corners of the room there waited, as actors stand within the wings beside the waiting stage, figures in crinoline and hooped muslin and silk; in stocks and flowing coats, in gray too, with crimson sashes and sabers in gallant, sheathed repose; Jeb Stuart himself, perhaps, on his glittering garlanded bay or with his sunny hair falling upon fine broadcloth beneath the mistletoe and holly boughs of Baltimore in '58" (pp. 60-61). Miss Jenny sometimes deflates all this with hard and even contemptuous common sense; but at certain moments, notably when she remembers dancing with Stuart in Baltimore, she falls as helplessly victim to the charms of the past as anyone else.

The ghost image is again invoked when old Bayard goes to the attic storeroom where the unused heirlooms are kept, in order to record in the family Bible the deaths of John and of young Bayard's first wife and infant son. The storeroom is "cluttered with indiscriminate furniture—chairs and sofas like patient ghosts holding lightly in dry and rigid embrace yet other ghosts—a fitting place for dead Sartorises to gather and speak among themselves of glamorous and old disastrous days. The unshaded light swung on a single cord from the center of the ceiling" (pp. 89-90). There is an ambivalence suggested by the incongruous juxtaposition of the glamorous ghosts and the bare electric light, which is emphasized when old Bayard takes up "a rosewood case containing two dueling pistols with silver mountings and the lean, deceptive delicacy of race-horses, and what old man Falls had called 'that 'ere dang der'nger.'" The derringer is the weapon with which Colonel John killed at least four men; it is "a stubby, evil-looking thing with its three barrels, viciously and coldly utilitarian, and between the other two weapons it lay like a cold and deadly insect between two flowers" (p. 91). This juxtaposition suggests that beautiful heroism and ugly violence are perhaps merely two ways of looking at the same thing. A few pages farther on, the ghost image is thoroughly degraded in a description of a back yard "desolate with ghosts; ghosts of discouraged weeds, of food in the shape of empty tins, broken boxes and barrels; a pile of stove wood and a chopping-block across which lay an ax whose helve had been mended with rusty wire amateurishly wound" (p. 107).

The formula which many critics have tried to apply to this material—that it represents a contrast between the heroic past and the ugly present—is partial and misleading. That contrast is a sentimental trap into which young Bayard seems to have fallen, preventing his participation in the life of the present, the only life there is. According to Miss Jenny's theory, which is tinged with the same sentiment, young Bayard, as a true Sartoris, has to die a violent death. The family tradition, which to some extent typifies the traditional myth of the South, requires it. But we may also say that young Bayard's character is his fate. However it may be with other Sartorises, he is doomed by his inability to change. The "ghosts" that surround him symbolize, as they reinforce, his obsession with the past, which is dead and which brings death to him.

Another static character, almost a co-protagonist with young Bayard, is Horace Benbow. In his fashion, he is also home from the war, but he has been a YMCA worker, not a combat flyer. Instead of young Bayard's blighting memories of violence and death, Horace brings home a glass-blowing outfit from Venice, with which he "had had four mishaps and produced one almost perfect vase of clear amber . . . which he kept always on his night table and called by his sister's name in the intervals of apostrophizing both of them impartially in his moments of rhapsody over the realization of the meaning of peace and the unblemished attainment of it, as 'Thou still unravished bride of quietness' " (p. 182). In contrast to the "glamorous and old disastrous days" of the ghostly Sartorises, the peace which Horace believes he has found consists in "Old unchanging days; unwinged perhaps, but undisastrous, too" (p. 175). He is on occasion "amused at his own fantastic impotence" (p. 198), and on other occasions tormented by his inability to take any active part in life. His passive stasis provides a counterpoint to the violent stasis of young Bayard.

The more fundamental contrast, however, is between the stasis which they both represent and the dynamic aspects of life, which are emphasized by a great deal of the imagery in the book. The natural setting is full of vegetable and animal life, trees, flowers, birds, frogs, and insects, furnishing a continual accompaniment of sound and movement, as in *Soldiers' Pay*. This matter is epitomized in a description of the Sartoris garden in spring, where the narrator tries to transcend the particulars and provide a glimpse of the same esthetic vision that the sculptor, Gordon, is trying for in *Mosquitoes*. "The fine and huge simplicity of the house rose among thickening trees, the garden lay in sunlight bright with bloom, myriad with scent and with a drowsy humming of bees—a steady golden sound, as of sunlight become audible—all the impalpable veil of the immediate, the familiar; just beyond it a girl with a bronze swirling of hair and a small, supple body in a constant epicene unrepose, a dynamic fixation like that of carven sexless figures caught in moments of action, striving, a mechanism all of whose members must move in performing the most trivial action, her wild hands not accusing but passionate still beyond the veil impalpable but sufficient" (pp. 55-56). This passage is not particularly clear, but it is intensely eloquent in its attempted evocation of the moment of artificially stopped motion and of timeless esthetic contemplation.

Sometimes young Bayard seems to be moving toward a harmony with the motion of life in the world. In the spring after his return from the war, he takes a fling at agriculture, "and came in at mealtimes and at night smelling of machine oil and of stables and of the earth, and went to bed with grateful muscles and with the sober rhythms of the earth in his body and so to sleep." But he still has nightmares in which he feels like "a trapped beast in the high blue, mad for life, trapped in the very cunning fabric that had betrayed him who had dared chance too much, and he thought again if, when the bullet found you, you could crash upward, burst; anything but earth" (p. 203). When planting time is over and farm work slacks off, his partial assimilation into the life of the earth collapses: "It was like coming dazed out of sleep, out of the warm, sunny valleys where people lived into a region where cold peaks of savage despair stood bleakly above the lost valleys, among black and savage stars" (p. 205).

A particularly emphatic image of life is provided by a horse, "a haughty, motionless shape of burnished flame" (p. 130), which young Bayard, against advice, insists on riding. " 'That hoss'll kill him,' " the owner protests. But young Bayard's countryman friend Rafe MacCallum says, " 'Let him be . . . . That's what he wants.' " The horse, which "soared like a bronze explosion" and "swirled in a myriad flickering like fire" (p. 132; "myriad" is another of Faulkner's key words connoting life), is held and mounted, "rippling its coat into quivering tongues before exploding again" (pp. 132-33). Then "The beast burst like bronze unfolding wings; the onlookers tumbled away from the gate and hurled themselves to safety as the gate splintered to matchwood beneath its soaring volcanic thunder." As young Bayard rides it down the street, "The stallion moved beneath him like a tremendous mad music, uncontrolled, splendidly uncontrollable" (p. 133). Young Bayard in fact cannot control it or stay with it. His short ride ends in a fall and a rather severe head injury—but not, for that time, in death.

Another figure generally representative of life is Horace

Benbow's sister Narcissa. In *Sartoris* she is one of Faulkner's earth-mother figures, who move so harmoniously with the moving stream of life that they seem not to move at all. Because of "that aura of grave and serene repose in which she dwelt" (p. 30; cf. pp. 31, 33, 162, 175, 178, 301, 358, 371), her static brother associates her with Keats's marble urn. But he is mistaken, as he has to realize when she falls in love with young Bayard, whom Horace calls "'that surly blackguard ...'" (p. 303). When young Bayard becomes aware of her feeling for him, his isolation is melted: "Far above him now the peak among the black and savage stars, and about him the valleys of tranquillity and of peace" (p. 254); but this effect is only temporary. Soon after their marriage they go hunting together and he is reminded of his brother John, whose death has destroyed a greater and more faun-like potential for life than his own, "and again he had left her for the lonely heights of his despair" (p. 288).

Narcissa, however, refuses to be defeated. When young Bayard leaves her and dies, their son is born. Miss Jenny assumes that this new Sartoris will be called John. Narcissa says, "'He isn't John. He's Benbow Sartoris.'" Miss Jenny doubts that adding Benbow to the name will help. As she listens to Narcissa playing the piano, "the dusk was peopled with ghosts of glamorous and old disastrous things. And if they were just glamorous enough, there was sure to be a Sartoris in them, and then they were sure to be disastrous." The author's voice suggests that "perhaps Sartoris is . . . a game outmoded and played with pawns shaped too late and to an old dead pattern, and of which the Player Himself is a little wearied. For there is death in the sound of it, and a glamorous fatality, like silver pennons downrushing at sunset, or a dying fall of horns along the road to Roncevaux." Narcissa declines to be overcome by any such fatality. In answer to Miss Jenny's repeated question, "'Do you think . . . that because his name is Benbow, he'll be any less a Sartoris and a scoundrel and a fool?'" she only "turned her head and . . . smiled at Miss Jenny quietly, a little dreamily, with serene, fond detachment" (p. 380). On which note the book concludes.

Many critics have taken the phrase "a dying fall of horns along the road to Roncevaux" as the conclusive note, and have decided that nostalgia for a glamorous past is largely the theme of *Sartoris*, and of Faulkner's fiction generally. But the full context of *Sartoris* makes it clear that blowing a horn when it is too late to do any good is vanity, no matter how glamorous the tardy musician may be. Narcissa has a healthier and stronger relation to life in her apparently static passivity than the Sartorises with all their violence of apparent motion, which too often comes to nothing but their own violent death.

In *Sartoris* Faulkner bit off a good deal more than he chewed, and the published result is a poorly organized book. As in *Soldiers' Pay*, the images tumble in a profusion that is bewildering for lack of clear patterns. As in *Mosquitoes*, the action is crowded with people whose relations are complex but not entirely functional. There seem to be too many—not only Sartorises and Benbows, but Snopeses, MacCallums, and Mitchells, aristocrats and lawyers, bankers and clerks, doctors, merchants, farmers, and laborers, whites, and Negroes. It is as if Faulkner, having found his Eldorado, had tried to load it all on one cart, not knowing that he would come back again and again, often with stronger vehicles. He had not yet learned to fashion vehicle and load together, using the matter of Yoknapatawpha in the manner he had been trying to develop in the early poems and sketches. In the composition of *Sartoris* the right materials were only too abundantly present; but the dramatic encounter between the dynamic flow of life in nature and Narcissa and the artificial statis of the traditional South in Horace and young Bayard was not sufficiently concentrated. Something more, in the way of structural lines that would contain, channel, and direct the force against the obstacle, was needed.

Two / Tools: Structure

Although *The Sound and the Fury* is the first of Faulkner's master works, I have chosen to delay systematic discussion of it until the last part of this book. The usual order, proceeding by dates of publication from *Sartoris* through *The Sound and the Fury* and *As I Lay Dying* to *Sanctuary*, is perhaps the most legitimate. But nearly all of *Sanctuary* was written before *As I Lay Dying*,[1] and *Sanctuary*, not *The Sound and the Fury*, is the sequel to *Sartoris*. From a genetic point of view, *The Sound and the Fury* seems outside the line of Faulkner's development, as if the apprentice had suddenly leaped ahead of himself, inspired by some extraordinary pressure of creative energy to produce a kind of work that he did not yet know how to do. It is in *Sanctuary* that we can most easily and clearly see how Faulkner acquired the mastery which *The Sound and the Fury* demonstrates but does not explain. *The Sound and the Fury* deserves to be treated not as a stepping-stone but as the summit of Faulkner's artistic career. I want to approach it by way of a large amount of Faulkner's other work, and to discuss it at length from several points of view, in the light of what he wrote afterward as well as before.

[1] See James B. Meriwether, *The Literary Career of William Faulkner: A Bibliographical Study* (Princeton: Princeton University Library, 1961), pp. 65-66.

Having created his fictional world in *Sartoris*, Faulkner was able in later novels to concentrate on techniques, or what he liked to call, in interviews, his "tools." The one most urgently in need of improvement, as we have seen, was the technique of building an adequate structure. An aspect of the seeming miracle in *The Sound and the Fury* is that it has none of the structural weakness or inadequacy of its predecessors. But the development of this technique is more easily seen in *Sanctuary*, partly because it is not so strong, and partly because the published version can be more cogently compared to an earlier galley version and to *Sartoris*.

A few critics have suggested that Faulkner, at some point in his early career, may have encountered T.S. Eliot's essay "Ulysses, Order and Myth," which was published in *The Dial* for November 1923.[2] It seems to me very probable that he read this essay, that he studied Joyce's *Ulysses*, and that he agreed with Eliot's recommendation: "In using the myth, in manipulating a continuous parallel between contemporaneity and antiquity, Mr Joyce is pursuing a method which others must pursue after him. . . . It is . . . a way of controlling, of ordering, of giving a shape and a significance to the immense panorama of futility and anarchy which is contemporary history . . . . Psychology . . . ethnology and The Golden Bough have concurred to make possible what was impossible even a few years ago. Instead of narrative method, we may now use the mythical method."[3] I think it is also likely that Faulkner understood Eliot's own use of "the mythical method" in *The Waste Land* (1922), Fitzgerald's application of it in *The Great Gatsby* (1925), and Hemingway's adoption of the same technique in *The Sun Also Rises* (1926).[4]

---

[2] Notably Waggoner, p. 35; and Lawrance Thompson, *William Faulkner: An Introduction and Interpretation* (New York: Barnes and Noble, 1963), pp. 21-22.

[3] T.S. Eliot, "Ulysses, Order and Myth," *The Dial*, LXXV (November 1923), 483.

[4] See John M. Howell, "The Waste Land Tradition in the American Novel,"

Faulkner was trying all through his apprenticeship to use the kind of mythic parallels that Eliot advocated, but he had not used them systematically enough. He might have discovered or invented a "mythical method" of his own, sooner or later. The fact is, however, that his successful use of it followed the examples of Eliot, Joyce, Fitzgerald, and Hemingway both chronologically and methodologically. Joyce had used the structure of the *Odyssey*; the others had borrowed mainly from the tradition of fertility myth and ritual as it was traced by Jessie L. Weston in *From Ritual to Romance* (1920) and Sir James Frazer in *The Golden Bough* (1911-13; one-volume edition 1922). It is characteristic of Faulkner that he was not as prompt as some of his more urban contemporaries in adopting these resources. It is equally characteristic that, once he did so, he went far beyond his models.

Carvel Collins pointed out long ago that Faulkner used the method, and has specified some of the mythical patterns that appear in *The Sound and the Fury, As I Lay Dying*, and later works.[5] Other scholars have added many observations, but much work remains to be done before we can feel that we have adequately surveyed the extent, the variety, or the complexity of Faulkner's use of myth.

Sanctuary

The pattern Collins explored most fully in his discussion of *As I Lay Dying* was that of the Demeter–Persephone–Kore myth, which Faulkner used in a number of other novels as well, and which is especially conspicuous in *Sanctuary*.

According to Frazer in *The Golden Bough*, Demeter and Persephone were essentially the same goddess, an annually

---

Ph.D. Diss., Tulane University, 1963; and my "Sunrise out of the Waste Land," *Tulane Studies in English*, IX (1959), 119-31.

[5] Carvel Collins, "The Interior Monologues of *The Sound and the Fury*," *English Institute Essays*, 1952 (New York: Columbia University Press, 1953), pp. 29-56; and "The Pairing of *The Sound and the Fury* and *As I Lay Dying*," *Princeton University Library Chronicle*, XVIII (Spring 1957), 115-23.

renewed spirit of the corn, originally represented by bound sheaves of the corn itself. "But," says Frazer, "unfortunately the Demeter and Persephone whom we know were the denizens of towns, the majestic inhabitants of lordly temples; it was for such divinities alone that the refined writers of antiquity had eyes; the uncouth rites performed by rustics amongst the corn were beneath their notice. Even if they noticed them, they probably never dreamed of any connexion between the puppet of corn-stalks on the sunny stubble-field and the marble divinity in the shady coolness of the temple."[6] Frazer's contrast is meant to be mildly shocking; Faulkner gives us one which is far more so. Temple Drake is a savagely humorous caricature of the classical Persephone, and she undergoes a horribly uncouth rite amongst the Mississippi corn before her abduction by Popeye, who, as a king of the Memphis, Tennessee underworld, is an equally savage caricature of the Greco-Roman Pluto. The urban corruption represented by these two is commented upon by the small-town respectability of the role Narcissa Benbow plays in *Sanctuary*. In the galley version she is said to have "that quality of stupid serenity upon her brow that statues have,"[7] and in the published version she is described as "living a life of serene vegetation like perpetual corn or wheat in a sheltered garden instead of a field ..." (p. 103). Lee Goodwin's common-law wife, Ruby Lamar, although she has experienced urban corruption, remains a kind of rural Demeter, who demolishes the marble statue image by calling Temple " 'putty-face!' " (p. 57). The associations with corn provide the most outrageously ironic humorous situations. Temple is bedded at the Old Frenchman place on a corn-shuck mattress; then she is taken by Ruby to

[6] James G. Frazer, *The Golden Bough* (New York: Macmillan, 1922), p. 421.

[7] Galley 14. I gratefully acknowledge my indebtedness to Linton Massey and to the Alderman Library of the University of Virginia for allowing me to use the galleys.

the crib where corn and cottonseed have been stored; and there Popeye makes his ingenious use of the corncob, which, if Temple is an embodiment of corn, would seem to be appropriately placed. Zeus was the father of Persephone; when Temple tries to pray the only formula she can think of is " 'My father's a judge . . .' " (p. 50).

As Robert M. Slabey has noticed, the Memphis whorehouse of Miss Reba Rivers, to which Temple is taken by Popeye, has many resemblances to Hades; but Slabey's comparison of Popeye to Hermes overlooks the more obvious parallel.[8] Popeye, like Pluto, is associated with death, with darkness, with the color black, with money, and especially with shadows. Horace Benbow, looking at Ruby's baby, thinks "of Popeye's black presence lying upon the house like the shadow of something no larger than a match falling monstrous and portentous upon something else otherwise familiar and everyday and twenty times its size; of the two of them—himself and the woman—in the kitchen . . . and Goodwin and Popeye somewhere in the outer darkness peaceful with insects and frogs yet filled too with Popeye's presence in black and nameless threat" (pp. 116-17). Miss Reba's house is described as a shadowy realm like the land of the Cimmerians where Ulysses, in the *Odyssey*, goes to meet the shades of the dead. Temple sees herself "in a dim mirror, a pellucid oblong of dusk set on end" which makes her appear "like a thin ghost, a pale shadow moving in the uttermost profundity of shadow" (p. 144).

Horace, as his name would perhaps suggest, is a refined classicist who cannot, when it comes to the point, give himself to the demands of genuine fertility. He is attracted to Ruby, and he tries to help her, and incidentally Goodwin, but he shrinks from her offer to pay him with her body. He lets Narcissa bind him with her demand for conventional respectability, and he worships his concept of her marble serenity, in

[8] Robert M. Slabey, "Faulkner's *Sanctuary*," *Explicator*, XXI (January 1963), item 45.

Sanctuary as in *Sartoris*, with more devotion than he can give to any aspect of life. His character is sympathetically presented, but his virtues will not bear examination. The corruption which horrifies and sickens him is more alive than he is. By temperament as well as by training, he is devoted to a static, abstract justice, and that is probably why the legal rites which he performs on Goodwin's behalf result in Goodwin's lynching.

At least two of the organizing patterns in *Sanctuary* are supplied by the Bible. The first and more important is the story of the Fall of Man, which is directly referred to when Temple looks at the stopped clock in her Memphis room. Its single hand points to "half-past-ten-oclock. The hour for dressing for a dance"; and Temple recalls a dormitory conversation in which "The worst one of all said boys thought all girls were ugly except when they were dressed. She said the Snake had been seeing Eve for several days and never noticed her until Adam made her put on a fig leaf" (p. 147). The other girls, cruelly demanding to know how she knows, force her to assert that she has had sexual intercourse, whereupon "the youngest one" runs to the bathroom to vomit (pp. 147-48).

This recollection is merely an ironic comment on Temple's status as a fallen woman; the story of the Fall of Man has a larger relevance to the experience of Horace. It comes out clearly in his relation to his stepdaughter, Little Belle, whose manifest lack of innocence as she approaches sexual maturity shocks and offends him. The whole book reaches its emotional climax when he returns to Jefferson after interviewing Temple in Memphis and looks at a photograph of Little Belle which he has brought with him from his home in Kinston. As he gazes, its "quality of sweet chiaroscuro" subtly changes. "Communicated to the cardboard by some quality of the light or perhaps by some infinitesimal movement of his hands, his own breathing, the face appeared to breathe in his palms in a shallow bath of highlight, beneath the slow, smokelike tongues of invisible honeysuckle. Almost palpable enough to be seen, the scent filled the room and the small face seemed to swoon in a voluptuous languor, blurring still more, fading, leaving upon his eye a soft and fading aftermath of invitation and voluptuous promise and secret affirmation like a scent itself" (pp. 215-16). His vicarious experience of Temple's rape repeats itself in his imagination, and he, like the youngest girl, runs to the bathroom and vomits. What most dismays him is not the violence done to Temple, or her suffering, but his realization during the interview "that she was recounting the experience with actual pride, a sort of naïve and impersonal vanity" (p. 209), and that she has deliberately, though not quite consciously, offered the temptation that provoked the violence done both to her and to the innocent Tommy, whose murder by Popeye has been preliminary to the rape.

The suggestion that Horace's "own breathing" makes the photograph seem "to breathe" indicates that the corruption he sees in Little Belle may come at least partly from himself, and that, since breathing is often equivalent to life in Faulkner's imagery, the corruption is a quality of life. The added association with the smell of flowers is parallel to an earlier impression "of the delicate and urgent mammalian whisper of that curious small flesh which he had not begot and in which appeared to be vatted delicately some seething sympathy with the blossoming grape" (p. 162). On this earlier occasion, the photograph presents "a face suddenly older in sin than he would ever be" (p. 163); and this impression is prophetic. Horace is unable to assimilate the Fall of Man; he cries out at one point, " 'Dammit, say what you want to, but there's a corruption about even looking upon evil, even by accident; you cannot haggle, traffic, with putrefaction—' " (p. 125). If this is true, and it seems to be true of Horace, then it must follow that nothing can be done to mitigate evil or to correct injustice; and this is also true of Horace. He is one of Faulkner's static characters, who identify life, and especially sexual potency and fertility, with evil and corruption. By refusing to fall, he refuses to live. His desperate feeling that it would be better for Temple, Popeye, Ruby, Goodwin, the Goodwin baby, and himself if they were all dead (pp. 213-14) is the only logical conclusion he can arrive at. In a fallen world, the attempt to avoid evil does not make a man more than human, but less; and anyway the attempt is sure to fail.

The Eden story operates in harmony with the Demeter myth to help shape the strategy of the book; and much of the imagery, as the quotations above have shown, works in both contexts and helps to relate them. The other Bible story, that of Christ, is not so effectively used in *Sanctuary*, and Faulkner does not seem to have been sure what he wanted to do with it. In the galleys, it is associated with Tommy, the feeble-minded victim, who is explicitly compared with Christ,[9] and with Horace, who looks at the nails he has awkwardly driven ten years before in closing his and Narcissa's house in Jefferson and says, " 'I crucified more than me, then . . . .' "[10] Both of these references were cut before publication, although an obscure possibility remains that Tommy may be thirty-three years old when he is murdered (p. 44). In both versions, the Goodwin baby lies "in the attitude of one crucified" (p. 131),[11] Temple is described in Horace's imagination with "her chin depressed like a figure lifted down from a crucifix" (p. 216),[12] and Popeye, when he is arrested and tried for a murder he has not committed, says, " 'For Christ's sake . . .' " (pp. 302, 304). In the published version, Goodwin's lynching, which is only hinted at in the galleys, is described in terms that make it obviously though not explicitly parallel to the Crucifixion (pp. 287-89); and the new material on the biographical background of Popeye specifies that he was born on Christmas day (p. 296). Taken singly or together, these references do not seem to contribute significantly to the struc-

[9] Galley 19.
[10] Galley 23.
[11] Cf. Galley 29.
[12] Cf. Galley 79.

ture of the book. Faulkner evidently had the Easter story naggingly in mind, but he failed to make it work in *Sanctuary* as it does in *The Sound and the Fury* and several of his other novels.

A remarkably perceptive article by Lawrence S. Kubie, published twenty years before Carvel Collins's essay on *The Sound and the Fury*, points out a Freudian pattern in *Sanctuary*. The theme, Kubie says, "represents the working out in fantasy of the problems of impotence in men, meaning by impotence a frailty in all spheres of instinctual striving." This theme is dramatized as a struggle between the Id, represented by the underworld figures, and the Superego, represented by the lynch mob (and perhaps more obviously, although Kubie does not specify them, by Narcissa, the respectable ladies who persecute Ruby, the District Attorney, and Temple's father and brothers). In this socio-psychological drama Horace is seen, from Kubie's Freudian point of view, as "the weak representative of the much-battered 'Ego,' that fragment of the personality which is so often ground to pieces in the battle."[13]

This pattern is an effective device in the novel because it tends to concentrate the action in terms of Horace's point of view. The dramatic conflict is primarily inside Horace. His Superego suppresses his Id, and his Ego suffers; the other characters and the social situations they create can be regarded as projections of the conflicting elements in his divided and self-destructive mind. His attempt to escape from his marriage takes him to the Old Frenchman place, and his attraction toward Ruby involves him in Temple's adventures there and in Memphis. When his efforts to eradicate injustice by legal methods expose him to the repressive force represented by Narcissa and the District Attorney, who successfully plot the conviction of Goodwin for Popeye's crime, the real repressive

[13] Lawrence S. Kubie, "William Faulkner's 'Sanctuary,' " *Saturday Review of Literature*, XI (Oct. 1934), 225, 224, *et passim*.

force is within Horace, as a passage from the galley version
rather clearly indicates. In that version, when he tries to call
Temple in Memphis and discovers that she has left for an un-
disclosed destination, instead of taking vigorous measures
against the betrayal thus indicated, he only feels relief. "Thank
God, Horace said, thank God. He realised now that it was too
late, that he could not have summoned her: realised again that
furious homogeneity of the middle classes when opposed to
the proletariat from which it [sic] so recently sprung and by
which it is so often threatened. Better that he should hang, he
thought, than to expose . . . than to expose . . . I cannot even
face the picture, he told himself."[14]

This passage does not appear in the published version, perhaps because Faulkner decided that the Marxist terminology
was too abstract. But it helps to explain why Horace lets Temple's perjured testimony, without contradiction or cross-exam-
ination, determine Goodwin's fiery death at the hands of the
lynchers. The fault lies not so much in the corruption of society
(the judge delivers a mild reprimand on the weakness of
Horace's defense) as in Horace's own corruption, which results from his inability to resolve his inner conflict so as to
assert his identity and his potency as a man.

The Freudian pattern harmonizes with the Demeter myth
and reinforces the meaning of the Fall of Man. It also has the
valuable effect, in focusing the story through Horace's point of
view, of tinting all its events with the color of his impotence
and consequent frustration. It is Horace's frantic feeling which
justifies the cosmic implications of the ancient myths, and
which accounts for the extravagance of the rhetoric, about
which critics have often complained. The rhetoric is an expression of Horace's intensity of inner conflict, rather than a
description of the way things objectively are. We may disap-
prove of the tone (we are certainly not meant to approve of
Horace), but the strategy can be at least partly justified by its

[14] Galley 93; ellipses Faulkner's.

results. Everything in the book is more or less distorted by Horace's views, feelings, and opinions in such a way that the whole story is shaped and fitted together by his awareness and given to us in the context of his experience, and of his being the kind of character he is.

Like Hemingway, Fitzgerald, and Eliot, Faulkner also used the Grail legend, as Jessie Weston had interpreted it. The praise which Hemingway's narrator in *Death in the Afternoon* (1932) gives to Faulkner evidently refers to *Sanctuary*. "My operatives tell me," he says, "that through the fine work of Mr. William Faulkner publishers now will publish anything rather than to try to get you to delete the better portions of your works, and I look forward to writing of those days of my youth which were spent in the finest whorehouses of the land amid the most brilliant society there found." The Old Lady who acts as foil inquires, "Has this Mr. Faulkner written well of these places?" The narrator assures her, "Splendidly, Madame. Mr. Faulkner writes admirably of them. He writes the best of them of any writer I have read for many years. . . . Madame, you can't go wrong on Faulkner. He's prolific too."[15] These remarks, although they provide an unfortunate example of Hemingway's characteristic bad manners in personal criticism, are nevertheless high praise, which may have been motivated in part by a realization that Faulkner had succeeded in joining the select club of modern American novelists—previously including only Fitzgerald and Hemingway himself—who had mastered the mythical method and used the Grail legend as a symbolic structural device by means of which to communicate a feeling of sterility in modern civilization.

The appeal of the Grail legend to Faulkner, as to other modern writers, may be partly due to Weston's description of it as

[15] Ernest Hemingway, *Death in the Afternoon* (New York: Scribner's, 1932), p. 173.

a fusion of many myths, deriving from the fertility rituals of Sumeria, Egypt, Phoenicia, Greece, Persia, and Rome, and assimilated to some of the most ascetic and mystical traditions of the Christian Church. Weston asserts that some early Christians "boldly identified the Deity of Vegetation, regarded as Life Principle, with the God of the Christian faith." In their view, she says, "Attis was but an earlier manifestation of the Logos, Whom they held identical with Christ."[16] A more specific relevance of the legend to Faulkner's purposes in *Sanctuary* is suggested by a passage in *From Ritual to Romance* where Isidorus, an Alexandrian Neo-Platonist of the fifth century A.D., is quoted to the effect that in one of his dreams " 'Attis seemed to appear to me, and on behalf of the Mother of gods to initiate me into the feast called Hilario, a mystery which discloses the way of our salvation from Hades.' "[17] Weston's thesis is that the Grail legend is a progressively Christianized (and thereby corrupted) handling of this mixed material.

From Horace's point of view, as I have partly suggested in reference to the Persephone myth, the Eden story, and Kubie's Freudian parallels, the problem in *Sanctuary* is precisely that of discovering a way of "salvation from Hades," or from the waste land of the modern world as Horace's impotence defines it. If we regard Horace as being in some ways a seeker of the Grail, the quest is his effort to free himself from the waste land aspect of things by establishing his own fertility, or manly strength and creativity, and the fertility of the world as he is able to conceive it and present it to us.

His failure is emphasized by the even more obviously disgraceful behavior of Gowan Stevens, whose first name sounds a little like that of Sir Gawain. In the oldest versions of the Grail story cited by Weston, Gawain is the successful knight;

[16] Jessie L. Weston, *From Ritual to Romance* (Cambridge: Cambridge University Press, 1920), p. 192.
[17] *Ibid.*, p. 147.

68

but in later, more Christianized accounts (notably those of Malory and Tennyson), Perceval and then Galahad take over the principal role, and Gawain fails. Like Perceval in Wolfram von Eschenbach's version of the story, both Horace and Gowan fail to ask the right question; unlike Perceval, they get no second chance. When Gowan comes to the Old Frenchman place, he gets drunk and betrays all his responsibilities. Horace spends most of his time there talking about himself. Neither inquires what is wrong with Popeye (or the blind and deaf old man who seems to be Goodwin's father), or why the land is not productive. Ruby Lamar plays the role of a grail maiden (with some violent ironies from her past as a prostitute) by serving food (but not drink, since she regards whiskey as a kind of poison) and by finding the seekers deficient. " 'The fool,' " she says of Horace; " 'The poor, scared fool . . . .' " Horace freely acknowledges his weakness. " 'You see,' he said, 'I lack courage: that was left out of me. The machinery is all here, but it wont run' " (p. 16).

Horace's experience focuses all of the mythic parallels we have noted on the theme of sterility. In reference to the Grail legend, Horace is the cowardly knight who fails either to rescue the maiden in distress or to restore fertility to the Waste Land and its people. In the context of the Persephone myth, he fails to be initiated into the mysteries of fertility or to restore the goddess to the upper world. From the point of view of the Eden story, he refuses to acknowledge the Fall of Man, and therefore he is denied the salvation offered by the Passion of Christ. Each of the external patterns, including that of the Freudian psychodrama, implies the possibility of a rebirth, or a regeneration of physical and spiritual health and potency. But Horace, in whatever terms the test is presented to him, fails.

The many patterns of *Sanctuary* converge on the crisis which serves as Faulkner's artificial means of stopping the motion of life. When Temple, apparently recaptured from Popeye by her father and brothers, falsely testifies that Goodwin is guilty of raping her and murdering Tommy, Horace's effort to save Goodwin, serve Ruby, and restore their son to healthy life collapses. The repressive forces of respectable society, led by Narcissa, have been too much for his feeble power to overcome. Therefore the power of life, represented by the natural setting (which is by no means waste), by Ruby, by Temple (who is as potent as she is perverse), by Temple's lover Red, and by a gaggle of minor characters, mostly comic, is frustrated, and the book ends with the tableau of Temple sitting in the Luxembourg Gardens, gazing "across the pool and the opposite semicircle of trees where at sombre intervals the dead tranquil queens in stained marble mused, and on into the sky lying prone and vanquished in the embrace of the season of rain and death" (p. 309).

Sanctuary is not one of Faulkner's very best novels. The galley version is badly organized and seriously inconsistent in style and tone. The published version, although it is more cogently arranged, and although Faulkner managed, by judicious cutting, to eliminate some of the unevenness, is still not all that it might have been. It is reasonable to say, as Faulkner does in his introduction to the Modern Library edition of 1932, that in revising he "made a fair job";[18] certainly it is a better job than *Sartoris*; but it is not up to the level of quality that Faulkner had set in *The Sound and the Fury* and reached, or nearly reached, again in *As I Lay Dying*.

Sanctuary nevertheless remains an impressively powerful book. The crucial confrontation between the force of life and the static weakness of Horace Benbow as its pathetically inadequate would-be champion raises a compelling tension, which is emphasized by the extremities of the violence in which he is involved. His point of view provides a maximum of revulsion from the horrors of life, a maximum of outrage at the

[18] William Faulkner, *Sanctuary* (New York: Random House, 1932), p. viii.

injustices of life, and a maximum of amusement at the hilarious incongruities of life—although Horace, who is the butt of the whole grisly joke, is not the one to laugh.

As I Lay Dying

Structurally, *As I Lay Dying* seems more linear than most of Faulkner's other good books; but this appearance is deceptive. The chronology of events is interrupted by four substantial flashbacks, in which we learn of Dewey Dell's seduction by Lafe, of Jewel's successful effort to earn his horse, of Cora Tull's discussion with Addie about sin and about Addie's prophecy that Jewel will save her " 'from the water and from the fire' " (p. 160), and of Addie's recollection and analysis of her life. One section is chronologically displaced, so that we are given Whitfield's account of his good resolution, and subsequent failure, to confess his sin with Addie at a point in the story several days after the failure has occurred. There is also a continual overlapping or partial recapitulation of one section by another, or several others, particularly at the end of the book, as if the supposedly single stream of time were shown to be more like a many-stranded rope or braid of interweaving motion. This effect is reinforced by Darl's narration of several scenes and events as they happen, but at a time when he is somewhere else, out of sight and hearing. The cumulative result is a pervasive and fascinating sense, for the reader, of temporal and epistemological disorientation, which is further stimulated by Faulkner's frequent use of language that the characters in whose interior monologues it appears would be unlikely to articulate. These technical elaborations build a complexity of vision which contributes a good deal to the vibrancy of the story.

The same complexity of vision may tend to obscure the fact that *As I Lay Dying*, like *The Sound and the Fury* and *Sanctuary*, makes use of several externally provided structural patterns, or myths. One effect of these is to place the fictional

71

chronology of events in contrapuntal juxtaposition with a context of time so long past, or so generally conceived, as to seem universal, and therefore nonchronological, or static. Both the continual disturbance of chronology and the contrast of the smaller and the larger conceptions of time serve Faulkner's purpose of artificially stopping the motion of life. The stoppage and consequently the motion are rendered in *As I Lay Dying* with brilliant intensity.

Perhaps the most conspicuous of the external parallels, and the one Faulkner may have had most clearly in mind, is that of the traditional epic journey, which many critics have noted and which nearly all readers must feel. Faulkner remarked in the *Paris Review* interview, "I simply imagined a group of people and subjected them to the simple universal natural catastrophes, which are flood and fire, with a simple natural motive to give direction to their progress."[19] These epic associations are not really as simple as they may have felt to Faulkner. They involve considerable symbolic reference to all four of the classic elements, earth and air as well as fire and water, and they lend a cosmic dimension to many intrinsically trivial details about the Bundren family and their adventure.[20] The journey becomes, as symbolic journeys tend to do, a parable of creation, the motion of travel implying a process in which the separately inert materials or elements of the world combine into living forms.

When the epic journey involves a visit to some kind of underworld, as it often does, it is closely related to the Demeter–Persephone–Kore myth, which, as Carvel Collins has shown, works as an externally provided structural device in *As I Lay Dying*.[21] This association lends meaning and importance to the death of Addie, to Dewey Dell's pregnancy, and to Cora

[19] *Writers at Work*, p. 129.
[20] This point is well discussed in Millgate, pp. 109-10.
[21] Collins, "The Pairing . . . ," pp. 119-23.

Tull's obsessive concern about salvation and resurrection. Faulkner, however, in harmony with Frazer's opinion that the three Greek goddesses all represent essentially the same thing —the fertility of corn and pigs and the earth—makes no particular effort to associate Addie exclusively with Demeter, Dewey Dell with Persephone, or Cora (except in name) with Kore. The most emphatic image of fertility in this context is Dewey Dell's silent cry, "I feel like a wet seed wild in the hot blind earth" (p. 61), which aptly describes the ritual significance of Persephone's sojourn with Pluto as Frazer interprets it. All three women are variously associated with images suggesting fertility myth and ritual: with corn and the color yellow (the color of sunshine and also of sulphur, which is used in several images suggesting hell), with animals, especially cows, and with milk and eggs.

Faulkner twists, distorts, or reverses the values of these images whenever it suits his purpose to do so; and his celebration of fertility is often conducted in a sharply ironic spirit. Addie's attitude toward her own fertility and its results in the Bundren children seems more negative than positive. Dewey Dell's fertility is completely involuntary, at least so far as she is consciously aware. And Cora's relation to fertility, like that of Narcissa Benbow in *Sanctuary*, is so involved with the respectabilities of Southern Protestantism that it appears hypocritical and false. Although her husband, Vernon Tull, compares her to "a jar of milk in the spring" and says "you would rather have milk that will sour than to have milk that wont, because you are a man" (p. 132), she is generally presented in terms that recall the wife in Melville's "I and My Chimney." According to Addie, "Cora . . . could never even cook" (p. 166), and Cora's cakes, made with eggs that she has saved only with difficulty from the depredations of possums and snakes, are jettisoned in favor of a Sunday dress which Dewey Dell hopes will help her obtain an abortion in town.

Faulkner uses the Persephone myth, along with associated

fertility imagery, to shape his story so that the energy of actual and potential motion, or life, which the mythological and ritual images evoke, will be opposed by other images and by a variety of circumstances representing static principles that resist or artificially stop the motion. This effect is achieved with special vividness in descriptions of the flooded river. Vernon Tull sees the partly washed-out bridge, in terms that suggest the journey to the underworld, "going down into the moiling water like it went clean through to the other side of the earth, and the other end coming up outen the water like it wasn't the same bridge a-tall and that them that would walk up outen the water on that side must come from the bottom of the earth" (pp. 130-31).[22] This impression is confirmed when Vernon, having crossed, feels "Like it couldn't be me here, because I'd have had better sense than to done what I just done . . . . I knew it couldn't be, because I just couldn't think of anything that could make me cross that bridge ever even once" (pp. 131, 132).

Darl's impression of the same scene is more complex and contradictory than Vernon's. Looking at those on the other side, he says, "The river itself is not a hundred yards across, and pa and Vernon and Vardaman and Dewey Dell are the only things in sight not of that single monotony of desolation leaning with that terrific quality a little from right to left, as though we had reached the place where the motion of the wasted world accelerates just before the final precipice. Yet they appear dwarfed. It is as though the space between us were time: an irrevocable quality. It is as though time, no longer running straight before us in a diminishing line, now runs parallel between us like a looping string, the distance being the doubling accretion of the thread and not the interval between" (p. 139). The river symbolizes for both observers a

[22] For other citations of this image, see Collins, "The Pairing . . . ," p. 120, and Barbara M. Cross, "Apocalypse and Comedy in *As I Lay Dying*," *Texas Studies in Literature and Language*, III (Summer 1961), 256.

profound transformational experience, a rebirth involving a change of identity and a shifting of all individual relations to the world and time. When Darl has crossed, he too confirms his impression and closes the circle of association with the Persephone myth by saying that the river now "looks peaceful . . . . As though the clotting which is you had dissolved into the myriad original motion, and seeing and hearing in themselves blind and deaf; fury in itself quiet with stagnation. Squatting, Dewey Dell's wet dress shapes for the dead eyes of three blind men those mammalian ludicrosities which are the horizons and the valleys of the earth" (p. 156).

The motion of life is vividly represented by the river; but the men, instead of dissolving into it, as they might in death, or moving with it, as they should in life, resist it. They cross it and carry the corpse across. To them, the motion of fertility embodied by the pregnant girl, if they see it at all, seems ludicrous. The myth of fertility, in its encounter with the static character of the men, especially Darl, defines an almost perfect impasse. The lyric exuberance of the rhetoric perhaps reflects Faulkner's satisfaction at having accomplished the artist's aim so fully and so well.

The Christ story is used more confidently and successfully in *As I Lay Dying* than in *Sanctuary*. Some of the references are ironic, as when Whitfield approaches what he calls "the scene of my Gethsemane" (p. 170), but hypocritically evades crucifixion. Another equivocal instance is Jewel, the violent one, who betrays his brother and loves his horse with curses, but of whom his mother says, " 'He is my cross and he will be my salvation' " (p. 160). He confirms her prophecy by his efforts at the river, by letting Anse trade his horse in part payment for a team of mules to pull the wagon, and by manhandling the coffin out of Gillespie's burning barn, on which occasion, like Christ in a Byzantine mosaic, he "appears to be enclosed in a thin nimbus of fire" (p. 212). The dubious character of this salvation is in harmony with the fact that Jewel is not the son of his mother's husband but of the hypocritical man of God, Whitfield, and the fact that his mother has conceived him in a kind of religious, or rather sacrilegious, fervor. Addie says, "I believed that the reason was the duty to the alive, to the terrible blood, the red bitter flood boiling through the land. I would think of sin as I would think of the clothes we both wore in the world's face . . . the sin the more utter and terrible since he was the instrument ordained by God who created the sin, to sanctify that sin He had created. While I waited for him in the woods . . . . I would think of him as thinking of me as dressed also in sin, he the more beautiful since the garment which he had exchanged for sin was sanctified. I would think of the sin as garments which we would remove in order to shape and coerce the terrible blood to the forlorn echo of the dead word high in the air" (pp. 166-67). In this mixed logic, the Christian references encounter pagan fertility rituals in images appropriate to Addie's role as a Demeter figure: the land, the woods, and the flood. The pagan images seem stronger, but they do not entirely prevail; in the end of the story it is the "word" exacted from Anse by Addie, his promise to bury her in Jefferson, that controls events.

A less equivocal set of parallels has to do with Vardaman, the youngest member of the family. It is with him in mind that Vernon Tull quotes Christ's injunction "Suffer little children to come unto Me" (p. 70), and later Vardaman sleeps in a manger (p. 111). His association with fish and fishing also has Christian implications, as well as a possible reference to the Grail legend. A more significant parallel is present in Tull's account of the crucial river crossing. "It was that boy," Tull decides. "I be durn if it wasn't like he come back and got me; like he was saying They wont nothing hurt you. Like he was saying about a fine place he knowed where Christmas come twice with Thanksgiving and lasts on through the winter and the spring and the summer, and if I just stayed with him I'd be all right too" (p. 132). The implicit reference to Christ walking on the water and supporting St. Peter is somewhat ironic here, because the reason Vardaman wants to get across the river and on to Jefferson is that he remembers seeing a toy train at Christmas time, and he wants to see it again. Another irony is suggested by the explicit reference made by Darl in his description of the log which overturns the wagon and tips the coffin into the flood: "*It surged up out of the water and stood for an instant upright upon that surging and heaving desolation like Christ.*"

The fact that Darl also describes the same log as being bearded with foam like "an old man or a goat" (p. 141) may be a hint that Pan is also involved in this scene. The river crossing is, at any rate, an effective climax, partly because of the way it brings together images referring to the Christian tradition, to the Persephone myth, and to the theme of the epic journey. These references evoke mythic patterns which work together, mutually bracing one another in the structure of the book.

The psychological pattern of *As I Lay Dying* is as important as that of *Sanctuary*, and more complex. It is presented, with sharp variations, from the different points of view of the Bundren children, and it is seen in very different lights by the parents and by people outside the family. The great static obstacle in the book is the death of Addie, the mother. Each of the children whose lives originate in her feels threatened or cut off by her death. Each of them has to face the fact of death as a stop to life, and try to find some way to live in spite of it. For each of them the story is a kind of elegy, more or less pastoral. The typical pattern of pastoral elegy is a sequence in which the singer announces a death, mourns the dead person, despairs for himself and humanity, finds or invents some formula of reconciliation with the fact of death, and ends on a note of comfort or even rejoicing. Each of the Bundrens handles this pattern in his own peculiar way, and some with more emotional success than others, but all are involved in it, and their differences are significant in relation to it.

Cash, the oldest and most fully formed, relying on his craft as a carpenter (he, like Jewel and Vardaman, resembles Christ in some ways), maintains his identity in the face of change, rather than changing or renewing himself. By his meticulous care in building the coffin and preserving his tools during the journey, he keeps his sanity and his life.

Darl, who has no professional discipline, confronts the problems of death and identity and relationship and life without defense, partly because he is the most sensitive of them all to his own identity and the identities of other people and things. His analysis is more subtle than any other, drawn out as it is by his inability to arrive at any satisfactory solution. In his soliloquy during the night of Addie's death, he reasons mainly in terms of time, by playing, like Quentin in *The Sound and the Fury*, on the tenses of the verb *to be*: "In a strange room you must empty yourself for sleep. And before you are emptied for sleep, what are you. And when you are emptied for sleep, you are not. And when you are filled with sleep, you never were. I dont know what I am. I dont know if I am or not. Jewel knows he is, because he does not know that he does not know whether he is or not. He cannot empty himself for sleep because he is not what he is and he is what he is not. Beyond the unlamped wall I can hear the rain shaping the wagon that is ours, the load that is no longer theirs that felled and sawed it nor yet theirs that bought it and which is not ours either, lie on our wagon though it does, since only the wind and the rain shape it only to Jewel and me, that are not asleep. And since sleep is is-not and rain and wind are *was*, it is not. Yet the wagon *is*, because when the wagon is *was*, Addie Bundren will not be. And Jewel *is*, so Addie Bundren must be. And then I must be, or I could not empty myself for sleep in a strange room. And so if I am not emptied yet, I am *is*" (p. 76).

This elaborate logic is not convincing, least of all to Darl, who in the end loses hold of his identity. Describing the outset of his trip to the insane asylum at Jackson, he speaks of himself in the third person, and to himself in the second: "Darl has gone to Jackson. They put him on the train, laughing . . . . 'What are you laughing at?' I said" (p. 243). Darl is the most sympathetically presented character in the book, and the best observer. But he is also the most incorrigibly static. For him there is no reconciliation with the fact of death, and no rebirth. As Cash, with more than his usual shrewdness, remarks, "This world is not his world; this life his life" (p. 250).

Discussing the problem with Vardaman, Darl tries to define the children in terms of their different relations to Addie. He says that he himself has no mother, and therefore no identity. " 'But you *are*, Darl,' " Vardaman says; and Darl replies, " 'I know it . . . . That's why I am not *is*. *Are* is too many for one woman to foal.' " Jewel's identity, as Darl has already noted in his soliloquy, is not in question. Darl defines it by telling Vardaman that " 'Jewel's mother is a horse . . .' " (p. 95). By earning his horse without letting Addie know what he is doing, by transferring his love for her to the horse, and then by sacrificing the horse so that she can be buried in Jefferson, apart from all Bundrens, Jewel asserts and confirms, in a harshly isolated independence, his own bastard identity. The logic of this is not made explicitly clear, but Jewel is not a logical creature, and he survives.

Dewey Dell is saved, ironically, because she is in too much trouble over her pregnancy to worry about anything else. She is aware of the problem of death, but she cannot focus on it. "I heard that my mother is dead," she says to herself. "I wish I had time to let her die. I wish I had time to wish I had. It is because in the wild and outraged earth too soon too soon too soon. It's not that I wouldn't and will not it's that it is too soon too soon too soon. . . . *That's what they mean by the womb of time: the agony and the despair of spreading bones, the hard girdle in which lie the outraged entrails of events"* (pp. 114-15). The life she carries is carrying her too rapidly, in spite of her frantic desire to stop it with an abortion, for the static obstacle of death to stop her.

Vardaman, the youngest and most Christlike of the Bundrens, is the most heroic in facing the problem of death and the most successful in dealing with it. Like Darl, he confronts it directly, without any ready-made defense. Unlike Darl, he is sane, and he preserves and strengthens his sanity. As Faulkner explained in a Virginia interview, "He was a child trying to cope with this adult's world which to him was, and to any sane person, completely mad. That these people would want to drag that body over the country and go to all that trouble, and he was baffled and puzzled. He didn't know what to do about it."[23] He is too young to have acquired any of the comforting abstract formulas that grown people fall back on when irrational facts are too harsh to face. Groping among the recent events of his concrete experience, he creates a formula which is not conventionally logical but which is psychologically sound enough to save him.

His initial responses to the knowledge of Addie's death, although they are not adequate, are energetic and mostly positive. His first move is an appeal to Jewel's symbol of their mother's life, the horse. Rushing from the death bed to the barn and into the horse's stall, he says, "Then I can breathe again, in the warm smelling. . . . The life in him runs under the skin, under my hand, running through the splotches, smelling up into my nose where the sickness is beginning to cry, vomiting the crying, and then I can breathe, vomiting it. . . . I can smell the life running up from under my hands, up my arms, and then I can leave the stall" (p. 53). Next he

[23] *Faulkner in the University*, ed. F. L. Gwynn and J. L. Blotner (Charlottesville: The University Press of Virginia, 1959), p. 111.

takes revenge on Dr. Peabody, whom he blames for Addie's death, by chasing Peabody's horses off down the road. Returning to the barn, after sundown, he finds himself in danger of losing Jewel's horse in the darkness. "It is as though the dark were resolving him out of his integrity, into an unrelated scattering of components . . . . I see him dissolve—legs, a rolling eye, a gaudy splotching like cold flames—and float upon the dark in fading solution; all one yet neither; all either yet none." By an effort of what Coleridge called "secondary imagination," and by using senses other than sight, Vardaman recovers his "illusion of a co-ordinated whole of splotched hide and strong bones within which, detached and secret and familiar, an *is* different from my *is*. . . . I can see hearing coil toward him, caressing, shaping his hard shape—fetlock, hip, shoulder and head; smell and sound. I am not afraid" (p. 55).

Remembering his experience of being "shut up in the crib the new door it was too heavy for me it went shut I couldn't breathe because the rat was breathing up all the air" (p. 62), Vardaman defines death as inability to breathe, and he is horrified when he learns that Cash is going to nail the coffin up with Addie in it. He tries to persuade himself that "It was not her. . . . She went away when the other one laid down in her bed and drew the quilt up. . . . And so if Cash nails the box up . . . it is not her" (p. 63). But this is not convincing, and his efforts to help Addie breathe by opening the windows of her room and boring holes in the coffin lid are even less satisfactory. A further step in the process of nonlogical reasoning is needed. He remembers the fish he has caught earlier in the day, and he has an intuition of the temporal problem with which Darl unsuccessfully wrestles. "It was not her," he tells himself, "because it was laying right yonder in the dirt. And now it's all chopped up. I chopped it up. It's laying in the kitchen in the bleeding pan, waiting to be cooked and et. Then it wasn't and she was, and now it is and she wasn't. And tomorrow it will be cooked and et and she will be him [Peabody] and pa and Cash and Dewey Dell and there wont be anything in the box and so she can breathe" (pp. 63-64).

The formula at which he finally arrives is "My mother is a fish" (p. 79); and the importance of this statement is indicated by the fact that it is given a section of the book (the shortest and most emphatic section) to itself. It means everything that is meant by the parallel statement " 'Jewel's mother is a horse' " and a great deal more. Besides suggesting the Christ story and the Grail legend—which Vardaman partly reenacts by fishing (unsuccessfully) in the slough (p. 87)—it plainly refers to the old fertility ritual, reflected in the Grail legend according to Weston and refined in the Christian sacrament of communion, of transmuting the life of a dead totem animal or person into the lives of those who eat the flesh or drink the blood. Vardaman says in effect that, if Addie, in the form of the fish, can be assimilated into the other members of the family (and Peabody), she will be able to breathe, or live. Throughout the rest of the story, in spite of uncertainties and occasional inconsistencies, he clings to this belief and to the assurance it gives him: *"My mother does not smell like that. My mother is a fish"* (p. 187).

The structural patterns of *As I Lay Dying* converge, as do those of *Sanctuary*, to suggest the symbolic process of death and rebirth. The experience of the whole Bundren family is in this sense one, but the pattern is different for each individual member, and the book is extremely complex. It is also in many ways equivocal. The various myths to some extent retain their separate identities; they do not entirely coalesce. The same is true of the various points of view. No single pattern or point of view dominates or governs the whole. Each one contributes something to the energy of motion in the book, and this energy is embodied in much of the imagery. The image of the epic journey, which is perhaps the largest single image in the book, is particularly dynamic. This powerful tendency to motion is systematically opposed by static elements in each of the characters, and by the fact that the journey is a funeral. Darl, although he is presented with entire sympathy, is especially static, and his breakdown serves most effectively as an artificial device for stopping the motion.

As I Lay Dying is unlike *Sanctuary*, however, in that the motion of life is not entirely suppressed, as it seems to be in Horace's final situation (or Popeye's or Temple's). Although Addie is dead and Darl is insane, the rest of the Bundrens are conspicuously alive and still in motion when we see them last. The feeling we are left with after reading *As I Lay Dying* is a ruefully humorous conviction that no matter what happens life goes on.

The character of Anse Bundren, the father, is perhaps more important in the making of this impression than most critics have recognized.[24] Anse is absurd and often ridiculous. He is usually described in static terms. He seems to have evaded the curse of Adam, which is the doom of life, in that he never sweats. And yet it is Anse who decrees the journey (paradoxically by maintaining his "word" to Addie), drives the wagon (except at the river crossing), and overcomes some of the more difficult obstacles on the way—not always, to be sure, by strictly honorable means. He appears to have a kind of magic power over others. As Armstid remarks, "be durn if there aint something about a durn fellow like Anse that seems to make a man have to help him . . . . I be durn if Anse dont conjure a man, some way" (pp. 183, 184). His neighbors suggest, only half jokingly, that even God is trapped. " 'He's took care of Anse a long time now,' " says Quick. Armstid agrees; " 'Too long to quit now' "; and Uncle Billy Varner concludes, " 'He's done it so long now He cant quit' " (p. 84). Darl, whose clair-

---

[24] Robert W. Kirk, however, in "Faulkner's Anse Bundren," *Georgia Review*, XIX (Winter 1965), 446, maintains that "Anse is . . . the central figure in *As I Lay Dying* . . . ."

voyance gives his judgments a special authority, describes Anse's "humped silhouette partaking of that owl-like quality of awry-feathered, disgruntled outrage within which lurks a wisdom too profound or too inert for even thought" (p. 48). In the end it is Anse, looking "a foot taller" with his new teeth and his new wife, and even with a "graphophone" such as Cash has been longing for, who is most evidently renewed (p. 249). His rejuvenation, absurd though it is, provides a focus for the experience of the family as a whole.

Light in August

Critics have had a great deal of trouble in efforts to demonstrate any general unity in *Light in August*, and have sometimes concluded that it is an inferior book. The great majority, however, feel that, unity or no unity, it is one of Faulkner's greatest works. Evidently there is something in it that has not been adequately explained.

The problem presents itself most obviously in the fact that the stories of Lena Grove, Joe Christmas, and Gail Hightower are not connected logically in such fashion as to account for the degree of unity critics generally expect to find in a great work of art. Attempts to discover thematic and symbolic links among the three stories have met with only partial and unconvincing success. The harder such attempts are pressed, the more they tend to demonstrate that the stories are not meant to be linked in quite that way. A formula is needed that will account for the quality of the novel without compromising the separate identities of the stories within it.

A useful suggestion was made when James W. Linn and Houghton W. Taylor, only three years after the book was published, called it a "counterpoint of stories,"[25] which is what Faulkner later called *The Wild Palms*.[26] Linn and Taylor sug-

[25] J. W. Linn and H. W. Taylor, *A Foreword to Fiction* (New York: Appleton-Century, 1935), p. 157.

[26] *Writers at Work*, p. 133; *Faulkner at Nagano*, pp. 79-80; *Faulkner in the University*, p. 171.

gested that an author might compose a novel by placing two or more separate stories in juxtaposition, without close logical connections, and that the novel could be unified by unstated comparisons, involving differences as much as likenesses. This suggestion has not been developed very much in recent criticism of *Light in August*, perhaps because neither Linn and Taylor nor anyone else has succeeded in finding a common denominator in terms of which the structures of the constituent stories could be shown to cooperate in establishing a solid structure of the whole.

The materials for such a demonstration have, however, been made available. Many critics have noticed that Lena's story has parallels with fertility myths and that Christmas's is based (often in ironically reversed terms, to be sure) on the Christ story, and one critic, Beach Langston, has contended that Hightower's story is significantly related to the story of Buddha.[27] If these parallels are valid, and if Faulkner was using the mythical method, in conjunction with a contrapuntal technique, we may find the common denominator we need in the juxtaposition of the three religious stories, each of which carries its own distinct system of ritual symbolism, and each of which may contribute its archetypal structure to help organize the story Faulkner wanted to tell.

In an interview at Virginia, Faulkner said his conception of *Light in August* "began with Lena Grove, the idea of the young girl with nothing, pregnant, determined to find her sweetheart. . . . As I told that story I had to get more and more into it, but that was mainly the story of Lena Grove."[28] Later, in answer to a question about the meaning of the title, Faulkner explicitly associated the book, and particularly Lena, with Greek mythology, saying that "in August in Mississippi there's

[27] Beach Langston, "The Meaning of Lena Grove and Gail Hightower in *Light in August*," *Boston University Studies in English*, V (Spring 1961), 51-63.

[28] *Faulkner in the University*, p. 74.

a few days somewhere about the middle of the month when suddenly there's a foretaste of fall, it's cool, there's a lambence, a luminous quality to the light, as though it came not from just today but from back in the old classic times. It might have fauns and satyrs and the gods and—from Greece, from Olympus in it somewhere. . . . it reminded me of that time, of a luminosity older than our Christian civilization. Maybe the connection was with Lena Grove, who had something of that pagan quality of being able to assume everything, that's—the desire for that child . . . ."[29] The imagery used and the intention suggested here are strikingly similar to what Faulkner had been trying for in some of his earliest work, notably "Twilight" and "The Hill," where the quality of light at sunset is associated with the dancing of nymphs and fauns. Lena's story is roughly analogous to the typical myth of the fertility goddess—Cybele, Aphrodite, Demeter–Persephone—, and it seems to have particular affinities with the account of the Arician Diana given by Frazer in the opening pages of *The Golden Bough*.[30]

Faulkner seems, however, to have deliberately avoided giving too firm a structure to Lena's story. She serves as a representative of pure motion, tranquilly natural, comfortable, and inevitable, completely in harmony with the motion of life in the earth. She is never stopped or frustrated, and so her story has no dramatic conflict out of which a structural system of relations could be developed. She is so defined that she cannot serve by herself to effect the artificial stopping of motion at which Faulkner always aimed. Therefore Faulkner had to bring in at least one other story in order to provide the fric-

[29] *Ibid.*, p. 199.

[30] This similarity is convincingly demonstrated by Millgate, p. 136. Millgate seems excessively cautious in thinking that "These suggested correspondences . . . may be entirely accidental"; I prefer his alternative hypothesis that "such correspondences, like those linking characters in the book with the members of the Holy Family, may represent only one among several patterns of analogy which Faulkner pursued in the course of the novel . . . ."

tions, blockages, and tensions needed for the accomplishment of his artistic purpose.

Joe Christmas is the most direct foil and the most obvious antithesis to Lena. He experiences and represents frustration, denial of life, and failure to change or develop or, in any meaningful sense, to move. His situation, conceived in terms of continual conflict, within himself and between him and others, is rich in drama, and Faulkner exploits it richly. It occupies so much of the foreground of the book that most critics have taken Christmas to be the protagonist. Faulkner, however, according to the statement quoted above, regarded Christmas as only a means to an end. His function in the story is to stand over against Lena as a static contrast in relation to which her motion can be seen and her power of life appreciated.

This function defines his role as a Christ figure in a rather special way. He does not represent the Christ of the New Testament, but rather the rigid repressiveness which Faulkner had associated with Southern Protestant morality in *Sanctuary* and *As I Lay Dying*. Christmas is more the helpless victim of a pharisaical society than Christ was. He is not only persecuted and killed; he is also corrupted by being made to pattern himself on the models of repression, such as Doc Hines and Simon McEachern, who impose his alienation from life. Because the principle of static repression is as much within him as it is about him, he is unable to accept change, or survive disillusionment, without reacting destructively. Therefore he becomes a murderer, and his own death looks like suicide. He is a mirror image of the sterility that kills him. Hightower, meditating with helpless concern on the coming event, defines it as a "crucifixion" to which each of the town's three churches "will raise a cross. 'And they will do it gladly,' he says . . . . 'Since to pity him would be to admit selfdoubt and to hope for and need pity themselves' " (p. 348). It is the image of such churches that Christmas reflects when, being religiously beaten by McEachern, he looks "like a monk in a picture" (p. 140), and a little later when "The boy's body might have been wood or stone; a post or a tower upon which the sentient part of him mused like a hermit, contemplative and remote with ecstasy and selfcrucifixion" (p. 150). The same expression is seen on the face of that other murderer, Percy Grimm, as he pursues Christmas to kill him: "that serene, unearthly luminousness of angels in church windows" (p. 437). In Hightower's final meditation, the faces of Christmas and Grimm "fade and blend" into one (p. 466). Christmas embodies all the static and sterile intolerance from which he suffers. His death, like his punishment by McEachern, is actually a "selfcrucifixion."

Several other kinds of intolerance are associated with Protestantism in the book, and they are developed in ramifications and subramifications of Christmas's story. The intolerance of Doc Hines is not so much religious as it is racial and sexual. The Burden family's intolerance of slavery is as dogmatic and as violent as the doctrine it opposes. And Christmas's own intolerance of experience, or of life, is demonstrated over and over in his encounters with women: the dietician at the orphanage, Mrs. McEachern, his prostitute sweetheart Bobbie Allen, the anonymous prostitute who is tolerant of Negroes as customers, and Joanna Burden.

The religious parallels in *Light in August* are not used to inculcate any religious belief that Faulkner himself may have had, nor are they intended primarily to express his criticism of other people's beliefs. Their function is to help build the artificial static obstacle to the motion of life that Faulkner needed if he was to succeed in telling the story of Lena. They tell us nothing at all about Faulkner's personal feelings or opinions about anything except the art of fiction, in the exercise of which he made them serve as tools.

Hightower, according to Beach Langston, is an incarnation "of the recurring figure of the Buddha, or, more accurately, of a Bodhisattva."[31] That is, he tries by meditation and passive suffering to emulate the Buddha in spiritual purification, to escape the cycle of life, and to achieve Nirvana, a nothingness or a loss of identity, a static condition in which he can be at peace. Langston's hypothesis is supported in the text by Faulkner's use of the word "avatar" (pp. 5, 213, 244),[32] by the image of "the wheel of thinking" in Hightower's final revery (pp. 462-66), and by the description of Hightower, on two occasions, sitting like "an eastern idol . . ." (pp. 83, 298).[33] Langston notes that Hightower, like a disciple of Buddha, has two possibilities of salvation: the passive way of withdrawal, the Lesser Vehicle, Hinayana; or the way of Mahayana, the Greater Vehicle, a life of responsible action such as the Buddha led after his enlightenment under the Bo-Tree.

In his last session of sunset meditation, Hightower is forced to realize that his effort to escape the responsibilities of present life by a process of passive withdrawal has been disastrously unsuccessful. He sees that, by using his wife as a means of retreating into the past, he has driven her to sexual debauchery and probably to suicide; that he has been " 'her seducer and her murderer, author and instrument of her shame and death' " (p. 462). His withdrawal, instead of being passive and virtuous, has been a negative action, for the results of which he has to acknowledge a criminal responsibility.

He is able to arrive at this realization partly because he has been forced, by the insistence of Byron Bunch, to take an active part in life, after twenty-five years of isolation. It is he who delivers Lena's baby; and for a time he feels that the

---

[31] Langston, p. 47.

[32] The word "avatar" is never applied directly to Hightower, however.

[33] The probable source of this image in the last paragraph of Conrad's *Heart of Darkness* is more explicit: Marlow "sat apart, indistinct and silent, in the pose of a meditating Buddha."

waste land aspect of his world has been overcome. He is sorry for Joanna Burden chiefly because she has " 'not lived only a week longer . . . . Until luck and life returned to these barren and ruined acres.' It seems to him that he can see, feel, about him the ghosts of rich fields, and of the rich fecund black life of the quarters, the mellow shouts, the presence of fecund women, the prolific naked children in the dust before the doors; and the big house again, noisy, loud with the treble shouts of the generations" (p. 385). The momentum of this feeling carries him to the point of offering the alibi that Byron has asked him to furnish for Christmas, trying to stop Percy Grimm and his followers by telling them, " 'He was here that night. He was with me the night of the murder' " (p. 439). When Hightower acknowledges that he himself is, in effect, a murderer, the tormenting weight of "the wheel of thinking" is lifted. "The wheel, released, seems to rush on . . . . going fast and smooth now, because it is freed now of burden, of vehicle, axle, all. In the lambent suspension of August into which night is about to fully come, it seems to engender and surround itself with a faint glow like a halo. The halo is full of faces. . . . They are peaceful, as though they have escaped into an apotheosis; his own is among them" (p. 465).

According to Langston, this description indicates Hightower's attainment, by the way of Mahayana, the Greater Vehicle, of the Buddhist "*pari-nirvana.* Hightower has bought his immunity through crucifixion on the martyr's wheel, has worked out his karma, has attained the peace that passeth understanding, has finally on this August night turned the Wheel of the Law and become, momentarily at least, an enlightened Bodhisattva. He has been released from the chain of reincarnations which required that he should continually re-enter the world as an avatar of his grandfather and the romantic religion of the Civil War."[34] Faulkner's text confirms the view that Hightower experiences a kind of release: "Then

[34] Langston, p. 60.

it seems to him that some ultimate dammed flood within him breaks and rushes away. He seems to watch it, feeling himself losing contact with earth, lighter and lighter, emptying, floating. 'I am dying,' he thinks" (p. 466). But the nature of this experience is more dubious, more complex and equivocal, than Langston's account seems to recognize. Faulkner has said in an interview that Hightower "didn't die. . . . He had to endure, to live," and that he still had "the memory of his grandfather, who had been brave."[35]

Hightower's ultimate vision is the same one into which he has been retreating from life for twenty-five years, the vision of his grandfather's cavalry troop charging into Jefferson in a gallant and successful effort to destroy a cache of supplies intended for Grant's army. As his imagination recreates the scene, "They rush past, forwardleaning in the saddles, with brandished arms, beneath whipping ribbons from slanted and eager lances; with tumult and soundless yelling they sweep past like a tide whose crest is jagged with the wild heads of horses and the brandished arms of men like the crater of the world in explosion" (pp. 466-67). This vision hardly seems an appropriate representation of the Buddhist pari-nirvana, which Langston describes as "that infinite and eternal peace into which the enlightened Bodhisattva may enter when he has worked out his karma and thus broken the chain of reincarnation."[36] On the contrary, it is a vision of war and violent action, in which two of Faulkner's favorite images of life in motion, the horse and the flood, are energetically combined.

It seems very probable that Faulkner did use the story of Buddha as a basis for his characterization of Hightower. But he was no more confined by it than he was by the story of Christ, and Hightower is no more like the Buddha than Christmas is like the Savior. Hightower's symbolic value in

---

[35] *Faulkner in the University*, p. 75.
[36] Langston, p. 55.

the structure of *Light in August* lies somewhere between those of Lena Grove and Joe Christmas. Hightower is not wholly static, like Christmas, but neither is he wholly dynamic, like Lena. His effort to enter the current of life is too reluctant and it comes too late to be more than partly successful. He falls back on his vision of the past. But it is a dynamic vision, and perhaps now he is able to see it less as a retreat from life and more as an encouragement to help him endure whatever life remains with a better grace than he has had before.

The pattern of individual personal development in *Light in August* is most clearly seen in the experience of Byron Bunch, which has generally been regarded by critics as part of Lena's story rather than a story in its own right, but which nevertheless provides a major element in the structure of the book as a whole. Byron begins by being as isolated as Hightower in his Hinayana phase, and as static as Christmas in his rejection of any fertile relations with women. But Byron falls in love with Lena, and finds himself launched, willy nilly, in the current of life. Unlike Christmas, he falls from innocence into involvement, into acceptance of sin, guilt, responsibility, and all the other burdens of creative activity.

To assume that Christmas is the protagonist of *Light in August*, as critics have generally done, is to classify the story as a tragedy and to find, as many critics have found, that it is lacking in unity, faulty in structure, and full of irrelevancy. Faulkner pointed to the error in an interview by saying that *Light in August* does not argue "for the acceptance of an inevitably tragic view of life" (his questioner's phrase) and by remarking that "the only person in that book that accepted a tragic view of life was Christmas . . . . The others seemed to me to have had a very fine belief in life, in the basic possibility for happiness and goodness—Byron Bunch and Lena Grove, to have gone to all that trouble."[37] On another occasion, in

[37] *Faulkner in the University*, pp. 96, 97.

answer to the more general question, "Mr. Faulkner, do you consider human life basically a tragedy?" he said, "Actually, yes. But man's immortality is that he is faced with a tragedy which he can't beat and he still tries to do something with it."[38] Byron Bunch says much the same thing when he sees Lucas Burch, Lena's other lover and the biological father of her baby, running away from the opportunity and the responsibility of marrying her: " 'I took care of his woman for him and I borned his child for him. And now there is one more thing I can do for him. I cant marry them, because I aint a minister. And I may not can catch him, because he's got a start on me. And I may not can whip him if I do, because he is bigger than me. But I can try it. I can try to do it' " (p. 403). If we regard Byron as the protagonist, rather than Christmas, the book becomes comedy instead of tragedy, and its structure makes more sense.[39]

The book is framed, as well as permeated, by the story of Byron and Lena, and it ends on a note of humorous absurdity which has been particularly embarrassing to critics of the Christmas-as-protagonist-of-a-tragedy school. Hyatt H. Waggoner indicates the proper corrective when he says that the function of Byron and Lena in opening and closing the novel "seems to me crucial and not to have been given sufficient weight in most interpretations." But Waggoner considers the ending "an anticlimax," and reaches out, rather desperately, to suggest that "the final implication of the book is a kind of Christian existentialism which could be explicated in terms of the theology of a Tillich or a Bultmann."[40] We need not go so far afield as that. We need only look at the whole structure to see that the book is not a tragedy with an inappropriate bit of farce tacked on at the end, but a comedy which contains a

[38] *Faulkner at Nagano*, p. 4.
[39] Cleanth Brooks, in *William Faulkner: The Yoknapatawpha Country* (New Haven: Yale University Press, 1963), pp. 71-74, argues convincingly for the view that *Light in August* is comic rather than tragic.
[40] Waggoner, pp. 113, 114.

tragedy and assimilates it, as life assimilates disease and death.

Byron's function is rather like that of Anse Bundren in *As I Lay Dying*, except that Byron's result is more clearly optimistic. It is not easy. Byron, having accepted the loss of his innocence, the end of his friendship with Hightower, the death of Christmas, and Lena's lack of virginity, must also accept his own weakness and absurdity, as he has partly done in his unsuccessful fight with Burch. In the final sequence, as narrated by the anonymous furniture dealer, Byron walks off twice, once after Lena ignores his roundabout proposal of marriage and again when she puts him out of the truck " 'like she would that baby if it had been about six years old . . .' " (p. 477). But he persists, and his success has been foretold, with misgiving, by Hightower, who says to himself, after delivering the baby, *"She will have to have others, more . . . . That will be her life, her destiny. The good stock peopling in tranquil obedience to it the good earth . . . . But by Byron engendered next. Poor boy"* (p. 384). The furniture dealer, whose humor goes along with a shrewd objectivity of judgment, supports the same view, concluding that Lena probably has no intention " 'of finding whoever it was she was following. I dont think she had ever aimed to, only she hadn't told him yet. . . . I think she had just made up her mind to travel a little further and see as much as she could, since I reckon she knew that when she settled down this time, it would likely be for the rest of her life' " (p. 480).

In assimilating the stories of Lena, Christmas, and Hightower more or less closely to Byron's experience of change and growth, Faulkner has been careful not to compromise their identity as separate stories. They remain distinct, and they represent sharply different aspects of human nature and the world. Each is insulated from the others by its own particular mythological ambience; each has its own time dimension, different from and incompatible with the others; and each has its own protagonist, who is not a complete human being but a typical Faulkner caricature, or grotesque. Lena is so fully immersed in the flow of life, and so slightly developed in the dimensions of conscious thought and feeling, as to seem almost subhuman. Christmas, isolated by his refusal either to identify himself in relation to other people and the world or to be content with anonymity, lacking the ties of tenderness and mutual dependency that keep normal people from going beyond the bounds, becomes inhuman. Hightower, retreating from life in the present, exiles himself to an extrahuman region from which even Byron's exigencies cannot quite rescue him. Because they resist a too-complete assimilation, either in Byron's experience or that of the reader, they serve to dramatize the artificial stoppage of motion at which Faulkner aims. The motion, the stoppage, and the artificiality of the dramatic confrontation are all emphasized by the counterpoint. The total impression aroused by the tension between the motion and the stoppage is greatly enhanced by the stubbornly maintained independence of the separate materials.

Pylon

By comparison with the other novels discussed in this chapter, including *Sanctuary*, *Pylon* is a failure. Its deficiencies might be accounted for from various points of view. It does not use the Yoknapatawpha setting, but takes place almost entirely in New Valois, Franciana, which is a paper-thin and cellophane-transparent disguise for New Orleans, Louisiana. It is based too closely on the actual events of the dedication of Shushan Airport, which took place in February 1934, a little more than a year before the book was published.[41] It was apparently written in an interlude of diversion from the writing of *Absalom, Absalom!*, on which Faulkner worked longer and harder.[42] But such reasons are external to the book. The internal reason is that *Pylon* does not have a strong enough

[41] For parallels between the fiction and the reality, see Millgate, pp. 138-41.
[42] See Millgate, p. 142.

structure, and that it is therefore deficient in the qualities of organized complexity that we have found in the other books.

We may reasonably assume that Faulkner, whatever his need for relaxation at the time, did not mean to write an unsuccessful novel. He must have believed that he could apply the technical resources he had developed over the preceding years to his knowledge and experience of flying—an activity in which he was intensely interested—in such a way as to produce an artistically satisfactory story. The trick would be to use the mythical method on this class of material, something which he had not done in *Sartoris*. The nature of the attempted strategy is partly indicated by Faulkner's review, published about eight months after *Pylon*, of *Test Pilot*, by Jimmy Collins. Faulkner said he had hoped to find in that book "a folklore not of the age of speed nor of the men who perform it, but of the speed itself, peopled not by anything human or even mortal but by the clever willful machines themselves carrying nothing that was born and will have to die or which can even suffer pain, moving without comprehensible purpose toward no discernible destination, producing a literature innocent of either love or hate and of course of pity or terror, and which would be the story of the final disappearance of life from the earth."[43] Such a folklore would indeed provide the basis for a cosmic arrest of motion.

In *Pylon* the motion of life is again represented by a woman. Laverne Shumann, like Lena Grove, Ruby Lamar, and Dewey Dell Bundren, is a rural fertility figure. She is associated with corn by her "mealcolored . . . Iowacorncolored, hair" (p. 22). She is also, though somewhat equivocally, identified as earth; her two consorts, one of whom (but no one knows which) is the father of her son, are described by the unnamed newspaper reporter as " 'two farmers' boys, at least one from Ohio . . . . And the ground they plow from Iowa; yair, two farmers' boys

43 "Folklore of the Air," *American Mercury*, XXXVI (November 1935), 372.

downbanked; yair, two buried pylons in the one Iowadrowsing womandrowsing pylondrowsing. . .'" (p. 110; last ellipsis Faulkner's). In one aspect, the two fliers, Roger Shumann and Jack Holmes, are gods of the air, like Zeus. But, unlike Zeus, they depend for their dominance on a complex of mechanical and mechanistic arrangements, at the airport, in the city, and among such institutions as the sewage board, the Ord-Atkinson Aircraft Corporation, the American Aeronautical Association, and the federal government. The reporter, whose feelings color *Pylon* as pervasively as those of Horace Benbow color *Sanctuary*, identifies the fliers with their machines. He thinks " 'they aint human. It aint adultery; you can't anymore imagine two of them making love than you can two of them airplanes back in the corner of the hangar, coupled. . . . Yair; cut him and it's cylinder oil; dissect him and it aint bones: it's little rockerarms and connecting rods. . .'" (p. 231; last ellipsis Faulkner's).

The evidence in the text indicates that the reporter himself, rather than the fliers, is meant to embody the new folklore and to illustrate its moral. His most intense moment occurs when he rides inside the fuselage of the airplane that is going to kill Shumann, acting as ballast to keep it in trim. After landing, "he lived and relived the blind timeless period during which he lay on his stomach in the barrel, clutching the two body-members, with nothing to see but Shumann's feet on the rudderpedals and the movement of the aileron balancerod and nothing to feel but terrific motion—not speed and not progress —just blind furious motion like a sealed force trying to explode the monocoque barrel in which he lay from the waist down on his stomach, leaving him clinging to the bodymembers in space" (pp. 216-17). He is repeatedly described, at other times, as a corpse or a skeleton; and Haygood, the editor for whom he works, complains that, although he has an uncanny faculty of being present when things happen, his reporting is " 'not the living breath of news. It's just information. It's dead before you even get back here with it' " (p. 42).

This quality is not peculiar to the reporter but is attributed to various media of mass, long-distance, high-speed mechanical communication. A telephone, as the editor listens between an answer and a question, gives "only dead wirehum, as if the other end of it extended beyond atmosphere, into cold space; as though he listened now to the profound sound of infinity, of void itself filled with the cold unceasing murmur of aeon-weary and unflagging stars" (p. 75). The public address system at the airport, as the reporter goes into the air-conditioned lobby, sounds "as though it were the voice of the steel-and-chromium mausoleum itself, talking of creatures imbued with motion though not with life and incomprehensible to the puny crawling painwebbed globe, incapable of suffering, wombed and born complete and instantaneous, cunning intricate and deadly, from out some blind iron batcave of the earth's prime foundation . . ." (pp. 28-29). The description of the airplanes as "creatures imbued with motion though not with life" states an important reservation: life is motion, but motion is not always life. In fact, the faster it goes, the more it depends on mechanical power, and the more inimical to life it seems.

The deadliest machine of all is the newspaper which the reporter and the editor serve. Its freshly printed headlines record a "crosssection out of timespace as though of a lightray caught by a speed lens for a second's fraction between infinity and furious and trivial dust" (p. 75). Two hours later the same headlines are "that cryptic staccato crosssection of an instant crystallized and now dead two hours . . . ." But the omniscient author at this point remarks that it is "only the moment, the instant," that is dead: "the substance itself not only not dead, not complete, but in its very insoluble enigma of human folly and blundering possessing a futile and tragic immortality . . . ." A watch, lying face-down on top of a stack of these headlines, presents "the blank backside of the greatest and most inescapable enigma of all" (p. 85); that is, time. The newspaper provides an image of an artificial arrest of motion which not only does not really bring life to a stop but which may have the artistic effect of emphasizing the dynamic power of life by contrast to what is called, in a third passage, "the fragile web of ink and paper, assertive, proclamative; profound and irrevocable if only in the sense of being profoundly and irrevocably unimportant . . . the dead instant's fruit of forty tons of machinery and an entire nation's antic delusion" (p. 111; ellipsis Faulkner's).

The artistic strategy of the book is to juxtapose the motion of life, embodied in Laverne, with the mechanical motion represented by the airplanes, by the mass media of communication, and above all by the reporter. This mechanical motion is out of phase with the motion of life, and therefore it is equivalent to stasis or death. When the reporter intervenes in the affairs of the fliers, the results are always futile, mischievous, or disastrous. He takes them for endless taxi rides, he gets their mechanic drunk, and he arranges acquisition of the airplane in which Shumann crashes and dies.

Laverne tries consistently, gallantly, and unsuccessfully to prevent all this, just as she has tried for several years to sustain the unorthodox family, to make a home, and to care for her son. In particular, she protests against Roger's decision to fly the cranky airplane that the reporter is helping to get: " '. . . all I want,' " she says, " 'is just a house, a room; a cabin will do, a coalshed where I can know that next Monday and the Monday after that and the Monday after that . . .' " (p. 165; last ellipsis Faulkner's). When the reporter urges her to watch Roger win the big race, her only response is " 'Yes. The money will be fine' " (p. 233). When the airplane breaks in two, she says, " 'Oh damn you, Roger! Oh damn you! damn you!' " (p. 234). And when the reporter runs with her and the boy toward the seawall, "she turned, still running, and gave him a single pale cold terrible look, crying,

" 'God damn you to hell! Get away from me!' " (p. 235). With Roger Shumann dead, she still goes on to do the best she can. Pregnant again, this time by Holmes, the parachute jumper, she leaves her first child with Shumann's parents and departs, in the proverbial snow, with Holmes.

Pylon is the story of Laverne Shumann in somewhat the same fashion that *Light in August* is the story of Lena Grove. But it is also parallel to *Sanctuary* in that the story of Laverne is colored by the reporter's point of view, as that of Temple Drake is by Horace Benbow's; and the reporter's effect on Laverne is like that of Horace on Ruby Lamar. In respect to its organization, however, *Pylon* is more like *Sartoris*. The materials for a symbolic or mythic structure are there, but the pattern is not strong enough to assimilate them effectively. The counterpoint of dynamic versus static images is not contained and concentrated as it ought to be.

Weaknesses are hard to prove, but perhaps the kind of weakness that undermines *Pylon* can at least be illustrated by reference to an inconsistency in its time scheme. The dedication of Feinman Airport is planned (as was that of Shushan Airport) so that the last day of racing will be Mardi Gras day. But the story is planned so that the races will take place on Thursday, Friday, and Saturday; and in the book Mardi Gras falls on Saturday, in defiance of language and tradition. Evidently Faulkner wanted to make simultaneous use of the pattern of carnival and the pattern of Easter, and brought them together by doing crude violence to the calendar.

The imagery is equally awkward, although there is no logical reason why it has to be. In *Light in August* the pagan imagery of fertility, focused on Lena, is sharply contrasted to the imagery of sterility associated in the story of Joe Christmas with the Christian tradition. In *Pylon* there is no such intense confrontation. Laverne, as we have seen, is provided with fertility symbols, and she is literally fertile, but she is not strongly related to any ritual that might be suggested by Mardi Gras.

The carnival itself is consistently described in terms of mechanization and sterility. A parade is called "Momus' Nilebarge clatterfalque" (p. 77; cf. p. 202), and the reporter describes the air race headquarters hotel as " 'tiered identical cubicles of one thousand rented sleepings,' " only to be corrected by Jiggs, who says, " 'Teared Q pickles. Yair; on one thousand rented . . . . . if you got the jack too. I got the Q pickle all right' " (p. 58); the points of the ellipsis represent five letters which were written out in Faulkner's manuscript.[44]

Instead of building an original system of symbolic relations, in accordance with the needs of his own story, as he usually did, Faulkner in *Pylon* seems to have borrowed wholesale, without sufficient modification, from T.S. Eliot. Feinman Airport, for example, is advertised as having been "Created out of the Waste Land at the Bottom of Lake Rambaud . . ." (p. 14). The reporter is "something which had apparently crept from a doctor's cupboard and, in the snatched garments of an etherised patient in a charity ward, escaped into the living world" (p. 20; cf. "The Love Song of J. Alfred Prufrock," l. 3). Some newsboys are "apparently as oblivious to the moment's significance as birds are aware yet oblivious to the human doings which their wings brush and their droppings fall upon" (p. 55; cf. "Sweeney among the Nightingales," l. 39). The reporter's eyes are "like two spots of dying daylight caught by water at the bottom of abandoned wells" (p. 135; cf. *The Waste Land*, l. 385). Laverne's father-in-law, Dr. Carl Shumann, asks for "some sign" of young Jack's paternity (p. 309; cf. "Gerontion," l. 17). The largest example is the chapter title "Lovesong of J. A. Prufrock" (p. 236; carried as a running head to p. 283). Thematic parallels have also been noted by critics between Eliot's uses of fire and water in *The Waste Land* and Faulkner's in *Pylon*, particularly in Shumann's death by water, which is not followed by a resurrection. But these elements do not cohere in *Pylon*; they only serve to in-

---

[44] See Millgate, p. 321, n. 20.

voke the coherent patterns of Eliot's works, which remain outside the novel and foreign to it. Instead of working Eliot's material into the fabric of his own story, Faulkner seems to have tried to make Eliot do his work for him. If so, Eliot has his revenge.

Pylon is a negative demonstration of the importance of mythic structural patterns in Faulkner's fiction. When they are weak, or incoherent, or insufficiently assimilated, they do not work. But when, as in *Sanctuary, As I Lay Dying*, or *Light in August*, they mutually interact, in contrapuntal tensions of harmony or opposition, they form extremely effective total structures in the service of Faulkner's artistic aim.

Critics have often observed that our contemporary culture lacks any stable system of belief on the basis of which its art forms can be defined. Hyatt H. Waggoner, applying this observation to Faulkner, says that "When *everything* becomes problematical, a matter of perspective or of the health of the unperceived unconscious, when one may choose one's assumptions for the construction of a geometry or an ego, when even the homeliest matters of status lose their translucence, it becomes impossible for the fully conscious man to write traditional fiction." This statement points to one of the most general problems of the modern mind. We cannot do anything with our experience—say anything intelligible about it, represent it in any way, or even conceive it in our minds—unless we come to it with some kind of formal or structural assumptions in terms of which to see, understand, and manipulate. We do not, as a matter of historical fact, have any one basic proposition on which we can agree to operate. Therefore it is often true that, as Waggoner goes on to say, "The novelist begins to write for a limited audience with whom he can share certain enabling assumptions; or he extends his idea of creation to include creation of belief."[45] The dilemma, thus defined, seems desperate.

[45] Waggoner, p. 260.

I suspect, however, that the relation of fiction to belief is more complex, and rather more uncertain, than this dilemma implies, and that the dilemma may therefore be false. The mythical method may serve as a way of suspending our belief as well as our disbelief, and of making familiar ritual patterns available to fiction in a pragmatic, functional fashion, justified not by their prior truth but by the effectiveness with which they work in the fictional context. A novelist armed with this method is indeed free to choose among a variety of generally known traditional patterns, and he can share his experience all the better with large audiences if he does not raise the question of belief. Faulkner avoids the question by reducing rituals to the status of "tools." For his purpose the Old Testament is as good as the New and Frazer or Freud as good as the Bible: a pattern is a pattern regardless of provenance. This does not mean that Faulkner has no beliefs; it only means that he does not require us to share them in order to enjoy his fiction.

E. M. Forster, in *Aspects of the Novel* (1927), lays down a criterion that Faulkner may have seen and adopted; at any rate his successful novels meet it. A good plot, Forster says, "may be difficult or easy, it may and should contain mysteries, but it ought not to mislead. And over it, as it unfolds, will hover the memory of the reader (that dull glow of the mind of which intelligence is the bright advancing edge) and will constantly rearrange and reconsider, seeing new clues, new chains of cause and effect, and the final sense (if the plot has been a fine one) will not be of clues or chains, but of something aesthetically compact, something which might have been shown by the novelist straight away, only if he had shown it straight away it would never have become beautiful."[46] Faulkner's structural designs are usually difficult. They force the reader to the labor of remembering, rearranging, reconsider-

[46] E.M. Forster, *Aspects of the Novel* (London: Edward Arnold & Co., 1927), p. 119.

ing, and finally discovering, perhaps almost creating, the compact beauty of that moment of concentrated life at which the whole activity is aimed.

It is in aid of this activity, and particularly of the reader's part in it, that Faulkner uses what Conrad Aiken called his "whole elaborate method of *deliberately withheld meaning*, of progressive and partial and delayed disclosure," as a way "to keep the form—and the idea—fluid and unfinished, still in motion, as it were, and unknown, until the dropping into place of the very last syllable."[47] For most readers, the forms of Faulkner's novels never do stop moving; the dull glow of memory hovers over them long after the last syllable is read, still rearranging, still reconsidering, and still discovering new lights and beauties.[48] There is much to be gained also in re-reading. Even Aiken, writing in 1939, considered *Light in August* a failure.

Faulkner, trying to answer a question as to why, in *Light in August*, he had put "the chapter about Hightower's early life in the end of the novel . . . rather than when Hightower first appears," said that, "Unless a book follows a simple direct line such as a story of adventure, it becomes a series of pieces. It's a good deal like dressing a showcase window. It takes a certain amount of judgment and taste to arrange the different pieces in the most effective place in juxtaposition to one another."[49] The result of such placement is not a straight line—even the phrase "series of pieces" is misleading—but a system or set of tensions in a pattern that tends to be geometrical rather than chronological.

[47] Conrad Aiken, "William Faulkner: The Novel as Form," *Atlantic Monthly*, CLXIV (November 1939), 652; reprinted in *William Faulkner: Three Decades of Criticism*, ed. Frederick J. Hoffman and Olga W. Vickery (East Lansing: Michigan State University Press, 1960), p. 138.

[48] Cf. Slatoff, p. 136: ". . . the 'last syllables' of Faulkner's novels, as much as any other part of them, seem designed to prevent resolution, to leave the reader with conflicting thoughts and feelings. Not only do the 'endings' fail to resolve most of the tensions generated by the novels but they often provide new ones."

[49] *Faulkner in the University*, p. 45.

Faulkner's use of arbitrary, externally provided structural forms generally has the effect of confronting the reader with several different and more or less incompatible patterns at once. Each of these has its own integrity, which it contributes to the whole story; and the whole, if the method succeeds, transcends all the parts. No one of the individual mythical patterns can be legitimately seen as the only dominant scheme of the work; the reader or critic cannot safely relax in the confidence that Faulkner's story is "nothing but" the Persephone myth, the Christ or the Eden story, the Buddhist way of salvation, or the Freudian or Jungian psychodrama. It is likely to be all of these and more, at the same time that it is none of them but is supremely itself. It remains a bit mysterious—alive, moving, refusing to be pinned down, defined, or formulated. There is always something more to be seen, felt, and said, if we could find how to say it. Ultimately something escapes, leaving us still with an intuitive sense of the compact beauty that Forster cannot define either.

Three / Tools: Texture

When Bayard Sartoris in *The Unvanquished* kisses his cousin Drusilla, who has become his stepmother, he thinks "of the woman of thirty, the symbol of the ancient and eternal Snake and of the men who have written of her,[1] and I realized then the immitigable chasm between all life and all print—that those who can, do, those who cannot and suffer enough because they can't, write about it" (p. 262). Faulkner, like his fictional novelist in *Mosquitoes*, Dawson Fairchild, distrusted words, much as he distrusted ideas, because words as words are abstract and therefore static and contrary to life. As Addie Bundren remarks, there is a "dark voicelessness in which the words are the deeds," and then there are "the other words that are not deeds, that are just the gaps in people's lacks, coming down like the cries of the geese out of the wild darkness in the old terrible nights, fumbling at the deeds like orphans to whom are pointed out in a crowd two faces and told, That is your father, your mother" (*AILD* 166). Paradoxically, this opposition between dynamic life and static word is a basic element of Faulkner's style, a principal means by which the motion of life is artificially—and artistically—stopped.

[1] Cf. Balzac's novel *La femme de trente ans*.

Texture

Conrad Aiken's account of Faulkner's style suggests one way in which the paradox works. Aiken said, "It is as if Mr. Faulkner, in a sort of hurried despair, had decided to try to tell us everything, absolutely everything, every last origin or source or quality or qualification, and every possible future or permutation as well, in one terrifically concentrated effort: each sentence to be, as it were, a microcosm."[2] Many later critics have followed Aiken's line, and Faulkner himself appears to have taken it on occasion. Asked, in one of the Virginia sessions, what was his "objective in using long sentences over short sentences," he answered, "That is a matter of the carpenter trying to find the hammer or the axe that he thinks will do the best job. Another thing is, everyone has a foreknowledge of death that is, he will have only a very short time comparatively to do the work and he is trying to put the whole history of the human heart on the head of a pin, you might say. Also, to me, no man is himself, he is the sum of his past. There is no such thing really as was because the past is. It is a part of every man, every woman, and every moment. All of his and her ancestry, background, is all a part of himself and herself at any moment. And so a man, a character in a story at any moment of action is not just himself as he is then, he is all that made him, and the long sentence is an attempt to get his past and possibly his future into the instant in which he does something. . . ."[3] The long sentence, then, by Faulkner's account as well as Aiken's, is a technique, or "tool," for compressing the greatest possible amount of time, or life, or motion, into the smallest possible space, in order to condense and stop it for contemplation.

In other statements about his style, Faulkner generally expressed a pragmatic attitude based on the literary theory of

[2] Aiken, p. 651; reprinted in *Three Decades*, p. 137.
[3] *Faulkner in the University*, p. 84 (ellipsis in the text); cf. *Faulkner at Nagano*, pp. 37, 94.

the romantic tradition. He said in a Japanese interview, "I think that the theme, the story, invents its own style,"[4] a formula that might have come directly from Emerson or Whitman or Coleridge. In a Virginia interview he put it somewhat more explicitly by saying, "Style, if it's—like anything else, to be alive it must be in motion too. If it becomes fixed then it's dead, it's just rhetoric. The style must change according to what the writer is trying to tell. What he is trying to tell in fact compels the style."[5] Faulkner's style—up until the 1940s, when it began to fall noticeably into mannerism—does change, and it commands a wide variety of resources in its rhythms, its imagery, and its rhetorical tactics, which are far too functional to be dismissed as "*just* rhetoric."

Much of Faulkner's texture consists of narrative in which motion is presented as directly as possible, in action and imagery that aim at overwhelming us with the sheer power of speed, noise, and confusion. The short story "Mule in the Yard" is amusing more for these qualities than for its improbably tricky plot, both in its original version (*Scribner's Magazine*, xcvi [Aug. 1934], 65-70) and as it is told by Charles Mallison (whose treatment is no improvement on the earlier anonymous narrator's) in *The Town* (pp. 321-56). A much later story, "Race at Morning" (*Saturday Evening Post*, ccxxvii [March 5, 1955], 26, 103-104, 106; reprinted, somewhat revised, in *Big Woods* [pp. 175-98]) is also memorable more for the sensation of speed it gives than for the interest of its events or its rather labored moral. Many passages in other stories and in the novels, some of which we have noted and some that we will glance at presently, are similarly used to convey the sense of motion as motion. As Karl E. Zink says, Faulkner's "impatient sensitivity to the quality of physical sensation, particularly to the fluid quality of experience in

---

[4] *Faulkner at Nagano*, p. 35; cf. pp. 36, 152-53, 164, and *Faulkner in the University*, p. 56.

[5] *Ibid.*, p. 279.

time, to the supremacy of change and process, to the living impact of the past on the evanescent present moment—this sensitivity, this concept of reality, accounts for the unique external shape which Faulkner has brought to the American novel."[6] This sensitivity is indeed important, because it does reach up to Faulkner's metaphysical feeling about the life of the whole universe. His use of textural techniques is important because it makes these values tangible in the fabric of the fiction.

In texture as in structure, however, it is not motion as motion that raises Faulkner's work to its highest levels of intensity but motion as we see it opposed and artificially stopped and heightened by static elements or devices. Walter J. Slatoff describes a number of related stylistic devices which Faulkner uses pervasively to accomplish this effect. These consist essentially in various kinds of rhetorical contradictions. In a chapter entitled "Stylistic Antithesis" Slatoff analyzes negative statements, "Neither . . . nor" pairs, antitheses involving past-present and present-future relationships, and what he calls "gratuitous" antitheses, which are denials of statements that have not been made.[7] He notes "that the simple negative is the next-to-the-most concise way in which polar opposites can be suggested and fused. The most concise way is in words like 'motionless,' 'immobile,' 'soundless,' and 'substanceless,' which are favorites of Faulkner's, words which simultaneously suggest and deny a polar opposition."[8] They also operate with admirable efficiency to suggest both the motion of life and the stopping of it. In an earlier chapter Slatoff discusses Faulkner's use of oxymorons involving "sharp polarity, extreme tension, a high degree of conceptual and stylistic antithesis, and the simultaneous suggestion of disparate or opposed elements."[9] Again we may observe that the opposition is very

[6] Karl E. Zink, "William Faulkner: Form as Experience," *South Atlantic Quarterly*, LIII (July 1954), 385.
[7] Slatoff, pp. 122-27.   [8] *Ibid.*, p. 125.   [9] *Ibid.*, p. 86.

often between dynamic and static terms, as in Slatoff's examples from *The Hamlet*: "active and lazy," "ceremonial and negligee," "two separate expressions—a temporary one of static peace and quiet overlaying a constant one of definite even though faint harriedness," "vague and intense," "cluttered desolation," "teeming vacuum," "corrupt and immaculate," "unchaste and inviolable," "seething and decorous," "furious ... amity," "implacable constancy and invincible repudiation," "both illogical and consistent, both reasonable and bizarre," "tranquil, terrifying," and "the deathless slain."[10]

The most characteristic, as well as the sharpest and most meaningful kind of antithesis in Faulkner is the imagery of dynamic stasis which we have noticed before and which many critics have discussed. It is the most condensed symbolic vehicle of Faulkner's purpose as an artist; when it succeeds, as it often does, it makes an extremely emphatic stoppage of motion. As we have seen, it occurs in his earliest writing, and we shall see that he continues to use it throughout his career. Zink is correct in saying, "It is obviously vital to the way he thinks about and looks at his world, having for him something fundamental to do with ultimate reality," because, as Zink also remarks, "flux or change is for Faulkner a primary condition of all Life," and when it encounters obstacles that stop it "we perceive the fluid world in static moments which follow one another in rapid sequence, each one intact and complete in itself—like the still frames of a motion picture." But Zink is wrong, I believe, when he says that "Such recognition of symbolic moments constitutes a degree of transcendence of inexorable change. It is a moment of insight into true meaning."[11]

Zink's description of this device is remarkably similar to what Bergson says about the "cinematographical" quality of abstract thinking. "We take snapshots, as it were," Bergson

[10] *Ibid.*, pp. 85-86.
[11] Zink, "Flux and the Frozen Moment," pp. 286, 287, 299.

says, "of the passing reality," and string them together to approximate the process of change which is our real experience. Motion is continuous, but the mental equivalent of it is a series of motionless impressions.[12] These static impressions are not moments "of insight into true meaning," but merely a somewhat mechanical and unsatisfactory way of representing motion, the "true meaning" of which cannot be described by any direct method. Faulkner is primarily interested in motion; the static moments are the "tools" with which he fixes the motion for esthetic contemplation.

The Wild Palms, although it is not one of Faulkner's best novels, has a rich texture of images and of the kind of rhetoric we are discussing. Both Harry Wilbourne and the tall convict are swept away from safe moorings, Harry by a flood of emotion, the convict by the Mississippi River flood of 1927. Harry ultimately makes his way, and the convict makes his way back, to the static safety of the prison. Most readers, including most critics, prefer the convict's part of the story to Harry's. One reason for this preference, which I share, may be that the literal flood provides more emphatic imagery of violent motion than the love affair of Harry with Charlotte Rittenmeyer does. Another may be that the tall convict is presented as a desperately static character from the beginning, whereas Harry seems to have some possibilities of motion and even of growth, which tend to blur and soften the opposition between the motion of his story and its stasis. We may also note that Charlotte is hardly the pure embodiment of motion that the river is. Unlike Lena Grove, she thinks too much, and she talks even more than she thinks. The river only moves.

The power of the flooding river is awesome, but no more so than the incredible tenacity with which the convict, exiled from prison as from a paradise, opposes its motion. His phys-

[12] Henri Bergson, *Creative Evolution*, tr. Arthur Mitchell (New York: H. Holt and Co., 1911), pp. 304-10. The quotation is from p. 306.

ical situation is greatly complicated by his responsibility for the pregnant woman whom he has rescued and in whom the motion of life is also more simply and consistently embodied than it is in Charlotte. The convict's only passionate desire is to escape from her, to find someone, somewhere, "anything he might reach and surrender his charge to and turn his back on her forever, on all pregnant and female life forever and return to that monastic existence of shotguns and shackles where he would be secure from it" (p. 153).

His encounter with the flood is wildly humorous, because the water is so completely a world in motion, and he is so completely incapable of accepting it or cooperating with it. When the current of the Yazoo River is reversed by the swelling Mississippi, a mighty wave is formed. "It reared, stooping; the crest of it swirled like the mane of a galloping horse and, phosphorescent too, fretted and flickered like fire. And while the woman huddled in the bows . . . he . . . continued to paddle directly into it . . . though the skiff had ceased to move forward at all but seemed to be hanging in space while the paddle still reached thrust recovered and reached again; now instead of space the skiff became abruptly surrounded by a welter of fleeing debris—planks, small buildings, the bodies of drowned yet antic animals, entire trees leaping and diving like porpoises above which the skiff seemed to hover in weightless and airy indecision like a bird above a fleeing countryside, undecided where to light or whether to light at all, while the convict squatted in it still going through the motions of paddling, waiting for an opportunity to scream. He never found it. For an instant the skiff seemed to stand erect on its stern and then shoot scrabbling and scrambling up the curling wall of water like a cat, and soared on above the licking crest itself and hung cradled into the high actual air in the limbs of a tree, from which bower of new-leafed boughs and branches the convict, like a bird in its nest and still waiting his chance to scream and still going through the motions of paddling though he no longer even had the paddle now, looked down upon a world turned to furious motion and in incredible retrograde" (pp. 156-57).

The next paragraph begins abruptly with the sentence "Some time about midnight, accompanied by a rolling can-nonade of thunder and lightning like a battery going into action, as though some forty hours' constipation of the ele-ments, the firmament itself, were discharging in clapping and glaring salute to the ultimate acquiescence to desperate and furious motion, and still leading its charging welter of dead cows and mules and outhouses and cabins and hencoops, the skiff passed Vicksburg" (p. 157). The animism, in its comic identification of the thunderstorm with a bowel movement, of the skiff with a cat, and of the wave with a horse,[13] and with its impression of dead animals and inanimate objects behaving as if they were alive, brilliantly succeeds, as an image, in describing the powerful currents of life by which the convict has been carried away.

When the woman gives birth, the convict is ruefully dis-illusioned. "*And this is all*," he thinks, looking at the baby. "*This is what severed me violently from all I ever knew and did not wish to leave and cast me upon a medium I was born to fear, to fetch up at last in a place I never saw before and where I do not even know where I am*" (p. 231). A similar feeling seems to prevent him from trying to have any sexual relations with the woman he has rescued, although he takes the first opportunity to get into trouble with another one. He remembers "how there were times, seconds, at first when if it had not been for the baby he might have, might have tried. But they were just seconds because in the next instant his whole being would seem to flee the very idea in a kind of savage and horrified revulsion" (pp. 334-35), and the woman with her baby seems to him like a "millstone which the force

---

[13] Cf. Stephen Crane's imagery in "The Open Boat."

and power of blind and risible Motion had fastened upon him . . ." (p. 335).

The word "risible" here provides a clue to the meaning of the wind which is a prominent image in Wilbourne's story, which sets "the palm fronds clashing with their wild dry bitter sound . . ." (p. 8; cf. pp. 295, 315, 324). This is an ironic sound of motion to the essentially static Wilbourne, and therefore, as we are told half a dozen times, it strikes him as being "risible" (pp. 281, 282, 283, 291, 294). It opposes itself, as a sign of the "bright wild passion" (p. 279) that has partly drawn Harry into the current of life, to the grimly static morality of the puritanical doctor who turns him over to the police for killing Charlotte. The doctor's morality is hardly more static than Wilbourne's own relative impotence, which keeps him chaste in the beginning of the story, which makes him submit to Charlotte's insistence that he perform an abortion to prevent her bearing their child, and which lets him decline Rittenmeyer's gift of cyanide only because he feels a duty to stay alive so that he can preserve the memory of Charlotte.

Charlotte herself, although she claims always to act in aid of freedom, is almost equally static. She is too much obsessed with her fear of static bourgeois values to ignore them, and therefore, try as she may, she cannot really reject them. She can no more let go and ride with the current than Harry can. The purism of her unorthodoxy makes her little more than a mirror image of the conforming people whom she detests, and her touchy revulsion from all conventional ways of making a living causes arbitrary difficulties which Harry is not strong enough to resolve. Finally, it is her own weakness, as much as Harry's, that brings about their downfall and her death. She refuses to bear Harry's child because, she says, " 'we both know we cant have it, cant afford to have it. And they hurt too bad, Harry. Too damned bad' " (p. 218). In contrast to Charlotte, the woman whom the convict takes from the tree in the flood bears her baby almost literally in spite of hell, and quite literally in spite of high water.

The texture of *The Hamlet* is richer than that of *The Wild Palms*, partly because it draws more heavily on mythological references for its imagery. Of Eula Varner, approaching the age of thirteen, we are told that "her entire appearance suggested some symbology out of the old Dionysic times—honey in sunlight and bursting grapes, the writhen bleeding of the crushed fecundated vine beneath the hard rapacious trampling goat-hoof. She seemed to be not a living integer of her contemporary scene, but rather to exist in a teeming vacuum in which her days followed one another as though behind soundproof glass, where she seemed to listen in sullen bemusement, with a weary wisdom heired of all mammalian maturity, to the enlarging of her own organs" (p. 107). The same "luminosity" which Faulkner described in explaining the title of *Light in August,* and which he associated particularly with Lena Grove, pervades the account of "The Long Summer" following Eula's marriage to Flem Snopes—the summer during which the idiot Isaac Snopes has his affair with Jack Houston's cow. The cow, like Eula, evokes a number of classical references, as when Ike looks into her eyes and "sees himself in twin miniature mirrored by the inscrutable abstraction; one with that which Juno might have looked out with, he watches himself contemplating what those who looked at Juno saw" (p. 208).

Like Benjy in *The Sound and the Fury,* Ike has little or no sense of time, and his impressions are immediate and extremely concrete. In rendering those impressions, however, Faulkner uses every rhetorical trick he can bring to bear. The technique expands in outrageous metaphors, as when a rainstorm is described in terms of an equine sexual encounter: "The pine-snoring wind dropped, then gathered; in an anticlimax of complete vacuum the shaggy pelt of earth became overblown like that of a receptive mare for the rampant crash, the furious brief fecundation which, still rampant, seeded itself in flash and glare of noise and fury and then was gone, vanished . . ." (p. 211; cf. *A Green Bough,* xxxvi). The ironic flavor of the exaggeration is needed, perhaps, as a medium in which to contain the idiot's ecstatic and almost perfect immersion in the motion of life in the cow, the vegetation, the earth, the air, the water, and even the grass fire that, together with a frightened horse, gives him his chance to play Quixote to her Dulcinea.

The set pieces in which the idiot's experience of sunrise and sunset are described are perhaps the most eloquent passages in the book, the most extravagantly allusive, and the most emphatic in their evocation of the moving world. "Now he watches the recurrence of that which he discovered for the first time three days ago: that dawn, light, is not decanted onto earth from the sky, but instead is from the earth itself suspired. Roofed by the woven canopy of blind annealing grass-roots and the roots of trees, dark in the blind dark of time's silt and rich refuse—the constant and unslumbering anonymous worm-glut and the inextricable known bones—Troy's Helen and the nymphs and the snoring mitred bishops, the saviors and the victims and the kings—it wakes, up-seeping, attritive in uncountable creeping channels: first, root; then frond by frond, from whose escaping tips like gas it rises and disseminates and stains the sleep-fast earth with drowsy insect-murmur; then, still upward-seeking, creeps the knitted bark of trunk and limb where, suddenly louder leaf by leaf and dispersive in diffusive sudden speed, melodious with the winged and jeweled throats, it upward bursts and fills night's globed negation with jonquil thunder" (p. 207). The other end of the day is seen in reflection as Ike drinks from a spring which serves as an image for the same contraction of time as was attempted in "Twilight" and "The Hill." "It is the well of days, the still and insatiable aperture of earth. It holds in tranquil paradox of suspended precipitation dawn, noon, and sunset; yesterday, today, and tomorrow—star-spawn and hieroglyph, the fierce white dying rose, then gradual and invincible speeding up to and into slack-flood's coronal of nympholept noon. Then ebb's afternoon, until at last the morning, noon, and afternoon flow back, drain the sky and creep leaf by voiceless leaf and twig and branch and trunk, descending, gathering frond by frond among the grass, still creeping downward in drowsy insect murmurs, until at last the complete all of light gathers about that still and tender mouth in one last expiring inhalation" (pp. 212-13).

The rhetoric of these extracts, and of the whole section of the book from which they are taken, develops a complex strategy for evoking the sense of motion and making it available for esthetic purposes. Like the early romantic poets, particularly Wordsworth, but with a rather more conscious and sophisticated awareness of what he is doing, Faulkner develops the intuition of "something far more deeply interfused" as it arises in the supposedly simple mind of a child or an idiot. Unlike many of the early romantics, Faulkner clearly understands that the mysterious "something" which is identified with "the life of things" and seen especially in "the light of setting suns" is not a transcendent moral quality, but the quality of motion pervading the universe. The supposedly simple mind, he shows, is not so simple after all, but it is less likely than the educated mind to obscure the dynamism of the world and of its own life. Faulkner, describing the Wye above Tintern Abbey as it were from the point of view of the Idiot Boy, out-Wordsworths Wordsworth both in the intensity of the vision and in the concrete immediacy with which it is conveyed.

At the same time Faulkner avoids the pitfall of sentimentalism by making the whole incident ridiculously absurd. The love affair is doomed to be short because of the very conventions of human relationship which are parodied in the high-flown language of courtly love which he uses to describe it. The same conventions, when Eula's growing organs occasion her illegitimate pregnancy, marry her to "the froglike creature which barely reached her shoulder" (p. 169), Flem

Snopes. Flem has been prophetically visualized by Labove, the schoolmaster, as "the crippled Vulcan to that Venus, who would not possess her but merely own her by the single strength which power gave, the dead power of money, wealth, gewgaws, baubles, as he might own, not a picture, statue: a field, say. He saw it: the fine land rich and fecund and foul and eternal and impervious to him who claimed title to it, oblivious, drawing to itself tenfold the quantity of living seed its owner's whole life could have secreted and compounded, producing a thousandfold the harvest he could ever hope to gather and save" (p. 135).

The hamlet of Frenchman's Bend, "which wombed once by chance and accident one blind seed of the spendthrift Olympian ejaculation and did not even know it" (p. 169), sees her off (for the most part vicariously), on the train to Texas, and Ratliff contemplates his remembered glimpse of her face in the train window, "the calm beautiful mask seen once more beyond a moving pane of glass, then gone." He wonders just how badly life has been betrayed. "Of course there was the waste, not wasted on Snopes but on all of them, himself included—Except was it waste? . . . He looked at the face again. It had not been tragic, and now it was not even damned, since from behind it there looked out only another mortal natural enemy of the masculine race. . . . and now as he watched, the lost calm face vanished. It went fast; it was as if the moving glass were in retrograde, it too merely a part, a figment, of the concentric flotsam and jetsam of the translation, and there remained only the straw bag, the minute tie, the constant jaw" (p. 171) which characterize Flem Snopes. This passage is followed immediately by Ratliff's allegory of Flem in hell, dispossessing the devil on a technicality. Flem is presented as a Pluto who is the epitome of the conventional, and as such he is the perfect agent for the frustration of Eula's cosmic fertility.

Ratliff sees Eula in another window later on, when he and

some other men go to fetch her father to set Henry Armstid's broken leg, the night the spotted horses escape. The image this time is like a parody of Poe's early poem "To Helen": "She did not lean out, she merely stood there, full in the moon, apparently blank-eyed or certainly not looking downward at them—the heavy gold hair, the mask not tragic and perhaps not even doomed: just damned, the strong faint lift of breasts beneath marblelike fall of the garment; to those below what Brunhilde, what Rhinemaiden on what spurious river-rock of papier-mache, what Helen returned to what topless and shoddy Argos, waiting for no one" (pp. 349-50). The marble-statue image here gives appropriate emphasis to the betrayal of fertility, and it also has its usual function of stopping motion. It serves as contrast to the horses, which directly represent the energy of life.

The four most prominent incidents in the middle part of *The Hamlet* all follow essentially the same thematic pattern, and all involve frustration of life. Eula's "Olympian" sexuality and potential fertility, Ike Snopes's courtly feeling for and behavior with the cow, Houston's relations with his wife and his horse, and the sale of the spotted horses to the community at large all lead to dead ends. So, for that matter, does Mink Snopes's revenge on Houston (at least in *The Hamlet*), and so does Ratliff's running battle with Flem. Every hopeful green stalk of life that appears in this paradoxically burgeoning waste land is sooner or later blighted: the whole pattern of the book, especially as it is carried out in the imagery, systematically blocks fertility, which is the motion of life, with sterility, stasis, and death.

Too many critics, seeing this pattern partially, have decided that Faulkner was a pessimist, or that he was a failure as an artist. Neither conclusion is necessary. The purpose of the whole pattern is not to lead us to a feeling of despair but, as Faulkner said in the Nobel Speech, "to help man endure by lifting his heart, by reminding him of the courage and honor

and hope and pride and compassion and pity and sacrifice
which have been the glory of his past."[14] Eula has a child,
Ike has a toy cow, Houston has the only kind of release possible for him, Mink has another target for revenge, Ratliff
has a recovered sense of humor and balance, and we might
even note, as Faulkner may have wryly meant, that Flem has
all Jefferson before him, where to choose. Life is not always
pretty, and Faulkner never says it is, but it does go on. In *The
Hamlet* the obstacles serve to demonstrate its power, as it
swarms and scurries so abundantly and so amusingly that
nothing can really keep it down, least of all perhaps the sterile
and impotent Flem.

Humor, as we have briefly noted in connection with *As I
Lay Dying*, is one of Faulkner's most useful ways of expressing the energy of life in the face of frustration. In the texture
of the work it is one of his best tools for shaping the quirks
of paradox and sudden surprise in which the dialectic of
dynamism and stasis is so often seen. In the exuberance of its
exaggerations, and in its rendering of sheer speed and multi-
plicity of movement, it serves to communicate the bewildering and overwhelming power with which life sweeps around,
past, over, and through all obstacles.

The doom of the convict in the flood is a clear example of
both the dynamic and the static aspects of this humor. In the
flood, the whole world comes alive (or perhaps "awake" is a
better word, since it is never dead); everything is in motion,
and the convict is forced, by the urgency of the woman's pregnant condition and the brute force of the current, into frantic
motion too, in spite of his best efforts during most of the story
to return to the peace and quiet of the prison. In the Atchaf-
alaya Basin, as he tries to keep ahead of a second wave and
find solid ground on which to deliver the baby, he finds himself "driving the splintered board furiously now, glaring at her

14 *Essays*, p. 120.

out of his wild swollen sleepless face and crying, croaking,
'Hold on! For God's sake hold on!' . . . He told it, the un-
believable: hurry, hasten: the man falling from a cliff being
told to catch onto something and save himself; the very telling
of it emerging shadowy and burlesque, ludicrous, comic and
mad, from the ague of unbearable forgetting with a quality
more dreamily furious than any fable behind proscenium
lights . . ." (p. 171). The wild outrageousness of the humor
makes a substantial contribution to the picture we get of life,
or motion, rushing the convict along in spite of his desire for
peace, or stasis. From his point of view, the ten years added to
his sentence when he returns to the prison would seem to
be no injustice at all but rather a reward of that much more
static peace to compensate for the extreme suffering which the
motions of the river and the woman's pregnancy have inflicted
on him.

The Hamlet is the most obviously humorous of Faulkner's
books, and V.K. Ratliff is generally the happiest humorist.
As Faulkner said in one of the Virginia interviews, Ratliff is
the character "least troubled by change," or progress. "That
he had accepted a change in culture, a change in environment,
and he has suffered no anguish, no grief from it. In—for that
reason, he's in favor of change, because it's motion and it's
the world as he knows it, and he's never one to say, I wish
I had been born a hundred years ago, or I'm sorry I was born
now and couldn't have put it off a hundred years. Ratliff will
take what's now and do the best he can with it because he is
—possesses what you might call a moral, spiritual eupepsia,
that his digestion is good, all right, nothing alarms him."[15]
This interview took place after Ratliff had been corrupted by
Gavin Stevens' anti-Snopes campaign; but most of the statement applies fairly enough to the Ratliff of *The Hamlet*.
Except at the end of the book, when, in a surprising lapse of
his usual good sense, he falls for the salted mine trick, he is

[15] *Faulkner in the University*, p. 253.

master of himself and sufficiently of the situation to come off materially even with Flem, and morally far ahead. He is therefore free to develop the humor that arises when people, sometimes including himself, are figuratively or literally run over by something that moves too fast for them.

Ratliff's narrative of his encounter with Eck Snopes's spotted horse in the boarding house provides a humorous moment of dynamic stasis in which both time and space are collapsed. " 'Maybe there wasn't but one of them things in Mrs. Littlejohn's house that night, like Eck says. But it was the biggest drove of just one horse I ever seen. It was in my rooms and it was on the front porch and I could hear Mrs. Littlejohn hitting it over the head with that washboard in the back yard all at the same time.' " One of his listeners says, " 'I wonder what that horse thought Ratliff was . . . . Jumping out windows and running indoors in his shirt-tail? I wonder how many Ratliffs that horse thought he saw.' " Ratliff says, " 'I dont know . . . . But if he saw just half as many of me as I saw of him, he was sholy surrounded. . . . And that boy there [Eck's son Wallstreet Panic], he stayed right under it one time to my certain knowledge for a full one-and-one-half minutes without ducking his head or even batting his eyes. Yes sir, when I looked around and seen that varmint in the door behind me blaring its eyes at me, I'd a made sho Flem Snopes had brought a tiger back from Texas except I knowed that couldn't no just one tiger completely fill a entire room' " (pp. 353-54). This comic subversion of the categories of both space and time stops the motion effectively for a kind of bemused contemplation. Without such artificial intervention, the motion carries us along too ruthlessly to permit our conscious awareness of anything but its sound and fury.

The sentence in Ratliff's narrative about the immobility of Wallstreet Panic is more than matched by the anonymous narrator's account of Wall's behavior when the horses, frightened by their first sight of shelled corn, break out of the barn.

Eck and two others run for the comparative safety of a wagon in the lot. "Several voices from the fence were . . . shouting something but Eck did not even hear them until, in the act of scrambling madly at the tail-gate, he looked behind him and saw the little boy still leaning to the knot-hole in the door which in the next instant vanished into matchwood, the knot-hole itself exploding from his eye and leaving him, motionless in the diminutive overalls and still leaning forward a little until he vanished utterly beneath the towering parti-colored wave full of feet and glaring eyes and wild teeth which, overtopping, burst into scattering units revealing at last the gaping orifice and the little boy still standing in it, unscratched, his eye still leaned to the vanished knot-hole" (p. 323). This is essentially the same wave that overwhelms the convict in his skiff, and essentially the same comic contrast is developed with the static human figure, the function of which is to make the motion emphatically apparent.

The version of the spotted horses incident in *The Hamlet* (but not the version published in *Scribner's Magazine* nine years earlier) makes the same use of trees, birds, moonlight, dust, and shadows as some of Faulkner's apprentice works in order to emphasize the pervasiveness of motion and fertility. The evening before and the evening following the sale of the horses are brightly moonlit, and the conversations and activities of the characters are punctuated by references to this cluster of images. When Ratliff warns the men against buying any of the spotted horses, the anonymous narrator notices "the dreaming lambence of the moonlight beyond the veranda. The pear tree across the road opposite was now in full and frosty bloom, the twigs and branches springing not outward from the limbs but standing motionless and perpendicular above the horizontal boughs like the separate and upstreaming hair of a drowned woman sleeping upon the uttermost floor of the windless and tideless sea" (p. 316). Later, "A bird, a shadow, fleet and dark and swift, curved across the moon-light, upward into the pear tree and began to sing; a mock-ingbird" (p. 317). Again, "In the pear tree the mockingbird's idiot reiteration pulsed and purled" (p. 318). As evening falls on the following day, the men stand "along the fence, looking quietly into the lot where the ponies huddled, already begin-ning to fade a little where the long shadow of the house lay upon them, deepening. . . . A noisy cloud of sparrows swept across the lot and into a chinaberry tree beside the house, and in the high soft vague blue swallows stooped and whirled in erratic indecision, their cries like strings plucked at random" (p. 335). After supper, "The pear tree before Mrs. Littlejohn's was like drowned silver now in the moon. The mockingbird of last night, or another one, was already singing in it . . ." (p. 342). As Eck's horse runs away, after its adventure in Mrs. Littlejohn's house, "the road gashed pallid and moony be-tween the moony shadows of the bordering trees, the horse still galloping, galloping its shadow into the dust . . ." (p. 347).

The meaning of this imagery is most clearly seen as Ratliff and the others go to fetch Will Varner and as they return with him to treat Henry Armstid's broken leg. "They went up the road in a body, treading the moon-blanched dust in the tremulous April night murmurous with the moving of sap and the wet bursting of burgeoning leaf and bud and constant with the thin and urgent cries and the brief and fading bursts of galloping hooves" (p. 349), as the buyers chase their horses through the countryside. This passage is followed by the vision of Eula in the window. On the return trip, "The moon was now high overhead, a pearled and mazy yawn in the soft sky, the ultimate ends of which rolled onward, whorl on whorl, beyond the pale stars and by pale stars surrounded.[16] They walked in a close clump, tramping their shadows into the road's mild dust, blotting the shadows of the burgeoning

---

[16] Cf. Vincent Van Gogh, "La nuit étoilée" (1889), New York Museum of Modern Art.

trees which soared, trunk branch and twig against the pale sky, delicate and finely thinned. They passed the dark store. Then the pear tree came in sight. It rose in mazed and silver immobility like exploding snow; the mockingbird still sang in it. 'Look at that tree,' Varner said. 'It ought to make this year, sho' " (pp. 350-51). It is essentially the same tree as the one in the rector's garden in *Soldiers' Pay* and the one in the Sartoris garden in *Sartoris*; it works better in *The Hamlet* because *The Hamlet* is better organized to contain Faulkner's strong metaphysical awareness of a simultaneously local and universal energy of life.

The use of rhythm is another fundamental way to communicate a sense of life pervading people and the world, and Faulkner uses rhythm lavishly in many ways. We have noted his unusual sensitivity to seasonal change and to the cycles of the day, especially sunrise and sunset. Events and characters in his work are strongly influenced by these "biological clocks," which generally represent the motions of fertility in people, animals, and the plant life of the earth. These rhythms are especially strong in *The Hamlet*, a fertility comedy with a serious meaning.

A closely related technique is Faulkner's frequent use of visceral and kinesthetic imagery, which, as Walter J. Slatoff points out, is typically presented in rhythmic patterns of tension and release. Slatoff remarks "that there is undoubtedly a profound kinship between the responses we call 'kinesthetic' and 'visceral' and our fundamental sense of life and of our own being; certainly there is a deep kinship between those responses and the experiences of the kind of inmost self Faulkner assumes."[17] In many passages of Faulkner's fiction, eating and breathing are equivalent to living, whereas the feeling of suffocation or a refusal of food, and especially the act of vomiting, suggest an inability to live or a rejection of life.

[17] Slatoff, pp. 246-47; see also pp. 60-66 and 243-44.

This association is particularly strong when Horace Benbow in *Sanctuary* and Joe Christmas in *Light in August* vomit because they are horrified by their discovery of sexual maturity in Little Belle and Bobbie Allen. Joe's refusal of food on several occasions is a refusal of growth or change, as well as of social relations. His final abnegation of life makes him act "as though he desires to see his native earth in all its phases for the first or the last time." But we are told by the anonymous narrator that "he remained a foreigner to the very immutable laws which earth must obey." Then "suddenly the true answer comes to him. . . . 'I dont have to bother about having to eat anymore,' he thinks. 'That's what it is'" (*LIA* 320). In *The Hamlet*, similarly, when Mink Snopes realizes that he cannot escape the consequences of his murder of Houston, we are told that "he stopped being hungry" (p. 260). This imagery contrasts with the hearty eating of Lena Grove and Eula Varner, who embody and accept the motion of life.

Both eating and breathing are continually and conspicuously mentioned throughout the long description of Mink's efforts to conceal his crime, to evade his cousin Launcelot, or Lump, Snopes and the sheriff, to get rid of Houston's corpse, and to kill Houston's dog. Let down by the sudden fall of the corpse inside the hollow tree where he tries to hide it, Mink scrambles frantically to get out; "but the shell crumbled . . . and he climbed interminably, furiously perpetual and without gain, his mouth open for his panting breath . . ." (p. 259). He recognizes the dog as often by the sound of its breathing as by any other sign; and, when it howls in the swamp where the corpse is hidden, "It seemed to him that he had even heard the intake of breath before the first cry came up . . ." (pp. 259-60). He forces himself to eat raw corn meal, the only food he has, only so that he can continue his futile efforts. When he succeeds in shooting the dog, "the tremendous silence which had been broken three nights ago when the first cry of the hound reached him and which had never once been restored, annealed, even while he slept, roared down about him and, still roaring, began to stiffen and set like cement, not only in his hearing but in his lungs, his breathing . . ." (p. 264). But the dog is not dead, and Mink's breathing goes on, as does the life of the world around him, "his head and lungs filled with that roaring silence across which the random and velvet-shod fireflies drifted and winked and beyond which the constant frogs pulsed and beat, until the . . . sky . . . began to turn gray and then primrose, and already he could see three buzzards soaring in it. Now I must get up, he told himself . . ." (p. 265). The motion of life in Mink, as in nature, pulses and beats in many rhythmic patterns, which are evoked by Faulkner's descriptions, by the imagery he uses, and by the rhythms of his prose.

Breathing and eating continue to be prominently mentioned. Talking with his wife, Mink feels "her hard, hot, panting breath on his face," and she scolds him for killing Houston " 'when you had no money to get away on if you ran, and nothing to eat if you stayed' " (p. 275). Meeting his cousin Lump, he hears "the faint rasp of the repressed breathing at his shoulder" (p. 276), and Lump asks querulously, " 'Aint you even got nothing to eat?' " (p. 279). When he escapes from Lump and tries to get the decaying corpse out of the tree, "he knew now it was not imagination he had smelled and he dropped the axe and began to tear at the shell with his hands, his head averted, his teeth bared and clenched, his breath hissing through them . . ." (pp. 290-91). As he is being taken to Jefferson after his capture by the sheriff, he almost manages, with the help of a deputy, to break his neck in the framework of the surrey in which they are riding, but the officers extricate him and throw water on him to revive him, and he has to return to life. ". . . after a while he could breathe again all right, and the faint wind of motion had dried the water from his face and only his shirt was a little damp, not a cool wind yet but just a wind free at last of the unendurable

sun, blowing out of the beginning of dusk, the surrey moving now beneath an ordered overarch of sunshot trees, between the clipped and tended lawns where children shrieked
and played in bright small garments in the sunset and the
ladies sat rocking in the fresh dresses of afternoon and the
men coming home from work turned into the neat painted
gates, toward plates of food and cups of coffee in the long beginning of twilight" (p. 295). When he smells the food being
brought to the other prisoners in the jail, he thinks indig-
nantly, "Are they going to feed them niggers before they do a
white man?" (p. 296).

Faulkner is not always successful in his use of rhythm,
especially in his early work. In "The Priest," one of the
sketches published in *The Double Dealer* in 1925, he is
crashingly offensive. "The twilight is like the breath of contented kine, stirring among the lilacs and shaking spikes of
bloom, ringing the soundless bells of hyacinths dreaming
briefly of Lesbos, whispering among the pale and fronded
palms" (*NOS* 38-39). But in *The Hamlet*, using the same
material to evoke the same mood, he brings it off triumphantly. Ike Snopes is bedding down with the cow in the
woods. "The swale is constant with random and erratic fireflies. There is the one fierce evening star, though almost at
once the marching constellations mesh and gear and wheel
strongly on. Blond too in that gathering last of light, she owns
no dimension against the lambent and undimensional grass.
But she is there, solid amid the abstract earth. He walks
lightly upon it, returning, treading lightly that frail inextricable canopy of the subterrene slumber—Helen and the bishops,
the kings and the graceless seraphim" (p. 213). Aside from
the difference between the New Orleans setting of the sketch
and the Yoknapatawpha location of *The Hamlet*, neither of
which is very specific in these passages, the technique is essentially the same, even to the use of some rather esoteric literary

allusions in both. The difference in the results is due to a greater tact in the use of language—Houston's cow is more concrete than "contented kine"—and a greater skill in the weaving of rhythms. In *The Hamlet* the rhythms are complex and various, and they work together with the meaning, the rhetoric, and the imagery to persuade us into close empathy with the life that is being described.

It is this empathic sense of life that Faulkner uses all of his tools to evoke. As he says, "the carpenter don't build a house just to drive nails,"[18] and "you don't write a story just to show your versatility with your tools. . . . It's man in the ageless, eternal struggles which we inherit and we go through as though they'd never happened before, shown for a moment in a dramatic instant of the furious motion of being alive, that's all any story is. You catch this fluidity which is human life and you focus a light on it and you stop it long enough for people to be able to see it. . . ."[19] Technique, in Faulkner's view, is functional or it is nothing. His intent is always to communicate the motion of life, never the static concepts, images, rhetorical devices, sentences, or words in which the communication has to be cast. The motion is stopped, artificially, and emphasized by means of these "tools," so that we can see it as motion, and feel in ourselves the force and tension, the sweat, the agony, and the exaltation of living.

[18] *Faulkner in the University*, p. 50.
[19] *Ibid.*, p. 239; second ellipsis in text.

Four / Moral

The fiction that Faulkner published after 1940 is, in general, less well organized and artistically less successful than the great works of his middle period. There is a weakening of artistic imagination, and the style more and more gives way to mannerism. At the same time, perhaps because of the artistic weakening, the moral implications which were always present are brought out more explicitly.[1] The increasing thematic explicitness provides an opening that a critic may legitimately use in trying to explain what Faulkner is about; and the eagerness with which the later works have been discussed, in spite of their relatively low esthetic quality, is testimony to the critics' gratitude, if not always to their literary perspicacity. The interviews Faulkner gave and the public statements he made during the late period offer further useful material— granted that it has to be used with care.

The logic of Faulkner's moral meaning is fairly simple, once his premises are understood. Its emotional aspects, however, are complex, and they have proved difficult for many critics to accept. Confronted with what Faulkner explicitly

---

[1] Joseph Gold, in *William Faulkner: A Study in Humanism: From Metaphor to Discourse* (Norman: University of Oklahoma Press, 1966), pp. 4-20, describes this change at length. His second subtitle aptly characterizes it.

said, and sometimes tediously repeated, the critics have not always been able to believe that he really meant it.

One of the difficulties is the distinction, which is not always clear but which must be made, between the moral purpose of the work and the technical use of moral values within the work. On the technical side of the writer's job, as Faulkner pointed out, "A message is one of his tools, just like the rhetoric, just like the punctuation";[2] but this technical neutrality did not keep him from remarking with equal emphasis, "I like to think of the world I created as being a kind of keystone in the universe; that, small as that keystone is, if it were ever taken away the universe itself would collapse."[3] The writer, like other men, has a right to as much freedom as he needs in order to discharge his responsibilities. If the work is to be morally effective, the method cannot be restricted by moral formulas.

One of the interviews indicates that Faulkner had his own difficulties with the logic of this distinction, but that his grasp of the substance was firm. The session was with the Department of Psychiatry at the University of Virginia, and one question, naturally enough, contained the phrase "irrational human behavior," which evidently made Faulkner uncomfortable. He said, "I think the writer is not really interested in bettering man's condition. . . . He's interested in all man's behavior with no judgment whatever. That it's motion, it's life, the only alternative is nothingness, death. And so to the writer, anything man does is fine because it's motion." This answer did not satisfy the audience, a member of which pressed the psychiatrist's problem of relating a scientific objectivity of method with the value system implied by a therapeutic purpose. Faulkner was constrained to admit that "Maybe the writer has . . . . a hope that what he does may improve man in the sense that it will give man some instance of man's

---

[2] *Faulkner in the University*, p. 239.
[3] *Writers at Work*, p. 141.

fine record, being fragile and frail and not his own boss by any manner of means, yet out of that he has managed somehow to endure, to have accomplished a few things which have lasted. Maybe in that sense the writer has got to work for man's betterment, even if he's not deliberately trying to."[4]

Actually, the moment he assumed that motion, or life, is better than nothingness, or death, Faulkner had justified the writer's active role in the betterment of man. The formula "Life is motion" has, in fact, strong moral implications, about which Faulkner was never neutral. They are present in all of his work, from *The Marble Faun* to *The Reivers*. Stated simply, the moral is that in a world that changes man must also change. Mere endurance is not enough. To prevail is to live, to move, to do something positive. It is the moral duty of the writer to help man prevail by compressing the energy of life in his work so that others can release and use it even after the writer's personal life is done.

These considerations are obviously related to Faulkner's handling of time and his use of history; and there has always been a strong and very proper interest on the part of critics in these aspects of the work. But the critics have been wrong more often than right in their interpretations. Jean-Paul Sartre, noticing that "Faulkner appears to arrest the motion at the very heart of things," arrives at the conclusion that (like Proust, according to Sartre) he decapitates time: "they have taken away its future—that is to say, the dimension of free choice and act."[5] André Malraux makes a similar point in slightly different terms when he says that in *Sanctuary*, which he calls "the intrusion of Greek tragedy into the detec-

---

[4] *Faulkner in the University*, pp. 267, 268.

[5] Jean-Paul Sartre, "Time in Faulkner: *The Sound and the Fury*," *Three Decades*, pp. 227, 230. The original reads, "Il semble que Faulkner saisisse, au coeur même des choses, une vitesse glacée," and "Proust et Faulkner l'ont simplement décapité, ils lui ont ôté son avenir, c'est-à-dire la dimension des actes et de la liberté." *Situations, I: essais critiques* (Paris: Gallimard, 1947), pp. 73, 77.

tive story," Faulkner creates a world where man is always crushed, where, in effect, "There is no 'man' . . . or any values, or even any psychology, in spite of the interior monologues of his first books. But there is a Destiny standing, single, behind all these different yet similar beings, like death behind a ward for the incurable." Malraux suggests further that, "as Lawrence envelops himself in sexuality, Faulkner escapes into the irremediable," and that "An inexorable, sometimes epic force is released in his work whenever he succeeds in bringing one of his characters up against the irremediable. And perhaps the irremediable is his only true subject, perhaps his only aim is to crush man."[6] These interpretations deserve respect both for their intrinsic intelligence and because they supported some of the earliest authoritative recognitions of Faulkner's greatness; nevertheless their conclusions are completely wrong. They confuse Faulkner's means with his ends; they assume that the arrest of motion is his final purpose and not, as Faulkner himself in later interviews insisted, a technique or tool for achieving a diametrically opposite result.

The fact is that such terms as "doom," "fate," and "irremediable" in Faulkner's work almost always refer in one way or another to the inevitability of change in the world as he imagined it.[7] In that world a man is crushed if he is unable to move along with the motion of life; and certainly many of

[6] Preface to *Sanctuaire* (Paris: Le Livre de Poche, Gallimard, 1949), pp. 9, 6, 7-8 (my translation). In the original these passages read: "*Sanctuaire*, c'est l'intrusion de la tragédie grecque dans le roman policier." "Monde où l'homme n'existe qu'écrasé. Il n'y a pas d' 'homme' de Faulkner, ni de valeurs, ni même de psychologie, malgré les monologues intérieurs de ses premiers livres. Mais il y a un Destin dressé, unique, derrière tous ces êtres différents et semblables, comme la mort derrière une salle des incurables." "Et, comme Lawrence s'enveloppe dans la sexualité, Faulkner s'enfouit dans l'irrémédiable.

"Une force sourde, parfois épique, se déclenche chez lui dès qu'il parvient à affronter un de ses personnages et l'irrémédiable. Et peut-être l'irrémédiable est-il son seul vrai sujet, peut-être ne s'agit-il jamais pour lui que de parvenir à écraser l'homme."

[7] This point is well demonstrated in Karl E. Zink, "Flux and the Frozen Moment," p. 301, and "Faulkner's Garden: Woman and the Immemorial Earth," *Modern Fiction Studies*, II (Autumn 1956), 144.

Faulkner's characters are crushed. It is also true that in Faulkner's world, as in Bergson's, human consciousness can never be immediately aware of anything that is not already past, and therefore "irremediable." But Faulkner's truth is not limited to these considerations. We have seen that some of his characters, such as Lena Grove and eventually Byron Bunch, do move with the motion of life, and they are not crushed. Moreover, their motion in the present carries them toward the future, which they cannot clearly foresee, to be sure, precisely because it is the future, but to which they are completely and powerfully committed.

One of Faulkner's comments makes this point very fully and sensibly. In answer to a questioner in Japan, who wanted to know if he did not regard the present period as being unusually dark, Faulkner said, "Well, the darkness of the world, I agree with you it is darker at times than at other times, and this is a very dark time. But I am still convinced that man is tougher than any darkness. That man's hope is the capacity to believe in man, his hope, his aspiration toward a better human condition. . . . He knows that since his own yesterday showed him today that he endured, was capable of hope, was capable of believing that man's condition can be bettered, is his assurance that after he is gone someone will read what he has done and see what man yesterday was capable of believing and of hope that man's condition can be changed; and man's condition does change. . . . There will be a time when the older people that get the world into wars won't be able to get the world into wars any more for the young people to get killed in. That will come, it will take time, it will take patience, and it will take a capacity of people to believe that man's condition can be improved, not as a gift to him, but by his own efforts. That he can do it."[8] Man's fate, according to Faulkner, is that he must and will change; man's hope is that, "by his own efforts," he can change for the

[8] *Faulkner at Nagano*, pp. 157, 158-59.

better.[9] It would be hard to imagine an attitude with more emphasis on the future than is implied in this reasoning.

Faulkner's handling of history generally bears on the agrarian myth of the South, according to which that region before the Civil War was an Eden of simplicity and innocence, ruined by the war and Reconstruction, now a waste land where the aristocratic virtues of the old order have been abandoned and largely forgotten, creative fertility lost, and the meaning and value of human life corrupted by money, mechanization, and moral relativity. George Marion O'Donnell, Malcolm Cowley, Robert Penn Warren, Allen Tate, and most recently Cleanth Brooks, although they have all made valuable contributions to the growth of interest in Faulkner, have also, with varying degrees of intelligence, misinterpreted his relation to this popular myth by overestimating the extent to which he agreed with its premises and values.

Faulkner has assimilated this myth into a larger context than that of *Gone with the Wind*. He has seen it as a regional version of what R.W.B. Lewis describes as the myth of the American Adam, and he has seen that myth in turn as an American version of a myth of modern civilization generally —a myth of the fall of man from a simple, primitive, rural or even nomadic way of life into a modern, complex, urban, industrial way. He has also integrated it with the still more general myth of the individual's development from childhood to maturity: the fall of man from innocence defined as childish ignorance, weakness, and dependency into the greater strength, responsible independence, and possible wisdom of maturity. When these assimilations are fully worked out, they mean that, in order to grow up at the present time, a young Southerner must put away whatever unduly sentimental attachment he may have for the Old South (or rather for the

---

[9] Faulkner's use of the phrases "man's hope" and "human condition" in this passage makes me suspect that he was thinking specifically of Malraux, whose novels *L'espoir* and *La condition humaine* were translated under the titles *Man's Hope* and *Man's Fate*.

unrealistic legends about it with which he is likely to be stuffed) and become a citizen of the world as it is now and as his efforts may be able to help shape it for the future.

Faulkner made his intellectual understanding of this pattern perfectly clear in a number of interviews. When a questioner asked him, point-blank, "do you like the Old South or the New South better?" he said, "Well, the New South has got too many people in it and it is changing the country too much. It's—has—it gets rid of the part of Mississippi that I liked when I was young, which was the forest. Though it's foolish to be against progress because everyone is a part of progress and he'll have no other chance except this one so he —it's silly not to cope with it, to compromise with it, cope with it. Probably anyone remembers with something of nostalgia the—his young years."[10]

The emotional ambivalence reflected by this statement is present almost everywhere in Faulkner's fiction, and it has doubtless contributed to the critical misinterpretations of his relation to the agrarian myth. But such ambivalence need not be surprising or confusing. Because Faulkner's basic assumption is that of continual change, the feeling of nostalgia is practically inevitable. In a world where the only moral imperative is that men must change, for the better if possible, the unforgivable sin is innocence. The necessity of choosing among alternative possibilities of change involves not only regret for what must be rejected, but guilt as well. Therefore the most ardent advocate of change may be, for quite logical reasons, the keenest appreciator of the treasured but abandoned values of an older time. The man who responsibly lives and moves, and thereby destroys the past as he creates the future, is the very man to look back with most love and longing to that irrevocably lost time before the decision was taken, before we were driven out of whatever Eden, before

[10] *Faulkner in the University*, p. 98.

we brought whatever new kind of death and woe into the
world that we have made.

Go Down, Moses is generally regarded as the last of Faulkner's great works. The book as a whole has not received much
notice, although a part of it, "The Bear," has been a popular
topic of criticism, sometimes in connection with one or more
of the other stories in the volume and sometimes not. Discussions of "The Bear" almost always include consideration of
the fourth section, which Faulkner never published in any
version of the story except that of *Go Down, Moses.*

Most discussions have assumed that, as Irving Howe puts it,
"The fable of 'The Bear' falls within the broad stream of the
pastoral which courses through American writing, pastoral
suggesting the conscious turn to simplicity as a desired way
of life and the nostalgia for a time which could more fully
realize that desire." Moreover, says Howe, "That Isaac Mc-
Caslin is meant and deserves to gain our moral admiration,
seems beyond doubt."[11] As we have seen, Faulkner's general
statements do not support the first of these opinions, and several critics, increasingly in recent years, have had strong
doubts about one or both of them.[12]

In his explicit statements Faulkner supports the doubters
more than he does Howe, although he often shows his emo-

[11] *William Faulkner: A Critical Study* (revised edn., New York: Vintage
Books, 1962), pp. 95, 96.

[12] See William Van O'Connor, *The Tangled Fire of William Faulkner*
(Minneapolis: University of Minnesota Press, 1954), pp. 133-34; Ursula
Brumm, "Wilderness and Civilization: A Note on William Faulkner," *Partisan
Review*, XXII (Summer 1955), 340-50, reprinted *Three Decades*, pp. 125-34;
Olga W. Vickery, *The Novels of William Faulkner* (revised edn., Baton
Rogue: Louisiana State University Press, 1964), pp. 132-34; Leonard Casper,
"The Square Beatific," *America*, CIII (1960), 515; Herbert A. Perluck, " 'The
Heart's Driving Complexity': An Unromantic Reading of Faulkner's 'The
Bear,' " *Accent*, XX (Winter 1960), 23-46; Stanley Sultan, "Call Me Ishmael:
The Hagiography of Isaac McCaslin," *Texas Studies in Literature and Lan-
guage*, III (Spring 1961), 50-66; Melvin Backman, "The Wilderness and the
Negro in Faulkner's 'The Bear,' " *PMLA*, LXXVI (December 1961), 595-600;
and Brooks, pp. 418-19.

tional ambivalence. In one interview he said that Ike's wilderness experiences "didn't give him success but they gave him something a lot more important, even in this country. They gave him serenity, they gave him what would pass for wisdom —I mean wisdom as contradistinct from the schoolman's wisdom of education."[13] But in another interview, about a year later, when he was asked if Ike represented the predicament of modern man unable to "find a humanity that he can fit in with," he said, "Well, there are some people in any time and age that cannot face and cope with the problems. There seem to be three stages: The first says, This is rotten, I'll have no part of it, I will take death first. The second says, This is rotten, I don't like it, I can't do anything about it, but at least I will not participate in it myself, I will go off into a cave or climb a pillar to sit on. The third says, This stinks and I'm going to do something about it. McCaslin is the second. He says, This is bad, and I will withdraw from it. What we need are people who will say, This is bad and I'm going to do something about it, I'm going to change it."[14]

Faulkner's insistence on the feeling of regret for what is left behind could be accounted for on technical grounds alone. It serves him well in his efforts to oppose images of stasis to the motion of change. But he also insists on the moral principle that we must wisely govern change in order to insure that something good will be created to replace the good things we leave behind. When he uses the pastoral feeling, therefore, he gives the nostalgia that Howe observes full emphasis, but he does so in aid of something more complex. He almost always adds an ironic dash of what Richard Chase has called "antipastoral," an attitude in which, as Daniel Hoffman remarks, "the contrast between the 'pastoral idyl' and 'real life' " is "likely to . . . work to the disadvantage of the claims of per-

[13] *Faulkner in the University*, p. 54.

[14] *Ibid.*, pp. 245-46; for an earlier statement of the three-man formula, see *Writers at Work*, pp. 132-33.

fection made for the bucolic idyl."[15] Faulkner seldom lets a passionate shepherd say very much to his love without giving someone a chance to object. Ike McCaslin, the pastoral spokesman of *Go Down, Moses,* is not a complete spokesman for Faulkner, or an ideal hero in the book, and he does not have the last word.

The wilderness Ike loves is morally neutral, according to Faulkner. "To me, the wilderness was man's past, that man had emerged. The bear was a symbol of the old forces, not evil forces, but the old forces which in man's youth were not evil, but that they were in man's blood, his inheritance, his impulses came from that old or ruthless malevolence, which was nature. His dreams, his nightmares; and this story was to me a universal story of the man who, still progressing, being better than his father, hoping that his son shall be a little better than he, had to learn to cope with and still cope with it in the terms of justice and pity and compassion and strength."[16] Ike, however, learns to cope only with the wilderness, and not with the increasingly industrial civilization that is displacing it. When Faulkner was asked "What characters in general . . . in your novels, do you think respond best to . . . progress," he answered, in a way to surprise most readers, "The Snopes have responded to it and have coped with it pretty well."[17] Ike puts himself in such a position that he cannot cope with it at all.

The balance of Faulkner's attitude is most carefully struck, perhaps, in his answer to the direct question whether he intended his readers "to sympathize more with Old Ben . . . or . . . the hunters . . . ." He said, "What the writer's asking is compassion, understanding, that change must alter, must happen, and change is going to alter what was. That no matter how fine anything seems, it can't endure, because once it stops,

---

[15] Hoffman, p. 204.

[16] *Faulkner at Nagano,* pp. 50-51; cf. pp. 58-59; 92-93.

[17] *Faulkner in the University,* p. 253; cf. pp. 80, 283.

abandons motion, it is dead. It's to have compassion for the anguish that the wilderness itself may have felt by being ruthlessly destroyed by axes, by men who simply wanted to make that earth grow something they could sell for a profit, which brought into it a condition based on an evil like human bondage. It's not to choose sides at all—just to compassionate the good splendid things which change must destroy, the splendid fine things which are a part of man's past too, part of man's heritage too, but they were obsolete and had to go." He added, after another question, that "Change if it is not controlled by wise people destroys sometimes more than it brings."[18] Ike has gained a kind of wisdom from his experience of the wilderness; but he deliberately refuses to use that wisdom to help control the changes that are inevitably taking place.

The popular concentration on "The Bear" has tended to obscure the fact that *Go Down, Moses* is not just about Ike, but about the whole McCaslin family, which consists of three branches. The male white line of legitimate inheritance descends from the founder, Lucius Quintus Carothers McCaslin, through his son Theophilus (Uncle Buck) to Ike, in whom it ends. The female white line apparently runs through a daughter of old Carothers who marries a man named Edmonds; their grandson, McCaslin Edmonds, runs the plantation during Ike's minority, and he and his descendants continue to run it after Ike's refusal to inherit. The Negro line stems from old Carothers' miscegenation with his slave Eunice, compounded by his incest with their daughter, Tomasina, or Tomey; this match produces a son, Terrell, or Turl, who marries Tennie, a slave of the Beauchamp family, and the Negro line takes the name of Beauchamp after emancipation. Because Turl is both the son and the grandson of old Carothers, the Negro line begins, paradoxically, with fifty percent more of the founder's blood than either of the white

[18] *Ibid.*, pp. 276, 277.

140

lines. It is also the most prolific and varied of the three, while
the male white line, conventionally the "purest," is the shortest
as well as the thinnest, an irony which, although it is never
explicitly stated, pervades the novel. The female line and the
Negro line rejoin in the affair between young Carothers
(Roth) Edmonds, the founder's great-great-great-grandson,
and an unnamed great-granddaughter of Turl and Tennie.

"The Bear," as Faulkner apparently wrote it first, and as he
consistently said it should be printed independently of *Go
Down, Moses*, is about Ike's initiation as a hunter in the wilderness. The added fourth section, in the *Go Down, Moses*
version, is concerned with Ike's renunciation of his inheritance
of the "tamed land" and his reasons, or rationalizations, in
support of that gesture. In *Go Down, Moses*, "The Bear" is
preceded by "The Old People" and followed by "Delta Autumn," which frame it with accounts of Ike's earlier and later
experience in the wilderness. This triad is in turn framed by
four other stories, three before and one after, in which relations between Negroes and white people, mainly Negro and
white descendants of Carothers McCaslin, are dramatized.
Lying at the heart of all this framing, the fourth section of
"The Bear" is the climax of the book. The other four sections
and the other six stories are used, in Faulkner's contrapuntal
fashion, to balance, oppose, and comment on one another and
on the climactic section.[19]

The general tone of *Go Down, Moses* is comic, in Faulkner's usual complex and serious way; and all of the stories in
it are comic, although they vary considerably in the degree of
their seriousness. The comic effect of the first story, "Was,"
arises because the slave, Turl, who is hunted like an animal
by Uncle Buck and the boy Cass Edmonds, is the only char-

[19] For differing views on the success of this procedure, see Marvin Klotz,
"Procrustean Revision in Faulkner's *Go Down, Moses*," *American Literature*,
XXXVII (March 1965), 1-16; and Jane Millgate, "Short Story into Novel:
Faulkner's Reworking of 'Gold is Not Always,'" *English Studies*, XLV
(August 1964), 310-17.

acter who gets exactly what he wants, and not by accident. He not only marries Tennie, in spite of violent opposition to the match by her owner and his, but he is instrumental in saving Uncle Buck, for that time, from a much more dangerous hunter, Miss Sophonsiba Beauchamp.

The next story, "The Fire and the Hearth," is more complex. The protagonist, Lucas Beauchamp, grandson of Turl and Tennie, is tempted by the earth, or the power of life, somewhat as Job was by God and the devil, to betray the earth and life. While trying to hide his whiskey still, in order to forestall competition from one George Wilkins, and incidentally to forestall George's marriage to Nat, his daughter, Lucas is almost buried under the side of an old Indian mound. The scene is described in almost supernaturally dynamic terms: ". . . it was probably only a sigh but it sounded to him louder than an avalanche, as though the whole mound had stooped roaring down at him . . . . It drummed on the hollow kettle, covering it and the worm, and boiled about his feet and, as he leaped backward and tripped and fell, about his body too, hurling clods and dirt at him, striking him a final blow squarely in the face with something larger than a clod— a blow not vicious so much as merely heavy-handed, a sort of final admonitory pat from the spirit of darkness and solitude, the old earth, perhaps the old ancestors themselves." The object "even as he lifted it crumbled again and deposited in his palm, as though it had been handed to him, a single coin" (p. 38). Even in almost total darkness, he knows that it is gold.

Precisely and paradoxically at this point, fertility wins its first victory over, and because of, his awakened greed. Hearing "something" which "crashed into flight" from a thicket, he leaps in pursuit, "the quarry fleeing like a deer" (pp. 40, 41), and discovers that his daughter Nat has been watching. Before he can be free to hunt the treasure he assumes must be hidden nearby, he has to accept Nat's engagement to George, provide money for the young couple's domestic needs, and even take George as his partner in bootlegging.

In the conduct of his search, Lucas has no serious difficulty in dealing with white men. He consistently outwits both the salesman of a gold-finding machine and Roth Edmonds, the master of the plantation, whose usual feeling in the story is of puzzlement, rage, and frustration because he never knows what is really going on or what he can or should do about it, although he conscientiously tries (according to his lights) to discharge his responsibilities to the plantation and its people. Lucas' wife, Molly, is a much more formidable champion. As long as Lucas is merely wasting his energy and neglecting his farming in a futile search, Molly refrains from interfering. But she becomes afraid that he may succeed, breaking his own relation to the land and corrupting George as well; and Nat is now pregnant with her first child. Lucas is not deterred by Molly's asking for a divorce, but when she almost kills herself trying to hide the gold-finding machine in the thickets along the creek, he surrenders and asks Roth to get rid of it.

The meaning of this story in the whole context of *Go Down, Moses* lies in the fact that Ike McCaslin commits the same error, or sin against fertility, from which Lucas is rescued, against his will, by his wife and daughter. Lucas states the case when he silently expresses his opinion of "old Isaac who in a sense, say what a man would, had turned apostate to his name and lineage by weakly relinquishing the land which was rightfully his to live in town on the charity of his great-nephew . . ." (pp. 39-40). Although this view is not entirely just, Ike has long before had to acknowledge its essential truth. In a scene described from Ike's point of view, later in the text, we see Lucas, forty-six years earlier in time, coming on his twenty-first birthday to Ike's house in town to claim his inheritance, a sum of money left to Turl by old Carothers and tripled in transmission by Uncle Buck and Uncle Buddy.

Lucas says, " 'I want to know I can go when I decide to.' "
Ike protests, " 'You could have done that at any time. Even if
Grandpa hadn't left money for Tomey's Turl. All you, any of
you, would have had to do would be to come to me . . . .' his
voice died. He thought, *Fifty dollars a month. He knows
that's all. That I reneged, cried calf-rope, sold my birthright,
betrayed my blood, for what he too calls not peace but oblit-
eration, and a little food*" (pp. 108-109; ellipsis Faulkner's).
Ike, having rejected his inheritance on his own twenty-first
birthday, has deprived himself of the power to be a Moses
who could tell the Pharaoh of the South to "let my people
go."

Ike's wife, like Molly Beauchamp, tries to save her husband
by forcing him to return to the land, but she fails. She has
received bad moral marks from critics, and also from Faulkner, who said once that "She was ethically a prostitute" because she uses her body as a bribe,[20] but Ike may be as much
to blame for her ethical deficiency as she is. When Lucas
appears, Ike is aware of his wife's bitterness, and silently asks
her forgiveness, thinking that "it was all right. . . . husband
and wife did not need to speak words to one another, not
just from the old habit of living together but because in that
one long-ago instant at least out of the long and shabby
stretch of their human lives, even though they knew at the
time it wouldn't and couldn't last, they had touched and become as God when they voluntarily and in advance forgave
one another for all that each knew the other could never be"
(pp. 107-108). But the Biblical parallel suggests that it is not
all right. When Adam ate the apple, "the Lord God said, 'Be-
hold, the man is become as one of us, to know good and evil:
and now, lest he put forth his hand, and take also of the tree
of life, and eat, and live forever': Therefore the Lord God sent
him forth from the garden of Eden, to till the ground from

[20] *Faulkner in the University*, p. 275; see also p. 276.

whence he was taken."[21] Lucas has accepted the curse of Adam by staying on the plantation when he could have left it at the age of twenty-one, and he reaffirms his acceptance when he gives up his search for gold. Ike, refusing to "till the ground," becomes a carpenter, but his imitation of Christ is limited; as we have seen, he is impotent as a would-be savior. In fact, because he refuses to be persuaded by his wife's request, he fails to carry out even God's first command, "Be fruitful, and multiply ...."[22]

Some critics have found the next story, "Pantaloon in Black," digressive because the only member of the McCaslin family identified by name, Roth Edmonds, takes no part in the action. Faulkner, however, told Malcolm Cowley that "Rider," the protagonist, "was one of the McCaslin Negroes."[23] The story is linked with others in the book by its intense dramatization of Rider's humanity and the failure of the rather brutal but genuinely troubled sheriff's deputy to recognize humanity when he sees it. This juxtaposition heightens the feeling previously brought out in "The Fire and the Hearth" by the estrangement of Zack Edmonds and Lucas Beauchamp, which is repeated in that of their sons Roth and Henry. The theme, the damage that slavery and segregation do to the moral qualities of the master class, and the moral superiority that is almost inevitably conferred on the Negroes, is dominant in *Go Down, Moses,* and it is an important aspect of Faulkner's fiction generally.

The next story, "The Old People," and the four narrative sections of "The Bear" describe Ike's initiation into the disciplines of woodcraft and hunting, and into an organic relation with the wilderness and the life it contains. The body of the

[21] *Genesis* 3:22.

[22] *Genesis* 1:28.

[23] Malcolm Cowley, *The Faulkner-Cowley File* (New York: Viking Press, 1966), p. 113.

mystery is nature, the living universe; its priest is Sam Fathers; and its grand focus and representative is the bear, Old Ben, who, like the whale in *Moby Dick*, symbolizes the universal principle of life. In the same way that Lucas Beauchamp feels the power of the wilderness in the "admonitory pat" which presents its temptation, Ike senses, as he watches Sam treating the wounds of a bitch mauled by Old Ben, that "it was still no living creature but only the wilderness which, leaning for a moment, had patted lightly once her temerity" (p. 199).

Ike's wilderness initiation seems to place him in an Eden older than that of Adam, a paradise of hunters instead of farmers. His god is no gardener but a spirit of "Nature, red in tooth and claw," of a world in which the human animal is not sharply distinguished—and certainly not by any moral superiority—from the rest. Ike is accepted into it when, in "The Old People," he kills his first buck and Sam smears its blood on his face. As they leave the campsite for that year, the moment of his crisis and change is statically preserved in Ike's mind: "the wilderness watched them pass, less than inimical now and never to be inimical again since the buck still and forever leaped, the shaking gun-barrels coming constantly and forever steady at last, crashing, and still out of his instant of immortality the buck sprang, forever immortal . . . the moment of the buck, the shot, Sam Fathers and himself and the blood with which Sam had marked him forever one with the wilderness which had accepted him . . ." (p. 178). The success of the initiation is ratified by the appearance of the spirit buck which seems to be Sam's totem, as it is saluted by Sam, but not by Ike, in the Indian language, " 'Oleh, Chief .... Grandfather' " (p. 184).

The wilderness initiation is further ratified in the first section of "The Bear" when, abandoning his gun and then his compass and watch, Ike sees Old Ben. Ike has become completely lost, and the bear's fresh tracks lead him back to the bush on which his watch and compass hang. There is another dynamically static moment when, like Jewel's horse for Vardaman in *As I Lay Dying*, "the wilderness coalesced. It rushed, soundless, and solidified—the tree, the bush, the compass and the watch glinting where a ray of sunlight touched them." In the next moment Ike sees the bear. "Then it was gone. It didn't walk into the woods. It faded, sank back into the wilderness without motion as he had watched a fish, a huge old bass, sink back into the dark depths of its pool and vanish without even any movement of its fins" (p. 209).[24] The situation here, however, seems a bit equivocal; perhaps the bear is accepting Ike into the wilderness, perhaps merely showing him the way out of it.

The image of Eden and the meaning of Ike's initiation into the wilderness are involved in greater complexities when his failure to salute the buck is implicitly accounted for in the last section of "The Bear." Revisiting the knoll where Sam and the dog Lion are buried, along with one of the bear's paws, Ike achieves an exalted mood in which he feels that this "was no abode of the dead because there was no death, not Lion and not Sam: not held fast in earth but free in earth and not in earth but of earth, myriad yet undiffused of every myriad part, leaf and twig and particle, air and sun and rain and dew and night, acorn oak and leaf and acorn again, dark and dawn and dark and dawn again in their immutable progression and, being myriad, one: and Old Ben too . . ." (pp. 328-29). This is essentially the same formula that Shelley invoked as his pastoral elegiac mode of reconciliation to the fact of death in *Adonais*, immortality by diffusion into the life of the universe, which Old Ben symbolizes and into which Ike has presumably been accepted, at least as a candidate.

But, just at this point, Faulkner juxtaposes the Eden myth

---

[24] This image repeats the one used to help characterize Quentin Compson in *The Sound and the Fury* (pp. 144-49).

in an aspect that forces a startling shift of perspective. In the middle of an eloquent sentence, Ike encounters a big rattle-snake, "the once-bright markings of its youth dulled now to a monotone concordant too with the wilderness it crawled and lurked: the old one, the ancient and accursed about the earth, fatal and solitary and he could smell it now: the thin sick smell of rotting cucumbers and something else which had no name, evocative of all knowledge and an old weariness and of pariah-hood and of death" (p. 329). It is this animal, rather than bear or buck, that Ike, "speaking the old tongue which Sam had spoken that day without premeditation either," hails as " 'Chief . . . Grandfather' " (p. 330). So he is made to acknowledge not only that his Eden has its serpent, but the more personally significant belief that he is of the serpent's clan.[25]

Most readers of "The Bear" have apparently believed that the text supports Ike's theory that the curse on the South has been incurred largely as a result of the sin or crime of miscegenation. The evidence, however, is equivocal, and much of it is contrary. Sam Fathers, half Indian, three-eighths white, and one-eighth Negro, is a most admirable character who teaches Ike truly and well about the wilderness. The fyce who teaches him courage; Lion, who brings Old Ben to bay; and Boon Hogganbeck, who kills the bear, all have their virtues, and all are of mixed blood. The bear is pure of blood but obsolete and therefore doomed; but Sam Fathers, at the opposite end of the scale in his racial makeup, is equally obsolete and doomed. Ike thinks that Lucas Beauchamp, by declining old Carothers' first name, Lucius, has become, like the bear, "self-progenitive and nominate, by himself ancestored,

---

[25] For discussion of this point, see Alexander C. Kern, "Myth and Symbol in Criticism of Faulkner's 'The Bear,' " *Myth and Symbol: Critical Approaches and Evaluations*, ed. Bernice Slote (Lincoln: University of Nebraska Press, 1963), pp. 152-61. Kern reports (pp. 155-56) that the Chickasaw tribe, from whence Sam's Indian blood derives, had a deer clan, but no bear or snake clan.

as, for all the ledgers recorded to the contrary, old Carothers himself was" (p. 281); and Roth Edmonds, looking at Lucas in "The Fire and the Hearth," believes that he sees "*a man most of whose blood was pure ten thousand years when my own anonymous beginnings became mixed enough to produce me*" (p. 71). But Lucas is the son of Tomey's Turl, whose descendants are all mixed because of old Carothers' incest-compounded miscegenation. Lucas himself is at least three-eighths white and at most five-eighths Negro, so that purity of blood, whatever its color, can hardly be regarded as his dominant characteristic. If the South is cursed, the fault must lie in something other than, or at least in addition to, miscegenation.

Ike offers another explanation when he says in the fourth section of "The Bear" that old Carothers was guilty of exploiting the land, the earth itself, as well as his slaves and the Indians, because he bought it with money, or got it by some kind of chicanery. As soon as the land was owned, according to the tortured logic of Ike's argument, the American Eden ceased ever to have been. Ike tries to escape the guilt by saying "relinquish" rather than "repudiate" and by contending that the land never was really owned, by him or anyone else. He deplores the fall of man from the hunter's estate to those of the farmer and the manufacturer, and he tries to act as if, for him at least, there has been no fall. But the facts, as Cass Edmonds points out, are against him. The plantation exists, the lumber company operates, the Delta is cultivated, and the wilderness is steadily destroyed.

There seems to be no question here of a "fortunate fall," but only of a fall which has occurred, which is continuing to occur, and which is the inevitable result of the motion of life. Eden is an imaginary past condition, and never a present state. Faulkner once remarked that he was "inclined to think that the only peace man knows is—he says, Why good gracious, yesterday I was happy. That at the moment he's too busy. That maybe peace is only a condition in retrospect, when the subconscious has got rid of the gnats and the tacks and the broken glass in experience and has left only the peaceful pleasant things—that was peace. Maybe peace is not is, but was."[26] To try to restore such an imaginary past condition is to try to destroy creation, which is not a condition or a state but a process. To deny the fall, then, is to deny life itself, and that in effect is what Ike does.

The argument he offers to justify his repudiation, or relinquishment as he calls it, is so confused, so contradictory, and finally so weak that it is a wonder critics have not more generally rejected it. All Ike really says is that he refuses to accept responsibility for the crimes of old Carothers McCaslin, and Ike himself is not satisfied with that position. He makes a strenuous effort to deliver the thousand-dollar legacy of old Carothers to Tennie's Jim, the oldest child of Tomey's Turl. Failing in that, he succeeds, belatedly, in tracking down Fonsiba, the second child of Turl and Tennie, and forcing her to accept her inheritance. Her husband, whose half-hearted and wholly incompetent farming shows little prospect of keeping either of them alive and whose dependence on a pension only makes the matter worse, proclaims that " 'The curse you whites brought into this land has been lifted. . . . We are seeing a new era, an era dedicated, as our founders intended it, to freedom, liberty and equality for all, to which this country will be the new Canaan—' " Faced with this outrageous demonstration of irresponsibility, Ike plainly feels that a man's duty is to earn his own and his wife's bread, in the sweat of his brow, by tilling the land. " 'Freedom from what?' " he demands. " 'From work?' " (p. 279). Yet Ike says to his cousin McCaslin Edmonds two years later, " 'I am free' " (p. 299), meaning that he refuses to accept his own inheritance, or to till the earth, as his own wife wants him to do. What he really means is that he wants to be free from responsibility, and

---

[26] *Faulkner in the University*, p. 67.

from the conflicts that it engenders: " '. . . I have got myself to have to live with for the rest of my life,' " he says, " 'and all I want is peace to do it in' " (p. 288). But this is a kind of peace, and of freedom, that is not possible for a living man in a moving world.

Cass Edmonds is not so eloquent as Ike, but his logic is a good deal sounder. He has accepted, for better and for worse, the responsibility of running the plantation, "that whole edifice intricate and complex and founded upon injustice and erected by ruthless rapacity and carried on even yet with at times downright savagery not only to the human beings but the valuable animals too, yet solvent and efficient and, more than that: not only still intact but enlarged, increased; brought still intact by McCaslin [Edmonds], himself little more than a child then, through and out of the debacle and chaos of twenty years ago where hardly one in ten survived, and enlarged and increased and would continue so, solvent and efficient and intact and still increasing so long as McCaslin and his McCaslin successors lasted, even though their surnames might not even be Edmonds then . . ." (p. 298).

There is no brief made for injustice, rapacity, or savagery, for Zack's alienation of Lucas, for Roth's betrayal of Henry and later of his mulatto cousin and mistress and their son, or for the whole great web of discrimination imposed by a segregated society. But the Edmondses, with all their shortcomings, which the author exposes and they themselves acknowledge, are morally stronger than Ike. They till the land, they feed the people, and they work effectively, as Ike does not, to restore and improve the economy of the defeated South. They come considerably closer than Ike does to playing the role of Faulkner's third man, the one who does something positive about the intolerable evils of life.

Critics who have discussed *Go Down, Moses* as a whole have noticed, as they could hardly help doing, Ike's humiliating encounter in "Delta Autumn" with Roth's mistress, in which he proves his impotence not only to face the injustices of segregation but even, as the young woman scornfully suggests, to remember the value and meaning of love. But he has remembered, some hours earlier, in a passage which has less often been correctly read, what his impotence has cost him, first by his refusal to inherit the plantation and then by his refusal to return to it when his wife demanded that he do so as a condition of sexual relations between them. An old man now, lying awake in a hunting camp in the midst of the diminished wilderness, he thinks of "that day and himself and McCaslin juxtaposed not against the wilderness but against the tamed land, the old wrong and shame itself, in repudiation and denial at least of the land and the wrong and shame even if he couldn't cure the wrong and eradicate the shame, who at fourteen when he learned of it had believed he could do both when he became competent and when at twenty-one he became competent he knew that he could do neither but at least he could repudiate the wrong and shame, at least in principle, and at least the land itself in fact, for his son at least: and did, thought he had: then (married then) . . . himself and his wife juxtaposed in their turn against that same land, that same wrong and shame from whose regret and grief he would at least save and free his son and, saving and freeing his son, lost him" (p. 351). The ironic truth is that Ike has saved his son from the burdens of sin and responsibility in the only way that anyone can be saved, by failing to engender him. In trying to free himself he has repudiated more than a crime and a tract of land; he has repudiated life, and he has made himself the chief static obstacle to its motion in this novel.

"Go Down, Moses," the title story of the book, is one of the less successful parts. However, it has its function in relation to the whole, and an importance that is correctly indicated by its position at the end. It is there not as a denouement but rather as a contextual expansion of what has gone before. It records another victory for Molly (here inconsistently spelled "Mollie") Beauchamp, this time not merely over Roth Edmonds and Lucas, but over the whole town of Jefferson. Told from the point of view of Gavin Stevens, who is in a way its protagonist, the story is heavily weighted with ironies that bear contrapuntally on the rest of the book. It serves to complete the moral structure.

Molly's outrageous charge that " 'Roth Edmonds sold my Benjamin' " (p. 371) makes an eager Moses of Stevens, who mobilizes the town to bring home her grandson, Samuel Worsham Beauchamp, better known as Butch, who is being executed for the murder of a Chicago policeman. Stevens is keenly aware of the fact that Butch, whose personality is much like that of Popeye in *Sanctuary*, is beyond salvation. His main concern in providing for a proper funeral is that Molly should not learn the real circumstances of her grandson's death. Then, when it is too late, after he has arranged and largely paid for the ceremony, and has been humiliated by his inadequacy in the face of the family grief, he realizes that Molly has known the essential truth all along. "*Yes*, he thought. *It doesn't matter to her now. Since it had to be and she couldn't stop it, and now that it's all over and done and finished, she doesn't care how he died. She just wanted him home, but she wanted him to come home right. She wanted that casket and those flowers and the hearse and she wanted to ride through town behind it in a car*" (p. 383).

The evil of segregation comes full circle when Butch achieves equality with white gangsters like Popeye, and the white community is made to pay for the privilege of acknowledging him as its own. Progress of a sort is being made, but we are not to expect any quick or easy solutions to the problems of human relations, either between races, within families, or in society at large. The problems of hunters are superseded by the problems of farmers, and Ike McCaslin becomes obsolete. The problems of farmers give way to those of people in mechanized cities, and Edmonds is obsolete. Butch is dead and damned because, in his own words, he has been "'Getting rich too fast'" (p. 370); he has moved too quickly from the agrarian life of the plantation to the money-oriented life of the Chicago underworld. Only Molly, who plays an ironic Demeter to Butch's perverse Persephone, is enough in harmony with the motion of life to be neither obsolete nor damned. The principal irony of her position lies in the fact that it is she who has raised Butch, as she has also largely raised Roth Edmonds.

This story performs at least the negative function of preventing perceptive readers of *Go Down, Moses* from settling into any simple formula as a note on which to conclude. We are made to feel, if we read the book from beginning to end and try to keep it all in mind, that events are very complicated, paradoxical, and contradictory. Life, or man, as Faulkner says, goes on, pragmatically, ruthlessly, often cruelly, as regardless of static moral formulas as of any other static ideas, smashing them when they get in the way and leaving them behind as they become obsolete. But there are dynamic moral principles emerging from change itself and requiring change on the part of responsible men. The static formulas are often emotionally more attractive, probably to Faulkner as well as to many of his readers, than this uncomfortable dynamic imperative; but they are not for that reason more highly approved, either in Faulkner's recorded interviews or in his fiction. Change is the essence of Faulkner's work, in its moral as well as its artistic and technical aspects. The message is that we must go on with change, whether we like it or not.

In the fiction which he published after 1942, Faulkner tends to slide away from the moral deadlocks that characterize the best of his earlier output. He uses more linear plots and less counterpoint. The result is more emphasis on moral development, or melioration, and less on the intensely esthetic contemplation of the frenzied, apparently meaningless motion of life caught in moments of artificial stasis. It may be better preaching, but it is not so good art. It is useful, as I have suggested, not because it greatly raises our estimation of Faulkner's worth as a writer, but because it helps us to understand what he had been trying all along to mean.

Intruder in the Dust is a good example of these tendencies. Chick Mallison, like Huckleberry Finn, and unlike Isaac McCaslin, succeeds in freeing a Negro, again Lucas Beauchamp, from unjust bondage. Chick also succeeds in growing up toward a mature relation to society, mainly by rebelling against its most rigid moral taboos. After a period of trying to withdraw from the evils of segregation, as Ike does, Chick eventually takes action, which involves him in great labor and considerable danger, to overcome the evil. A degree of dramatic tension arises, particularly within Chick's own mind and feelings. It is hard for him, not yet a man, to defy the prejudice of his society, and it is even harder to clear himself of prejudice. Lucas has given him shelter when he badly needed it, as any neighbor would, and Chick has tried to assert his social superiority by paying for it. Lucas will not accept payment, but he will insist that, when his own life is in danger as a result of social injustice, Chick must come to his aid, as any responsible member of society should. When Chick does so, he admits that Lucas is his equal as a man, and he himself becomes a man in some ways equal to Lucas.

The motion of life is depicted more vividly by some of the imagery than it is by the structure of the book. Chick, for example, forced to go on long after he has exhausted what he thought were his last reserves of energy, is led to recognize "the need not to finish anything but just to keep moving not even to remain where they were but just desperately to keep up with it like having to run on a treadmill not because you

wanted to be where the treadmill was but simply not to be
flung pell mell still running frantically backward off the
whole stage out of sight ..." (p. 197). Moral maturity in
Faulkner's moving world does not consist in any particular
achievement, but rather in acceptance of this necessity to keep
moving.

The flood image, which Faulkner evoked so powerfully to
represent cosmic motion in *The Wild Palms*, is used in
Intruder in the Dust to suggest the collective life of humanity
in the motion of crowds of people. When Chick and his
uncle, Gavin Stevens, accompany the sheriff to town with the
body of Jake Montgomery, the people, "without even waiting
for the sheriff's car to get close enough to be recognised had
already turned and begun to flow back toward the Square like
the turn of a tide, already in motion when the sheriff's car
reached the jail, already pouring back into the Square and
converging in that one direction across it when first the sheriff
then the truck then his uncle turned into the alley beyond the
jail leading to the loading ramp at the undertaker's back door
where the coroner was waiting for them: so that moving not
only parallel with them beyond the intervening block but already in advance, it would even reach the undertaker's first;
and then suddenly and before he could even turn in the seat
to look back he knew that it had even boiled into the alley
behind them and in a moment a second now it would roar
down on them, overtake and snatch them up in order: his
uncle's car then the truck then the sheriff's like three hencoops and sweep them on and fling them at last in one inextricable aborted now-worthless jumble onto the ramp at the
coroner's feet . . ." (p. 181). As with the individual, so with
the race: it is no particular virtue or reform that saves it
from its own meanness and folly—not Chick's heroic demonstration in aid of justice, and certainly not his uncle Gavin's
fatuous abstractions about the race problem—so much as the
power of pure mobility, to which neither virtue nor vice is
much more than foam on the top of a wave.

In *Requiem for a Nun*, the plot concerns the salvation of a white person by a Negro. But neither the messianic quality of Nancy Mannigoe nor the reform of Temple Drake is convincing, and the attempted counterpoint between the dramatic scenes and the narrative chronicles is not successful. The crux of the story is Nancy's murder of one of Temple's children, and consequent sacrifice of her own life, in her effort to keep the rest of Temple's unstable family together as a functioning unit. The moral is expressed by Nancy's bare, intransitive injunction, "Believe." Her verb has no object because it is spoken in support of a process which, if it is truly dynamic, can only be that of motion itself, continually moving, never really ended by any object or objective. Her belief, which she states a little more explicitly, is that sin and suffering are inevitable, though never fortunate. The flaw in her logic, and in the plot, is that, somewhat like Isaac McCaslin, she demands acceptance of life on the part of other people while rejecting it for herself and for the murdered child.

The narrative sections of *Requiem for a Nun* extend and clarify the theme of *Go Down, Moses*. In general, they recount the changes in the land from the time of hunters through that of farmers into that of the urban masses. As the early settlers pour in, both the game and the hunters become "obsolete: anachronism out of an old dead time and a dead age; regrettable of course, even actually regretted by the old men," but making way for "the broad rich fecund burgeoning fields" and "the aggrandisement of harvest: the gold: the cotton and the grain" (pp. 39, 40), in short, the same violent fecundity that appalls Ike in "Delta Autumn." The hunter or forest man is seen in a very different light from that of "The Bear": "the Anglo-Saxon, the pioneer, the tall man, roaring with Protestant scripture and boiled whiskey . . . changing the face of the earth: felling a tree which took two hundred years to grow, in order to extract from it a bear or a capful of wild honey . . . turning the earth into a howling waste from which he would be the first to vanish," degenerating into the highwayman of the Natchez Trace and being "dispossessed" by the cotton farmer. Like the Indians, he is "Obsolete too" (p. 102), disappearing with the wilderness he helps to destroy or remaining, like Ike or Sam Fathers, as a functionless anachronism in the agricultural and ultimately industrial society for which he has unintentionally helped to clear the way.

If *Requiem for a Nun* is a poor sequel to *Sanctuary*, the later novels *The Town* and *The Mansion* are even more disappointing in their continuation of the Snopes saga begun in *The Hamlet* and related short stories. They, like the narrative sections of *Requiem*, are in large part recapitulation and summing-up of what Faulkner had written before about the county of Yoknapatawpha and the town of Jefferson. The unfortunate result is a great deal of tedious repetition, in which Faulkner's late style, with its prolixity and irritating mannerism, spoils the concreteness with which he had previously treated the material.

The grand theme of the "trilogy" is the purification of "Snopes," which is not just a family of exploiters but a symbol of exploitation permeating the modern world. The process of this purification is so complex in detail that few critics have been able to see it clearly as a whole, to arrive at sound conclusions about its essential nature, or to understand the roles played by the various characters. The easiest and most popular approach is made from the point of view of the characters who directly oppose Flem Snopes, that is, chiefly Gavin Stevens, Chick Mallison, and V.K. Ratliff. But actually, or "actively," as Ratliff would say, these people accomplish very little. Ratliff maneuvers Will Varner into purging Clarence Snopes out of politics. Gavin's only clear success is in a minor skirmish where he brings about the defeat of Res Snopes by Essie Meadowfill. Chick is never more than an interested observer. So the simple approach will carry us only a little way.

Ironically, it is Flem himself, regarded by Gavin as the principal enemy, who does more than anyone else to eliminate what Ratliff calls " 'Snopes out-and-out unvarnished behavior in Jefferson' " (*Town* 370), first by cooperating, after his fashion, with Gavin and the sheriff in the expulsion of Montgomery Ward, then by bribing I. O. to leave, and finally by sending Byron's half-Indian children back to Mexico.

Another irony is involved in the ability of Wallstreet Panic Snopes "to make money by simple honesty and industry" (*Town* 146), with the help of his wife, who refuses to let him borrow from Flem. There is a rumor that Wall's father, Eck, was a bastard and that therefore Wall is not really a Snopes at all. Gavin wonders why Wall's wife, who apparently never says "Snopes" without putting "damn" or "goddamn" in front of it, has not had the name changed. Ratliff says, " 'You dont understand. She dont want to change it. She jest wants to live it down. She aint trying to drag him by the hair out of Snopes, to escape from Snopes. She's got to purify Snopes itself. She's got to beat Snopes from the inside' " (*Town* 149-50). The point is that good cannot be imposed on evil, or substituted for it, but must evolve out of it and along with it. Ratliff helps the process by providing capital that Wall needs to save his business and by becoming Wall's silent partner.

The final purification of Snopes is indeed accomplished "from the inside" when Flem is killed by a bullet from a pistol in the hands of his cousin Mink, whose motive is revenge. However, from a wider point of view than his own, Mink is only an accessory, like the gambler in Stephen Crane's "The Blue Hotel." Flem's putative daughter, Linda, who is literally and certainly a bastard, has used Gavin Stevens to obtain Mink's release from prison two years before his extended sentence is up, knowing what the result will be. Further, she insists on letting Gavin know that she intended it. As Ratliff explains, " 'She could a waited two more years and God Hisself couldn't a kept Mink in Parchman without He killed him, and saved herself not jest the bother and worry but the moral responsibility too . . . . Only she didn't.' " According to Ratliff, Linda too has been motivated by revenge. Her mother, Eula Varner Snopes, has committed suicide in order to prevent the public exposure by Flem of her eighteen-year love affair with Manfred de Spain; and Ratliff suggests that Linda may go to heaven, where she would not want her mother to say, " ' "Why didn't you revenge me and my love that I finally found it, instead of jest standing back and blind hoping for happen-so? Didn't you never have no love of your own to learn you what it is?" ' " (*Man* 431).

The ultimate turn is back again to Flem himself. The evidence indicates that, as the reader has already been told by the omniscient narrator, Flem has made no attempt to save himself, even though Mink's pistol has misfired once. Flem's death, like Eula's, is apparently a suicide.

Eula, as an embodiment of sexual power and attractiveness, is obviously meant to represent some of the more important and creative energies of life. But these qualities are less convincing in *The Town* than in *The Hamlet*, because she talks too much and because she is less concretely described. In *The Town*, and reminiscently in *The Mansion*, she is presented almost entirely from the points of view of Ratliff, who is apparently sexless, Gavin Stevens, who flees ignominiously when she offers herself to him, and Chick Mallison, who is so young when she is alive that he hardly knows what the fuss is about. Neither Hoake McCarron, her first lover, nor Manfred de Spain is allowed to testify. The nearest thing to concrete evidence of her sexual potency is Mink's remark about "the hurrah and hullabaloo that Varner girl had been causing ever since she (or whoever else it was) found the first hair on her bump . . ." (*Man* 4). All we ever get on the subject in *The Town* or *The Mansion* is talk, and most of that from people who do not seem to know even in general what they are talking about.

The talk, moreover, is belied by much of what Eula actually does in these books. Although Manfred de Spain may be presumed both potent and fertile, Eula goes on living with the impotent Flem, for no better reason than to provide a conventionally respectable home for Linda. She is compared, dozens of times, to Helen of Troy and such other impressive women as Juliet, Isolde, Guenevere, Semiramis, Messalina, Judith, Lilith, Francesca, and Eve; but she behaves more like Narcissa Benbow. Her suicide, like the sacrifice of Nancy Mannigoe, is totally illogical, and its uselessness would appear to be tacitly acknowledged in the fact that Linda, whom the whole action is supposed to be intended to save, remains at the end of *The Mansion* deaf, static, and barren. The power of the motion of life is eloquently urged in abstract statements, but the concrete sense of it is lost.

A Fable is the most ambitious work Faulkner attempted in his later years, and perhaps the most ambitious of his career, in its intentions. Most readers seem to feel, however, that in its results it is largely a failure. It is an extremely difficult book to read, to reread, or to understand. At present there is so little agreement about it among critics that they are not even able to disagree very cogently, much less arrive at any confident conclusions about its moral or artistic value.

According to Faulkner, the basic theme is the dilemma of "the father who is compelled to choose between the sacrifice or saving of his son." He admitted, in terms that sound uneasy, that "It came, incidentally, out of a speculation which a lot of people besides me have probably wondered at: Who might have been in the tomb of the Unknown Soldier? And if that had been, if Christ had appeared again in 1914-15, he would have been crucified again. To tell that story, the thought was if I could just tell this in such a powerful way that people will read it and say this must not happen again, that is, if Providence, Deity, call Him what you will, had tried to save this world once, save men once by the sacrifice of His Son, that failed, He tried it again and that failed, maybe He wouldn't try it the third time, and so we must take warning because He may not try to save us again that way." But he concluded by insistently repeating that "that was incidental, I was primarily telling what to me was a tragic story, of the father who had to choose between the sacrifice or the saving of his son."[27] In a later interview he conceded that, once he had determined to indulge his speculation about the identity of the Unknown Soldier, "then it became *tour de force*, because I had to invent enough stuff to carry this notion."[28] But he was generally consistent in maintaining that even in *A Fable* the Christ story is used as a tool,[29] and that where "the pattern" of the traditional material conflicted with the shaping power of his own imagination "it was the pattern that bulged . . . that gave."[30]

Criticism of *A Fable* has generated a great deal of moral confusion, partly because the patterns of mythical and especially Biblical references in the book have suggested contradictory theological ideas to its readers. There is perhaps fairly general agreement that Faulkner, as he repeatedly said in the interviews, was not simply retelling the story of Christ's Passion, but there is as yet no general agreement on what he was doing.

One of the difficulties lies in the complexity and moral ambiguity of the Old General, who seems to combine the roles of God and Satan, and to whom, as Olga W. Vickery points out, some of Christ's experience is also assigned.[31] In

[27] *Faulkner at Nagano*, pp. 159-60; cf. pp. 46-47.
[28] *Faulkner in the University*, p. 27.
[29] *Faulkner at Nagano*, p. 23.
[30] *Faulkner in the University*, pp. 51-52 (ellipsis in the source).
[31] Vickery, pp. 213-14.

some very significant ways, he has the better of the argument with the Corporal, as Cass Edmonds has with Ike in "The Bear." Taking up the Old General's phrase " 'man and his folly—' " the Corporal says that they " 'Will endure' "; the Old General tops him by agreeing with Faulkner that " 'They will do more . . . . They will prevail' " (p. 354). But the Corporal illustrates better than the Old General most of the qualities that Faulkner attributed to the "soul" by which according to him "man will not merely endure: he will prevail."[32]

The dialectic of the Old General's relation to the Corporal is far more complex than any direct opposition. The two seem usually to be engaged not so much in conflict as in an indirect kind of cooperation, and they both seem to know it. Throughout the temptation scene the Old General acts as if he were offering his inducements more as tests than as persuasions, in the expectation and even the hope that they will be rejected. When they are rejected, he acts as if he were more pleased than disappointed, as if the result were what he had set out to prove, rather than a defeat for his side of an argument. Vickery suggests that there is an "inevitable and necessary . . . conflict" between the individual and society, and that salvation arises out of the continuing dialectic tension between "the two opposing forces of authority and freedom, explored through the complex relationship between the Corporal and the Marshal . . . ."[33] It seems to me that this concept points the right direction, and therefore I disagree with Vickery's statement that the Corporal's death is a defeat for the Old General.[34] The Corporal, in refusing to be bribed by the institutional values which the Old General offers him, paradoxically confirms the Old General's belief that man and his civilization will prevail. The Corporal proves by his death that the human soul will never be wholly extinguished by the institutions which are required in order to satisfy the physical needs of

[32] *Essays*, p. 120. [33] Vickery, pp. 226, 227.
[34] *Ibid.*, pp. 226-27.

civilized life. The Corporal resembles Nancy Mannigoe and Eula Varner Snopes in that he dies enjoining others to live; the Old General transcends the contradiction by enforcing the moral and by providing the means of life.

Most readers have assumed that the Corporal, who is the obvious Christ figure of the book, is trying to establish peace on earth by bringing the war to a halt. But the Corporal never says he has that aim; and we should perhaps recall that Christ is quoted by Matthew as having said, "Think not that I am come to send peace on earth: I came not to send peace, but a sword."[35] Life, in the gospel according to Faulkner, is motion; and motion often leads to conflict. Peace is nearly always (for example, when sought by Horace Benbow and when found by Joe Christmas) equated with lack of motion, or death. The Corporal's mutiny might be logically regarded, therefore, as a challenge or a test, to see if life, with all its difficulties, burdens, horrors, agonies, and responsibilities—in short, its conflicts, including its wars—can go on. The Old General may be regarded as accepting the challenge and passing the test. By sacrificing his son, whom he would spare if he could, he proves that life prevails in spite of everything. Conversely, but cooperatively, the Corporal, by refusing to let himself be spared, proves that man is worthy of survival. The two of them, in formal conflict with each other, are working together to demonstrate Faulkner's belief that life is both intolerable and inextinguishable. They love and respect each other, and each approves of what the other is doing.

This mutual approval is perhaps most clearly seen in the exchange between them after the return of Piotr, known as Pierre Bouc, a member of the Corporal's squad who has been released from confinement after denying the Corporal three times but who now asks forgiveness. The Old General translates what the Corporal says to Piotr in their native Zsettlani language, "'And you said, "Be a man," but he didn't move.

[35] *Matthew* 10:34.

Then you said "Be a Zsettlani" and still no move. Then you said "Be a soldier" and he became one. . . . No: returned to one. Good night, my child.'" The last two sentences are also "in the rapid unvoweled tongue," and the Corporal answers, in the same tongue, "'Good-bye, Father,'" to which the Old General objects, "'Not good-bye. . . . I am durable too. . . . Remember whose blood it is that you defy me with'" (p. 356). Piotr is not called a rock, but is made to move; he is not called upon to found a church, but to "'"Be a soldier,"'"" which must mean to fight in whatever human struggles may go on.

In the context of the whole book, the story of the Corporal and the Old General is the occasion for a more important dialectic development, in which neither of them plays the protagonist's role. Faulkner remarked in an interview that the Old General "was an implement, really," and that "What I was writing about was the trilogy of man's conscience represented by the young British Pilot Officer, the Runner, and the Quartermaster General. The one that said, This is dreadful, terrible, and I won't face it even at the cost of my life—that was the British aviator. The Old General [Faulkner meant the Quartermaster General] who said, This is terrible but we can bear it. The third one, the battalion Runner who said, This is dreadful, I won't stand it, I'll do something about it."[36] The largest question is not who wins an argument over material versus spiritual values, but how, in the presence of that argument and of all that is contradictory, conflicting, and destructive in the world, human life goes on.

Each member of this "trilogy" of protagonists is disillusioned when, after the Corporal's mutiny has brought about a tacit armistice, the Old General conspires with the commanders of the other armies, including the German, to get the war going again. Each of the three protagonists reacts in a different way.

Gerald David Levine, the British flier, commits suicide

[36] *Faulkner in the University*, p. 62.

because he thinks the war is over. He has volunteered, after the manner of Henry Fleming in *The Red Badge of Courage*, to satisfy a childish craving for glory in combat. Robbed, as he believes, of his chance to be a hero (like Cadet Julian Lowe in *Soldiers' Pay*), he gives way to despair.

The Quartermaster General has believed in the Old General as a savior of the "glory and destiny of France" (p. 247), impaired by the Franco-Prussian War of 1870-71. When he finds himself cooperating with the enemy command to suppress the mutinous enlisted men of both sides, he tries to resign his commission and thereby withdraw from the military profession, which he calls " 'our whole small repudiated and homeless species about the earth who not only no longer belong to man, but even to earth itself, since we have had to make this last base desperate cast in order to hold our last desperate and precarious place on it' " (p. 327).

This language is reminiscent of the way the Pariah-hood of the old rattlesnake is described in "The Bear." The possible reference to the serpent in Eden is supported by Faulkner's remark in an interview that "The Old General was Satan, who had been cast out of heaven, and—because God Himself feared him," and the added comment, in response to further questions, "That was a part of Satan's fearsomeness, that he could usurp the legend of God . . . . and then discard God. That's why God feared him."[37] Faulkner is not of the devil's party in a quarrel with God. He is making use, for his own quite conscious purposes, of a traditional romantic Manicheism, from which, according to Melville, "no deeply thinking mind is always and wholly free."[38] It is not a matter of seeking a devil to worship, but of understanding a world the creator of which made the lamb and the tiger, and perhaps, in making man, put both in the same skin.

[37] *Ibid.*, pp. 62, 63.
[38] Herman Melville, "Hawthorne and His Mosses, By a Virginian Spending July in Vermont," *Literary World*, No. 185 (August 17, 1850), 126.

When the Quartermaster General is tested in direct con-frontation with the Old General, he is found wanting. His de-sire to resign his commission is reduced to the level of Pilate's hand-washing. The Old General points out that the Corporal will be " 'murdered for that principle which, by your own bitter self-flagellation, you were incapable of risking death and honor for. Yet you dont demand that life. You demand in-stead merely to be relieved of a commission. A gesture. A martyrdom. Does it match his?' " (pp. 331-32). In defense of his own role in the drama, the Old General adds, " 'If he . . . keeps his life, he will have abrogated his own gesture and martyrdom. . . . By destroying his life tomorrow morning, I will establish forever that he didn't even live in vain, let alone die so' " (p. 332). The Quartermaster General walks out of the room, " 'With God,' " as the Old General helps him to say (p. 333), his commission still in his hand.

The British battalion Runner tries to extend the Corporal's mutiny by leading the men of his unit unarmed into no man's land, where they are met by unarmed men from the German line. As an artillery barrage from both sides falls on them, the last thing heard is "the runner's voice crying out of the sound-less rush of flame which enveloped half his body neatly from heel through navel through chin," saying, " 'They cant kill us! They cant! Not dare not: they cant!' " (pp. 321-22).

The Runner in fact is not killed, although he loses an eye, half an arm, and a leg. Later he visits the Corporal's two sis-ters, Marthe and Marya, who give him the Corporal's Médaille Militaire. They share his laughter, which seems, like that of Eugene O'Neill's Lazarus, to represent the immortality of man. Departing, he embodies an impressive static-dynamic image: "the single leg . . . strong and steady and tireless be-tween the tireless rhythmic swing and recover of the crutches. But moving . . . even if the infinitesimal progress was out of all proportion to the tremendous effort of the motion. Moving, unwearyable and durable and persevering, growing smaller and smaller with distance until at last he had lost all semblance of advancement whatever and appeared fixed against a panorama in furious progressless unrest, not lonely: just solitary, invincibly single. Then he was gone" (p. 431). Marya, who is supposed to be both feeble-minded and clairvoyant, remarks, " 'He can move fast enough. He will be there in plenty of time' " (pp. 431-32).

"There" is the Arc de Triomphe in Paris, where, six years after the war has been ended on the generals' terms, the funeral cortege of the Old General approaches the tomb of the Unknown Soldier, which probably but not certainly contains the body of the Corporal. The Runner, breaking suddenly out of the crowd, flings the Corporal's medal at the caisson carrying the coffin. " 'This is yours: take it!' " he cries. " 'You too helped carry the torch of man into that twilight where he shall be no more; these are his epitaphs: They shall not pass. My country right or wrong. Here is a spot which is forever England—' " (p. 436). Rescued from the outraged mob which attacks him, he recovers consciousness to hear someone say, " 'Maybe he will die this time,' " to which he replies, "laughing up at the ring of faces enclosing him . . . 'That's right . . . Tremble. I'm not going to die. Never' " (p. 437).

The Runner here, in the concluding scene of the book, emphatically reasserts the values of the rebellious individual human spirit, for which the Corporal has died. The scene, however, carefully maintains the ambiguity with which these values are treated in the Corporal's temptation by the Old General. Death is conspicuously present, and the conventions are fiercely upheld by the mob. The Runner's triumph is not to destroy conventions, much less to establish new ones in the place of old, as he might have done if he had succeeded in organizing the mutiny to enforce the peace. He triumphs rather in demonstrating that life, or motion, continues indomitably in spite of the most powerful repressions that conventional society can bring to bear. This is essentially the result

that the Old General has partly observed and partly predicted, with satisfaction, arising from the Corporal's martyrdom.

The Reivers is much less ambitious, and considerably more
successful, than *A Fable*. In it Faulkner returns to the main
theme of *Intruder in the Dust*, the successful development of
a boy's personality. In *The Reivers* this theme is largely freed
of social propaganda and rendered in a relatively simple,
straightforward comic narrative. *The Reivers* is not one of
Faulkner's greatest works, perhaps because it never creates
very much of the tension between motion and stasis that
gives the earlier and better novels their characteristic weight
and energy. But, as probably his most genial book, it makes an
agreeable conclusion to his career. It also makes a serious moral
point which is both amusingly paradoxical in itself and illuminating with regard to the earlier fiction.

The paradox is that the moral growth of Lucius Priest, at
the precocious age of eleven, results from his eager involvement in what he calls "Non-virtue," for which he feels an almost mystical vocation. When the adventure begins, with
Boon Hogganbeck's clumsy effort to corrupt him into stealing
his grandfather's automobile, Lucius has to acknowledge that
"I was as bent as Boon, and . . . even more culpable. Because
. . . I was smarter than Boon. I realized, felt suddenly that same
exultant fever-flash which Faustus himself must have experienced: that of we two doomed and irrevocable, I was the lead-
er, I was the boss, the master" (p. 53). His fate, however, is
more like that of Goethe's Faust than that of Marlowe's
Faustus. First, he becomes acquainted with some of the
seamier aspects of life: sexual activities in Reba Rivers' whorehouse and the legal and financial risks of gambling on horse
races. Then he has to accept a heavy share of responsibility,
under the guidance of the Negro Ned McCaslin, for getting
himself, Ned, Boon, and Boon's favorite whore and future

wife, Everbe Corinthia,[39] out of the mess he has helped to create. Finally he has to accept the guilt for his illicit activities and, as his grandfather tells him, "'Live with it,'" adding, when the boy protests, that "'A gentleman accepts the responsibility of his actions and bears the burden of their consequences ...'" (p. 302).

The moral is that, if we can break the rules we have to make in order to be civilized, and then bear the burdens of responsibility and of remorse that inevitably fall upon us as a result, we may succeed in living. The earlier and greater works imply the same moral, though usually in more negative terms: if we cannot accept the responsibility and the guilt—or worse, if we cannot break the rules—we are dead. Static formulas, however necessary or inevitable, must always in some way be surmounted, disregarded, or smashed, because they tend to smother life.

This moral is present in Faulkner's work from the early verse on. The "marble-bound" speaker of *The Marble Faun* and the unfortunate flier in "The Lilacs" who "didn't die" are excluded from life by their inability to move or develop. Donald Mahon in *Soldiers' Pay* has the same kind of frozen existence, and so, essentially, has young Bayard Sartoris, who, in addition, incurs a burden of remorse and guilt with which he cannot live. Horace Benbow in *Sanctuary* is prevented from living by his impotence, Darl Bundren in *As I Lay Dying* by his insanity, Joe Christmas in *Light in August* by the repressions of his childhood. Others, increasingly in the later works, are able to move and therefore to live. Januarius Jones does so, in his fashion, in *Soldiers' Pay*. In varying degrees, Hightower, Byron Bunch, and Lena Grove do so in *Light in August*. Eula Varner does in *The Hamlet*. And, as we have seen, many characters do in the works of Faulkner's later years. The mov-

[39] Everbe Corinthia is called Corrie, a name which recalls the use of the Demeter-Persephone-Kore myth in connection with Miss Reba's house in *Sanctuary*.

ing characters are not by any means always the easiest to like, and they seldom conform to conventional standards of virtue. But, because they move, in spite of or aside from the conventions, they are alive. They are the people in Faulkner's imaginary world who embody his belief that man will not merely endure but prevail.

Five / Work: *Absalom, Absalom!*

There is a strange uncertainty among critics as to whether Faulkner is or is not a novelist. Malcolm Cowley says that "All his books in the Yoknapatawpha saga are part of the same living pattern. It is this pattern, and not the printed volumes in which part of it is recorded, that is Faulkner's real achievement."[1] Irving Howe says that "Despite the virtuosity that goes into most of Faulkner's books, their fundamental source is less the artificer's plan than the chronicler's vision."[2] Leslie Fiedler suggests that Faulkner is "essentially a short story writer. . . . Only in *Absalom, Absalom!* and *The Sound and the Fury* has Faulkner worked out genuine full-length narratives by extension rather than patchwork; and even in these two books, he attains novelistic thickness not by inventing a long, complex fable, but by revealing in a series of strict 'point of view' accounts of the same experience the amount of narrative material proper to a short story."[3] On the other hand, Richard Chase says that Faulkner "is by instinct and practice *a novelist*, a master (if sometimes an unruly one) of the large

---

[1] Cowley, Introduction to *The Portable Faulkner*, p. 8.
[2] Howe, p. 30.
[3] Fiedler, "William Faulkner: An American Dickens," *Commentary*, X (October 1950), 385.

concerted novelistic effect."[4] There is some truth in each of these remarks, but most, I think, in the last. There must be something wrong with any definition that would exclude from the genre of the novel such works as *Sanctuary, As I Lay Dying, Light in August,* or even the admittedly less successful *Pylon* and *Mosquitoes.*

Because I agree with Chase in thinking that Faulkner is primarily a novelist, I want to conclude this study with a close examination of two novels. I have chosen to reserve *Absalom, Absalom!* and *The Sound and the Fury* for this purpose because I agree with Fiedler's evident feeling that these are the best organized of Faulkner's novels. I shall keep *The Sound and the Fury* for the last because it is the best, and also the most complex.

Absalom, Absalom! is usually approached as if it were essentially history, or at any rate as if Faulkner's method in it were essentially historiographical. Such an approach is plausible; but we become aware of a difficulty when we encounter critical flounderings such as that of Melvin Backman, who says that "For all its straining, its complexities and obscurities, *Absalom,* I would conclude, is Faulkner's most historical novel," although Backman has already questioned "whether such a work presents the best way of getting at historical truth."[5] The answer, as we have suggested in connection with other works, is that Faulkner is not using a story to teach us history. He is using history and historiography as tools in telling a story. More strictly, Faulkner is using the myth of the South, in much the same way that he uses the Persephone myth in *Sanctuary* or the Christ story in *Light in August,* as an organizing pattern for *Absalom, Absalom!*

The question then arises whether the story is about Sutpen,

[4] Chase, p. 205.

[5] Melvin Backman, "Sutpen and the South: A Study of *Absalom, Absalom!*," *PMLA,* LXXX (December 1965), 596.

as a representative and epitome of Southern history, or whether it may not be at least as much concerned with its chief narrator and historiographer, Quentin Compson, to whom it is a vehicle for the expression of his personality and his relation to the world. In a sense, the story of Sutpen is an explanation of Quentin's life, and Quentin's ability to tell it is a test of his ability to live.

Faulkner was asked at Virginia, "Who is the central character of *Absalom, Absalom!*?" His first reply was, "The central character is Sutpen, yes. The story of a man who wanted a son and got too many, got so many that they destroyed him. It's incidentally the story of Quentin Compson's hatred of the bad qualities in the country he loves. But the central character is Sutpen, the story of a man who wanted sons."[6] This answer was given at a time when Faulkner had to admit that his recollection of the book was dim. Later, when the same question came up again, after some talk about Quentin's roles in both *The Sound and the Fury* and *Absalom, Absalom!*, the answer had a somewhat different emphasis: "No it's Sutpen's story. But then, every time any character gets into a book, no matter how minor, he's actually telling his biography—that's all anyone ever does, he tells his own biography, talking about himself, in a thousand different terms, but himself. Quentin was still trying to get God to tell him why, in *Absalom, Absalom!* as he was in *The Sound and the Fury*."[7]

I suspect that even in this second answer Faulkner underestimated the importance of Quentin as the central intelligence through whom, with the help of Shreve McCannon, the story of Sutpen comes to us. Such a central intelligence almost inevitably emerges as a protagonist in his own right. He is so intensely involved in the process of assimilating the material of the story, making something out of it as he organizes it in and for the telling, and registering his reactions to it, that the

---

[6] *Faulkner in the University*, p. 71.
[7] *Ibid.*, p. 275.

resulting narrative becomes to a large degree the story of his own development in understanding and wisdom. Or it may be, as it mostly seems to be with Quentin, the story of his failure to develop those qualities and his consequent bafflement, frustration, and static exclusion from the moving world of experience, or life. The "history" in the book is perhaps more concerned with the fictional biography of Quentin than with that of Sutpen or, in any direct way, with the actual rise and fall of the plantation aristocracy of the South.

By his use of a sophisticated historiographical approach, with full awareness of the epistemological difficulties involved in the establishment and evaluation of all historical evidence, Faulkner shows us Quentin Compson exploring, not the actual past, but the myths about the past which have been made available to him. He uses these myths less to explain the past than to explain himself in the present. The outcome for Quentin is that he, like the speaker in *The Waste Land*, cannot connect the past with the present, and therefore he has no future. But for Faulkner the technique is a highly successful method. It is not, like some historical fiction, a way of escaping the complexities, confusions, and opacities of present experience, but a way of getting solidly into them and making them stick.

The germ of *Absalom, Absalom!* is the short story "Wash," first published in *Harper's Magazine* for February 1934. This story is concerned, in a relatively simple way, with the Southern aristocracy as seen by a poor white man, Wash Jones, and with Jones's bitter disillusionment when his ideal aristocrat, Colonel Sutpen, turns out not to be an honorable man. The status of Sutpen is given, rather than explained. He is the owner of much land, but nothing is said about how or why he got it. He has been cited for gallantry in the Civil War by General Lee. His wife has died and his son has been killed during the war, leaving him with only a daughter. His desire for a male heir is not explicitly stated or accounted for, except by the fact that he has an estate, or at least the remnant of one, to be inherited. The story is told by an omniscient narrator who stays mostly in or close to Jones's point of view, but who sometimes departs from it in order to provide information, a certain esthetic distance, and a degree of objective control. The inherent violence of the material is contained by the discipline of a clear exposition and a cool tone.

The climax occurs when Sutpen, who has got Jones's granddaughter Milly pregnant, passes by the cabin on his way back from supervising the birth of a colt and learns that Milly has given birth to a girl. He says, " 'Well, Milly . . . too bad you're not a mare. Then I could give you a decent stall in the stable.' "[8] He turns away to leave the child in the care of the Joneses and an anonymous Negro midwife. Jones kills him with a borrowed scythe.

The story is mainly concerned with Jones's illusion and with his feelings when the illusion is shattered. Initially, his reverence for Sutpen amounts to a kind of religious worship, oddly entangled with his concern about his own status in the hierarchical plantation society. Jones, we are told, "would see the fine figure of the man . . . on the fine figure of the black stallion, galloping about the plantation. For that moment his heart would be quiet and proud. It would seem to him that that world in which negroes, whom the Bible told him had been created and cursed by God to be brute and vassal to all men of white skin, were better found and housed and even clothed than he and his; that world in which he sensed always about him mocking echoes of black laughter was but a dream and an illusion, and that the actual world was this one across which his own lonely apotheosis seemed to gallop on the black thoroughbred, thinking how the Book said also that all men were created in the image of God and hence all men made the same image in God's eyes at least; so that he could say, as though speaking of himself, 'A fine proud man. If God Himself was to come down and ride the natural earth, that's what He would aim to look like.' "[9] Jones acquiesces in the seduction of his granddaughter, confident that the brave colonel will somehow " 'make hit right.' "[10]

His disillusionment is complete, and completely destructive. After killing Sutpen, he waits for the sheriff's posse, which he knows will be composed of "the curious, and the vengeful: men of Sutpen's own kind . . . men who had also shown the lesser ones how to fight in battle, who maybe also had signed papers from the generals saying that they were among the first of the brave; who had also galloped in the old days arrogant and proud on the fine horses across the fine plantations—symbols also of admiration and hope; instruments too of despair and grief. . . . It seemed to him that he had no more to run from than he had to run to. If he ran, he would merely be fleeing one set of bragging and evil shadows for another just like them . . . . It seemed to him that he now saw for the first time, after five years, how it was that Yankees or any other living armies had managed to whip them . . . . 'Brave,' he thought. 'Better if nara one of them had never rid back home in '65'; thinking *Better if his kind and mine too had never drawn the breath of life on this earth. Better that all who remain of us be blasted from the face of earth than that another Wash Jones should see his whole life shredded from him and shrivel away like a dried shuck thrown onto the fire.*"[11] When the posse arrives, Jones kills Milly and the baby, sets his cabin on fire, and runs at the aimed guns with the scythe uplifted.

[9] *Ibid.*, pp. 259-60. Cf. Emerson, "Self-Reliance": "The joyful loyalty with which men have everywhere suffered the king, the noble, or the great proprietor to walk among them by a law of his own, make his own scale of men and things and reverse theirs . . . was the hieroglyphic by which they obscurely signified their consciousness of their own right and comeliness, the right of every man."

[10] *Ibid.*, p. 261.

[11] *Ibid.*, pp. 264, 265.

This material is assimilated into *Absalom, Absalom!* to form an account, supposedly reaching Quentin through his father from his grandfather, General Compson, of Sutpen's death. But it is not the climax of the book, and its theme is only one strand or aspect of a more complex, obscure, and difficult theme.

The introduction to that larger theme is the question that Shreve asks, and repeats with variations, and that Quentin generalizes into a loaded and hostile demand made on him by his whole experience "in Cambridge since September" of trying to define himself among the outlanders of the North: "*Tell about the South. What's it like there. What do they do there. Why do they live there. Why do they live at all . . .*" (p. 174). Essentially, of course, the demand is being made by Quentin himself, who is grimly debating whether to be or not be, and who obsessively searches the story of Sutpen for an answer.

Shreve is not hostile but sympathetic, and more appalled by what he senses of Quentin's feelings than he will admit. After listening to part of what Quentin is able to tell him, and formulating his own summary of it, he says, " 'Jesus, the South is fine, isn't it. It's better than the theatre, isn't it. It's better than Ben Hur, isn't it. No wonder you have to come away now and then, isn't it' " (p. 217). After they have collaborated in the further development of the story, to which Shreve makes increasingly large and imaginative contributions, he asks the question in an expanded form. " 'Wait,' " he says. " 'Listen. I'm not trying to be funny, smart. I just want to understand it if I can . . . . What is it? something you live and breathe in like air? a kind of vacuum filled with wraithlike and indomitable anger and pride and glory at and in happenings that occurred and ceased fifty years ago? a kind of entailed birthright father and son and father and son of never forgiving General Sherman, so that forevermore as long as your childrens' children produce children you wont be anything but a descendant of a long line of colonels killed in Pickett's charge at Manassas?'"" Quentin, after correcting the name of the battle (which Shreve has very likely misstated on purpose), says, "'You cant understand it. You would have to be born there'" (p. 361). But Shreve will not accept that. "'Would I then?'" he demands. "'Do you understand it?'" (p. 362). Quentin has to admit that he does not know.

The question involves Faulkner's whole handling of time and the problem of the individual's relation to his environment as he and it develop out of the past and toward the future. Quentin's trouble is indicated in the first scene, where the author's voice informs us that Sutpen is only one among many "wraithlike" figures that haunt Quentin's imagination. "His childhood was full of them; his very body was an empty hall echoing with sonorous defeated names; he was not a being, an entity, he was a commonwealth. He was a barracks filled with stubborn back-looking ghosts still recovering, even forty-three years afterward, from the fever which had cured the disease, waking from the fever without even knowing that it had been the fever itself which they had fought against and not the sickness, looking with stubborn recalcitrance backward beyond the fever and into the disease with actual regret, weak from the fever yet free of the disease and not even aware that the freedom was that of impotence" (p. 12). Which, being translated, means that Quentin, like Hightower in *Light in August*, is so possessed by the past, and specifically by the Civil War, that he is unable to act in the present. His malady is more general and perhaps more severe than Hightower's because he is haunted not only by his own grandfather but by the whole class of people who, like Sutpen, tried and failed to establish an enduring aristocracy in the South. There are not just two Quentins, but hundreds, all dead.

The crux for Quentin is the murder of Charles Bon by his half-brother, Henry Sutpen, the act which visibly brings down the princely house their father has tried to build. We are told by the author's voice that, during the interview with Miss Rosa in September 1909, "He (Quentin) couldn't pass that" (p. 172). Again in January 1910, with the crucial question ringing in his mind, "he had something which he still was unable to pass: that door, that gaunt tragic dramatic self-hypnotized youthful face like the tragedian in a college play, an academic Hamlet waked from some trancement of the curtain's falling and blundering across the dusty stage from which the rest of the cast had departed last Commencement" (p. 174)—the scene, that is, in which Henry announces to his sister Judith that she cannot marry Bon because Bon is dead. If Quentin could find some explanation that would allow him to accept that scene and place it in a perspective of continuous time and moving life, he might be able to move in life himself. But, try as he does, and in spite of the inspired effort Shreve makes to help him, he never breaks the barrier it represents.

The historiographical method by which Faulkner manages the story has the effect of presenting the information Faulkner wants us to receive in the order in which he wants us to receive it, with vital bits held back until we are ready to use them as he wants them used to compose the picture he wants us to see. The effect is a kind of magic trick, performed with wonderful skill, in which the hand is tantalizingly slower than the eye and the reader is persuaded to expect and accept a climactic series of increasingly comprehensive views, none of which exhausts the energetic curiosity which has been aroused.

A parallel effect, which has not been sufficiently noted, is that the climactic series consists not only of added pieces of information but of increasingly complex patterns into which the pieces are made to fit. One of the most important functions of the various narrators is that they provide these patterns, develop systems of symbolic imagery to help flesh them out, and on occasion even invent a character who must have existed or an incident that must have happened in order to make a pattern seem plausible. The effect is finally not so much historiographical as mythical, aimed at developing a literary rather than a literal kind of truth. As Faulkner said in the Nobel Prize Address and confirmed in many interviews, he believed that a writer must deal with "the problems of the human heart in conflict with itself .... leaving no room in his workshop for anything but the old verities and truths of the heart,"[12] and not let himself be primarily concerned with social theories or propaganda.

Many mythical patterns operate in the novel, mostly drawn from the Bible, classical mythology, medieval legend, and modern literary works. The principal ones are the Gothic pattern imposed by Miss Rosa Coldfield, the pattern of classical and renaissance tragedy supplied by Mr. Compson, and the pattern of romantic narrative used by Quentin and Shreve.[13] The third of these patterns assimilates and dominates the other two but does not cancel or destroy them.[14] Critics who have tried to explain the structure of the story in terms of any one pattern have failed to understand its real complexity, and most of them have failed to discover its principal theme. Faulkner himself appears to have forgotten it by the time of the Virginia interviews. But the text, if I read it at all correctly, shows that the heart in conflict with itself is that of Quentin. Miss Rosa's frenzy, Mr. Compson's puzzlement, Sutpen's downfall, and

---

[12] *Essays*, pp. 119, 120.

[13] I am indebted here to the formulation proposed by Robert M. Slabey in "Faulkner's 'Waste Land' Vision in 'Absalom, Absalom!'" *Mississippi Quarterly*, XIV (Summer 1961), 155: "Depending on who the narrator is, Sutpen's story resembles a Gothic novel, a chivalric romance, or a fairy tale (when Miss Rosa is telling it), a Greek tragedy (when Mr. Compson is), or a romantic love story (when Quentin and Shreve are). The book is highly allusive, and the Southern past is filled with echoes of the Bible, Greek mythology, Shakespeare, and various literary fables." Slabey reasons, as I do, that "the novel cannot be read as a historical document of the Sutpen family, much less as a history of the South, although the story is an epitome of the rise and fall of a family and Sutpen embodies the social, economic, psychological, and moral evils of the Plantation system."

[14] Cf. *Moby Dick*, where it seems to me that Ishmael's romantic narrative, in somewhat similar fashion, assimilates the tragedy of Ahab, the epic of American whaling, and much Gothic matter and feeling.

the anguish of Charles Bon and Judith and Henry Sutpen are the more or less objective correlatives of Quentin's frustration and despair.

Even Quentin's view, however, is not final or adequate. It is further complicated and reinforced by Shreve's creative collaboration, controlled by the author's intrusions (which, though inconspicuous, are not infrequent), and ultimately weighed and judged by the reader in the light of all the points of view and all the evidence reported. Faulkner, apparently after re-reading the book, commented helpfully on this aspect of it. Someone at Virginia asked, "Mr. Faulkner, in *Absalom, Absalom!* does any one of the people who talks about Sutpen have the right view, or is it more or less a case of thirteen ways of looking at a blackbird with none of them right?" Faulkner said, "That's it exactly. I think that no one individual can look at truth. It blinds you. You look at it and you see one phase of it. Someone else looks at it and sees a slightly awry phase of it. But taken all together, the truth is in what they saw though nobody saw the truth intact. So these are true as far as Miss Rosa and as Quentin saw it. Quentin's father saw what he believed was truth, that was all he saw. But the old man was himself a little too big for people no greater in stature than Quentin and Miss Rosa and Mr. Compson to see all at once. It would have taken perhaps a wiser or more tolerant or more sensitive or more thoughtful person to see him as he was. It was, as you say, thirteen ways of looking at a blackbird. But the truth, I would like to think, comes out, that when the reader has read all these thirteen different ways of looking at the blackbird, the reader has his own fourteenth image of that blackbird which I would like to think is the truth."[15] Quentin's point of view, he added, in response to a follow-up question, "was just one of the thirteen ways to look at Sutpen, and his may have been the—one of the most erroneous. Probably his

[15] *Faulkner in the University*, pp. 273-74.

friend McCannon had a much truer picture of Sutpen from what Quentin told him than Quentin himself did."[16]

Taken in conjunction with Faulkner's continued insistence that *Absalom, Absalom!* is "Sutpen's story,"[17] this is still a bit misleading. In the text, the question of "truth," in any sense of historical accuracy, is hardly relevant. The issue is not what is true about Sutpen but what it is like to live in the South. The answer, primarily informed by Quentin's point of view, experience, and feelings, but enriched by a vast amount of historical, legendary, and mythological material, expands into an account of what it is like to live in the modern world. Faulkner's method forces the reader to participate in the efforts of all the narrators to work through layer after layer of interpretations to recover a story which is, to be sure, about a character named Sutpen; and this story is undoubtedly in some sense also about the social history of the South. But the reader should always remember that he is dealing with layers of fiction, not fact. To analyze the total structure of the book is to peel a very special kind of onion, a work of art in which the narrators are chosen not for their ability to understand history or solve social problems, but for their aptness in representing various ways of knowing and feeling human experience for the purpose of evoking an esthetic effect.

Miss Rosa's Gothic tale is thrust at the reader first. It is violent and melodramatic in feeling, but sparse in substance. Most of the essential "facts" that it contains are given in the first two paragraphs of the book by the author's voice, from Quentin's point of view, before Miss Rosa is directly quoted at all. When she is quoted, she communicates mainly her feeling of "the old insult" which Sutpen has in some unspecified way put upon her, and which she has been unable to avenge, "the old unforgiving outraged and betrayed by the final and complete affront which was Sutpen's death . . ." (p. 14). She pre-

---

[16] *Ibid.*, p. 274.   [17] *Ibid.*, p. 275.

sents him as a *"demon"* (p. 11), an "ogre-shape" (p. 13), a
"'fiend blackguard and devil'" (p. 15), and a brave man who
fought nobly in the Civil War but whose leadership was evidence of a "'fatality and curse on the South and on our family
. . .'" (p. 21). He and his class were "'men with valor and
strength but without pity or honor,'" and Miss Rosa cries out,
much like Jones in "Wash," "'Is it any wonder that Heaven
saw fit to let us lose?'" (p. 20). Worst of all, perhaps, to Miss
Rosa, "'He wasn't a gentleman. He wasn't even a gentleman'"
(p. 14).

   This colorful description is further colored by Quentin's re-
action to it. He resists Miss Rosa, partly because he resents
being drafted as her companion for a nocturnal visit to Sutpen's house. But, as her voice fades with his refusal to listen,
his own soundless vision pictures a godlike figure: "Immobile,
bearded and hand palm-lifted the horseman sat; behind him
the wild blacks and the captive architect huddled quietly, carrying in bloodless paradox the shovels and picks and axes of
peaceful conquest. Then in the long unamaze Quentin seemed
to watch them overrun suddenly the hundred square miles of
tranquil and astonished earth and drag house and formal gardens violently out of the soundless Nothing and clap them
down like cards upon a table beneath the up-palm immobile
and pontific, creating the Sutpen's Hundred, the *Be Sutpen's
Hundred* like the oldentime *Be Light*" (pp. 8-9).

   In herself Miss Rosa is an absurd comic character. But her
effect on the story is neither slight nor unimportant. In her
ridiculous way, she is a spokesman and bard of the Southern
myth; like Emmeline Grangerford in *Huckleberry Finn*, she
has "established herself as the town's and the county's poetess
laureate by issuing to the stern and meager subscription list of
the county newspaper poems, ode, eulogy and epitaph . . . ."
But her occasions have a larger reference than Emmeline's because she is a member of the war generation, writing "out of
some bitter and implacable reserve of undefeat" (p. 11), so

that her emotion, although it is often misdirected, is never in excess of the whole context of the story she helps to tell. It evokes a touch of the genuine old Gothic terror, which, as Poe rightly said, "is not of Germany, but of the soul . . . ."[18] This strain is kept alive, even as it is ridiculed, by Shreve later on, and it is nourished by occasional resemblances of the House of Sutpen to Poe's "House of Usher" and Hawthorne's *House of the Seven Gables*. The Gothic aspect of Sutpen himself, as critics have noted, is reminiscent of Hawthorne's Colonel Pyncheon and Ethan Brand, and of Melville's Captain Ahab.[19]

Mr. Compson's tragic version of the story associates the House of Sutpen with the House of Atreus (somewhat as Eliot associates Sweeney with Agamemnon), and uses dramatic terminology. He suggests that it was Sutpen who named his Negro daughter Clytemnestra, but " 'that he intended to name Clytie, Cassandra, prompted by some pure dramatic economy not only to beget but to designate the presiding augur of his own disaster . . .' " (p. 62). He says that Sutpen " 'acted his role . . . . while . . . behind him Fate, destiny, retribution, irony—the stage manager, call him what you will—was already striking the set and dragging on the synthetic and spurious shadows and shapes of the next one' " (pp. 72-73). He describes the chief characters of the story as being " 'people too as we are, and victims too as we are, but victims of a different circumstance, simpler and therefore, integer for integer, larger, more heroic and the figures therefore more heroic too, not dwarfed and involved but distinct, uncomplex who had

18 Preface to *Tales of the Grotesque and Arabesque, The Complete Works of Edgar Allan Poe*, ed. James Harrison (New York, 1902), I, 151.
19 Waggoner, p. 116, mentions Ethan Brand and Ahab; Harry Modean Campbell and Ruel E. Foster, *William Faulkner: A Critical Appraisal* (Norman: University of Oklahoma Press, 1951), p. 74, cites *The House of the Seven Gables*; Peter Swiggart, *The Art of Faulkner's Novels* (Austin: University of Texas Press, 1962), p. 149, names Ahab; Slabey, *op.cit.*, p. 156, notes that "Sutpen resembles Hawthorne's 'Men of science,' Ethan Brand, Dr. Rappaccini, and Aylmer, in whom the intellect is separated from the heart."

the gift of loving once or dying once instead of being diffused
and scattered creatures drawn blindly limb from limb from
a grab bag and assembled, author and victim too of a thousand
homicides and a thousand copulations and divorcements'"
(p. 89).

This way of talking, like Miss Rosa's, is carried over into
the other narrators' accounts and made to color the whole
book. The author, speaking from Quentin's point of view, calls
Miss Rosa "Cassandralike" (p. 22) before Mr. Compson does,
and Shreve as usual extends and deflates the reference by saying that Miss Rosa has found in Sutpen "'instead of a widowed Agamemnon to her Cassandra an ancient stiff-jointed
Pyramus to her eager though untried Thisbe . . .'" (p. 177).
Miss Rosa sometimes paraphrases Shakespeare, speaking
ironically of a *"summer of a virgin's itching discontent"*
(p. 145) and saying that Sutpen after the war *"was a walking
shadow"* (p. 171). Quentin, as we have already noted, sees
Henry as "an academic Hamlet . . ." (p. 174). All the chief
narrators refer now and then to the classical culture, literature,
and mythology that underlie both Greek and renaissance
drama.

The tragic pattern is no more "true" than the Gothic; if anything it is more abstract and therefore farther away from the
opaque complexity of actual events. Mr. Compson himself is
forced to admit that his version of the story is "'just incredible.
It just does not explain'" (p. 100). His actors, he complains,
"'are there, yet something is missing; they are like a chemical
formula . . . you bring them together in the proportions called
for, but nothing happens . . . just the words, the symbols, the
shapes themselves, shadowy inscrutable and serene, against
that turgid background of a horrible and bloody mischancing
of human affairs.'" The fault is that they are "'impervious to
time and inexplicable . . .'" (p. 101). A different kind of imagination is needed to fuse emotion and intellect into some-

thing that may impart at least an illusion of the concrete dynamism of life.

Quentin and Shreve, with some help from the author, make a determined effort to supply the dynamic quality and to add the dimension of continuous time which it must have in order to operate. They concentrate less on Sutpen in his aspect as an established plantation owner and aristocrat, and more on his childhood and on his children. The shift of emphasis and of sympathy does a good deal to bring out the potential of human development which has been frustrated and destroyed by the downfall of the Sutpen family and the South. The account of Shreve and Quentin is therefore more credible than either of the preceding versions. Miss Rosa, like Mr. Compson, has to admit her incomprehension, protesting that Judith's marriage to Bon, for example, was " 'forbidden without rhyme or reason or shadow of excuse . . .' " (p. 18). Quentin and Shreve explain this prohibition, Sutpen's previous abandonment of his first wife and their son, and the murder of Bon by Henry by discovering or inventing the "fact" that Bon is part Negro. This "fact" is seen as bringing the potential development of Sutpen and his children to a dead stop at every point.

The underlying obstacle, however, is what Quentin's grandfather, General Compson, has defined as Sutpen's " 'innocence' " (p. 220). This, Quentin says, was " 'his trouble, his impediment' " (p. 233), which he cannot outgrow because he never recognizes it for the unforgivable sin that it is. Quentin shrewdly suggests that it is not a natural quality; it is " 'that frank innocence which we call "of a child" except that a human child is the only living creature that is never either frank or innocent . . .' " (p. 246). The innocence, like the design which it allows Sutpen to formulate, has a fatally mechanical quality; it is " 'that innocence which believed that the ingredients of morality were like the ingredients of pie or cake and once you had measured them and balanced them and mixed them and put them into the oven it was all finished and nothing but pie or cake could come out.'" Sutpen does not ask General Compson what was wrong with his design ("'"Whether it was a good or a bad design,"'" he contends, "'"is beside the point"'"); he asks "'"Where did I make the mistake in it . . .?"'" (p. 263). His conscience is clear about his having "'put his first wife aside like eleventh- and twelfth-century kings did'" (p. 240) and refusing to acknowledge his first son, who could not further the design. He has made them a just and generous financial settlement. Quentin imagines General Compson, upon receipt of this information, "'saying, hollering maybe even: "Conscience? Conscience? Good God, man . . . . What kind of abysmal and purblind innocence could that have been which someone told you to call virginity? what conscience to trade with which would have warranted you in the belief that you could have bought immunity from her for no other coin but justice?"——'" (p. 265).

Quentin undertakes to explain the relation of the innocence to the conscience and the design by telling the story of Sutpen's childhood. He is building with materials he must have got largely from his father, who got them from General Compson, who got them from Sutpen. Quentin's handling of these materials, which have doubtless already become legendary, if not mythical, is shaped by the structure of the Eden story.

As Quentin tells it, when Sutpen, aged about ten years, is brought by his father from the mountains to the Tidewater region, "'he had hardly heard of such a world until he fell into it'" (p. 222). This fall, from a place where "'the land belonged to anybody and everybody'" into "'a place, a land divided neatly up and actually owned by men who did nothing but ride over it on fine horses or sit in fine clothes on the galleries of big houses while other people worked for them'" (p. 221), logically requires that young Sutpen, like Ike McCaslin in *Go Down, Moses*, should fall from the innocence of a primitive hunting society into the relative complexity and sophistication of the Southern plantation society. Sutpen, however, not only fails to fall but fails to realize that there is any complexity to fall into, until, at the age of thirteen or fourteen, he is turned away from the front door of the plantation house by the Negro butler. He suddenly sees " 'his own father and sisters and brothers as the owner, the rich man (not the nigger) must have been seeing them all the time—as cattle, creatures heavy and without grace, brutely evacuated into a world without hope or purpose for them' " (p. 235), and he realizes that " 'he would have to do something about it in order to live with himself for the rest of his life and he could not decide what it was because of that innocence which he had just discovered he had, which (the innocence, not the man, the tradition) he would have to compete with' " (p. 234).

Sutpen's analysis of the situation is considerably more intelligent than Wash Jones's. He resists the temptation to murder the plantation owner, and concludes rationally that " ' "to combat them you have got to have what they have that made them do what the man did. You got to have land and niggers and a fine house to combat them with" ' " (p. 238). So his "design" is born, to carry out which, he explains later to General Compson, " ' "I should require money, a house, a plantation, slaves, a family—incidentally of course, a wife" ' " (p. 263). His innocence prevents him from seeing that, in bringing himself up to the level of the plantation owner economically, he will bring himself down to that same man's moral level. " 'It was like that, he said, like an explosion—a bright glare that vanished and left nothing, no ashes nor refuse; just a limitless flat plain with the severe shape of his intact innocence rising from it like a monument . . .' " (p. 238). While he is making his first fortune in Haiti, " 'his innocence still functioned' " (p. 250), and it continues to function throughout the rest of his career, in his denial of Bon, his insult to Miss Rosa, and finally his rejection of Milly, which occasions his death.

Sutpen, in short, is prevented by his innocence from learning anything about the actual concrete relations that operate in a complex society, or in a family that belongs to such a society. All he can take in to shape a morality and a conscience with is an abstract and therefore static "design"—the word is well chosen—which then defines his character and identity. It is a monomania which enables him to become (twice) a rich plantation owner, the very pattern (in a sharply ironic sense) of the aristocrat, but which will never let him become a man, with human feelings, human virtues, and a human capability for the continual compromises imposed by human inconsistency, weakness, and error. Because he is unwilling or unable to bend, his doom in Faulkner's dynamic world is to be broken by the ubiquitous winds and floods of change.

In concentrating on the character and motives of Charles Bon and Henry and Judith Sutpen, Quentin and Shreve discover another highly important perspective. The original motive of the design, as Sutpen explains it to General Compson, was not " 'the boy-symbol at the door . . . because the boy-symbol was just the figment of the amazed and desperate child; that now he would take that boy in where he would never again need to stand on the outside of a white door and knock at it: and not at all for mere shelter but so that that boy, that whatever nameless stranger, could shut that door himself forever behind him on all that he had ever known, and look ahead along the still undivulged light rays in which his descendants . . . waited to be born without even having to know that they had once been riven forever free from brutehood just as his own (Sutpen's) children were—' " (p. 261). The irony is that, when Sutpen does finally stand " 'at his own door, just as he had imagined, planned, designed, and sure enough and after fifty years the forlorn nameless and homeless lost child came to knock at it and no monkey-dressed nigger anywhere under the sun to come to the door and order the child away' " (p. 267), the child is Charles Bon, who comes, as Sutpen says to General Compson, " ' "in such fashion as to be a mockery and a betrayal of that little boy who approached that door fifty years ago and was turned away, for whose vindication the whole plan was conceived and carried forward to the moment of this choice, this second choice devolving out of that first one . . ." ' " (p. 274).

The problem here is that Sutpen, in his innocence, has himself broken the father-son link which, in Quentin's mind, is the essence of time and life and history. When Shreve remarks that Quentin sounds like Mr. Compson, as Quentin has earlier charged Shreve with doing, Quentin thinks, "*Yes. Maybe we are both Father. Maybe nothing ever happens once and is finished. Maybe happen is never once but like ripples maybe on water after the pebble sinks, the ripples moving on, spreading, the pool attached by a narrow umbilical water-cord to the next pool which the first pool feeds, had fed, did feed, let this second pool contain a different temperature of water, a different molecularity of having seen, felt, remembered, reflect in a different tone the infinite unchanging sky, it doesn't matter: that pebble's watery echo whose fall it did not even see moves across its surface too at the original ripple-space, to the old ineradicable rhythm* thinking *Yes, we are both Father. Or maybe Father and I are both Shreve, maybe it took Father and me both to make Shreve or Shreve and me both to make Father or maybe Thomas Sutpen to make all of us*" (pp. 261-62). The effect of Sutpen's design is that it destroys his sons, and thereby, for him, the future. When Henry kills Bon, he seals his own previous repudiation of their father by condemning himself to exile, so that, when Sutpen returns from the war, as Quentin silently puts it, he finds Henry "*gone, vanished, more insuperable to him now than if the son were dead since now (if the son still lived) his name would be different . . . and whatever dragon's outcropping of Sutpen blood the son might sow*" would be "*under another name and . . . among people who will never have heard the right one . . .*" (pp. 181-

82). Even a female line of descent, which would not satisfy Sutpen anyway, is denied him because Judith has wholly given her love to Bon and will never marry anyone else.

These are the circumstances of life, change, and motion that overwhelm the static design. But ultimately, and essentially all along, Sutpen is defeated by time itself, which is the dimension of motion and change. General Compson sees, when Sutpen first appears in Jefferson, that he is "completely the slave of his secret and furious impatience . . . of a need for haste, of time fleeing beneath him, which was to drive him for the next five years—as General Compson computed it, roughly until about nine months before his son [Henry] was born" (p. 34). Because of the failure of his first marriage, which he never explains, he has to make up for what he calls " ' "these wasted years, these years which would now leave me behind with my schedule not only the amount of elapsed time which their number represented, but that compensatory amount of time represented by their number which I should now have to spend to advance myself once more to the point I had reached and lost" ' " (p. 264). Some years later still, the engagement of Judith to Bon brings Sutpen back again to the same impassable point: " 'no matter which course he chose, the result would be that that design and plan to which he had given fifty years of his life had just as well never have existed at all by almost exactly fifty years . . .' " (p. 272).

He never gives up, but his judgment gives way under the pressure, which increases as time inexorably moves on. Miss Rosa describes the *"fierce dynamic rigidity of impatience"* (p. 159) with which he sets to work after the war, and she is fascinated by *"his old man's solitary fury fighting now not with the stubborn yet slowly tractable earth as it had done before, but now against the ponderable weight of the changed new time itself as though he were trying to dam a river with his bare hands and a shingle . . ."* (p. 162). For a while even she is caught up in this *"prolonged and unbroken instant of tremendous effort"* (p. 163), and she accepts his proposal of marriage. He puts her sister's ring on her finger *"as though . . . he had turned all time back twenty years and stopped it, froze it"* (p. 165), and, she says, if he had taken her to bed that night, she would have submitted. Instead, he turns his attention back to the plantation, and two or three months later, according to Shreve's irreverent summary, revises his proposal to " 'suggest that they breed together for test and sample and if it was a boy they would marry . . .' " (p. 177). Here, Mr. Compson says, Sutpen's *"shrewdness failed him again. It broke down, it vanished into that old impotent logic and morality which had betrayed him before . . . . his morality which had all the parts but which refused to run, to move."* Driven harder than ever by *"the haste, the need for it; the urgency"* (p. 279), he provokes Wash Jones, as in "Wash," to kill him with his own scythe, which Shreve has called the " 'symbolic laurel of a caesar's triumph' " (p. 177), but which is even more obviously and appropriately the symbol of Sutpen's constant and implacable enemy, time.

In itself, as the omniscient author steps aside to remark, the version of Sutpen's story constructed by Quentin and Shreve is only another formula, albeit a good one: "the two of them, whether they knew it or not, in the cold room . . . dedicated to that best of ratiocination which after all was a good deal like Sutpen's morality and Miss Coldfield's demonizing . . ." (p. 280). Their version is more dynamic than the other two, however, because it expresses more sympathy for the youthful development of the characters and because it picks up the other two versions, puts them together, and goes beyond them. This process of assimilation develops a strong contrapuntal structure for the book as a whole, which finally has to be completed by the reader's "fourteenth image of that blackbird which," Faulkner said in the interview, "I would like to think is the truth." The reader moves with Quentin, and be-

yond Quentin with the aroused imagination of Shreve, with
frequent guiding touches of the author's hand, through all the
various points of view and all the layers on layers of changing impressions, feelings, and ideas, gradually building up the
esthetic effect of the work. The inconsistencies and the often
unresolved contradictions, so baffling to critics who try to
"make sense" of the book, are means by which the energy of
motion is developed and communicated. Its power is heightened and demonstrated by the tension between the dynamic
quality of motion through time, which is life, and the static
inertness of the formulas proposed by the characters to explain
or deal with their situations and by the narrators to explain
both the situations and the characters.

The reader is encouraged and instructed in his task by the
empathy that Quentin and Shreve come to feel with Henry
Sutpen and Charles Bon. This direct identification with the
characters enables the narrators to transcend their dependence
on the fragmentary and unreliable "facts" with which they
have been supplied, to bridge the gap of time which Mr.
Compson is unable to pass and the gap of emotional alienation
which Miss Rosa maintains, and to feel themselves participat-
ing so immediately and presently in the living action of the
story that they themselves, in a significant sense, become its
protagonists. These moments of empathy are always presented
from the point of view of the author, who frequently and explicitly calls attention to the dynamic energy they contain and
represent.

The series of these empathic moments is introduced, in the
midst of Shreve's effort to imagine the childhood of Charles
Bon, by the author's description of the relation between Shreve
and Quentin as they become emotionally involved in their mutual effort to develop the relation between Bon and Henry.
"There was something curious in the way they looked at one
another, curious and quiet and profoundly intent, not at all as
two young men might look at each other but almost as a youth

and a very young girl might out of virginity itself—a sort of hushed and naked searching, each look burdened with youth's immemorial obsession not with time's dragging weight which the old live with but with its fluidity: the bright heels of all the lost moments of fifteen and sixteen" (p. 299). At a point where Shreve is speaking, the author intervenes again to remark that "it might have been either of them and was in a sense both: both thinking as one, the voice which happened to be speaking the thought only the thinking become audible, vocal; the two of them creating between them, out of the rag-tag and bob-ends of old tales and talking, people who perhaps had never existed at all anywhere, who, shadows, were shadows not of flesh and blood which had lived and died but shadows in turn of what were (to one of them at least, to Shreve) shades too" (p. 303), that is, fictional characters whose life is created and lived in the cooperating imaginations of the teller and the hearer of the tale, whom the author fuses into one.

At this stage of the process, as the author's voice breaks in once more to specify, "all that had gone before" is "just so much that had to be overpassed"; and it is "not the talking alone which did it, performed and accomplished the overpassing, but some happy marriage of speaking and hearing where-in each before the demand, the requirement, forgave con-doned and forgot the faulting of the other—faultings both in the creating of this shade whom they discussed (rather, existed in) and in the hearing and sifting and discarding the false and conserving what seemed true, or fit the preconceived—in order to overpass to love, where there might be paradox and inconsistency but nothing fault nor false" (p. 316). What is meant here, as the context of the word "marriage" suggests and as the larger context in which the passage occurs clearly shows, is partly the homosexual attraction between Bon and Henry, which is paralleled if not created by that between Quentin and Shreve, and out of which, by their account, the attraction between Bon and Judith develops. This emotional complex contributes a good deal of energy and conviction to the sense which the author is building up of an understanding by the narrators and the reader of what must "really" have happened. The two parallel links fuse into one when the author again interrupts Shreve to tell us "that now it was not two but four of them riding the two horses through the dark over the frozen December ruts of that Christmas Eve: four of them and then just two—Charles-Shreve and Quentin-Henry . . ." (p. 334). Then there are "Four of them there, in that room in New Orleans in 1860, just as in a sense there were four of them here in this tomblike room in Massachusetts in 1910" (p. 336). Later, in still another intervention, the author says that "now neither of them were there. They were both in Carolina and the time was forty-six years ago, and it was not even four now but compounded still further, since now both of them were Henry Sutpen and both of them were Bon, compounded each of both yet either neither, smelling the very smoke which had blown and faded away forty-six years ago from the *bivouac fires burning in a pine grove*" (p. 351), the shift to italics marking the complete intermingling of "the two the four the two" (p. 346)—or five with the author and six with the reader—into a single timeless moment of awareness.

This awareness contains the whole experience of the book up to that point: all the secondary narrators, all the reported "factual" material, all the feelings, all the structural hypotheses, all the points of view from which information has come, and all the points of view into which Quentin and Shreve and several other narrators have projected themselves in order to explore and elaborate the story. The multiple assimilation makes for an extremely thick and many-dimensional texture. One bit of information (the only bit that would stand up in court as an eye-witness account) is directly known to Quentin and directly reported from his point of view to the reader: the fact that Henry Sutpen, Clytie, and Jim Bond, as well as Miss Rosa, are still alive in September 1909. There is also one document in this category, a letter from Bon to Judith, which Quentin has read and which the author quotes verbatim. A second and much more voluminous body of information reaches the reader through Quentin from Miss Rosa, Mr. Compson, and various unnamed townspeople, whose eyewitness accounts become hearsay as he reports them. Documents in this category are the tombstones of Charles and his son, Charles Etienne Saint-Valery Bon, bearing inscriptions ordered by Judith which are also seen by Quentin and quoted by the author. Further layers consist of information which is hearsay before it even gets to Quentin. Mr. Compson, for example, reports what General Compson has told him, which includes what General Compson has learned from observing or listening to Sutpen, Mr. Coldfield, the County Medical Officer, the French architect, Sutpen's Negroes, Wash Jones, Major de Spain, and unnamed townspeople; and Sutpen reports to General Compson what he has learned from the Tidewater plantation owner, white women and Negroes in that area, his father, his schoolteacher, and the Haitian planter.

Another category is created when one narrator imaginatively evokes some happening or impression as he infers it must have seemed from the point of view of another, giving or transmitting to the reader "information" for which there is no concrete evidence anywhere along the line. In a relatively simple instance, General Compson, not Sutpen, is made to tell how the Haitian slaves have suffered and how Sutpen's first wife feels about being set aside, although it is Sutpen and not General Compson who has had personal experience of these matters. The most extravagant user of imaginative license is Shreve, who has no personal knowledge of anything in the story of Sutpen and whose only source of information about it is Quentin, but who seems all the freer on that account to tell Quentin and the reader how things must have looked from the points of view of Miss Rosa, Sutpen, Henry, Bon, the New Orleans lawyer (a creature of Shreve's own invention),

Luster, Bon's mother, Ellen Coldfield Sutpen, Judith, and Bon's octoroon consort. Quentin, who as we have noted has very little personal knowledge, is almost as uninhibited in his projections from the points of view of Wash Jones, Judith, the Negro midwife who delivers Milly's baby, Sutpen, and the men of Sutpen's regiment. The author remarks of Quentin at one point that "he could see it; he might even have been there. Then he thought *No. If I had been there I could not have seen it this plain*" (p. 190). Mr. Compson also, in spite of his classical tone and his attitude of weary objectivity, gets carried away by his theory about the effect on Henry's feelings of Bon's liaison with the octoroon, and elaborates the details of Henry's visit to New Orleans with Bon in a fashion that the known or even halfway reliably reported evidence is quite inadequate to support.

The epistemology of all this becomes extremely complex. Information is given objectively and subjectively, directly and indirectly, sometimes in reports that seem to be publicly verified and agreed upon, sometimes in what are obviously pure fabrications, and sometimes in two or three different versions that seem incompatible if not downright contradictory. Often what is said is such a tangled web of direct testimony, hearsay, and imaginative embroidery that the reader can hardly tell where one leaves off and another begins. The situation is particularly confusing at precisely the moment when the narrative purports to be revealing most plainly and unequivocally what "really happened" to make Henry murder Bon. None of the narrators appears to have reliable information on the subject; it puzzles them all, from the beginning to almost the end of the book; yet in the next to last chapter we are given a highly circumstantial account, including what purport to be direct quotations from conversations between Sutpen and Henry and between Henry and Bon, which fully and plausibly explain the whole mystery.

The narrator of this crucial passage is the author, at a time when his voice is said to represent the combined points of view of Shreve and Quentin and Henry and Bon. Shreve and Quentin are "present" in imagination at the interviews and events which the author reports. But what their imagination has to work on in the way of reliable information, if any, we are never told.[20] The authority for the "fact" of Bon's Negro blood is therefore the whole tissue of hypothetical reasoning which Quentin and Shreve have woven and which Shreve in particular has pieced out with purely fanciful fabrications. There is nothing even as concrete as hearsay to back it up. The result is, in a paradoxical sense, entirely realistic; this is the way we are always reconstructing the past. From this point of view we may say, as several critics have said, that Faulkner has created in *Absalom, Absalom!* a highly sophisticated exercise in historiography. But it seems to me that he has done something far more important artistically. He has succeeded in doing what he tried to do in "Twilight" and "The Hill": he has frozen into one timeless moment of contemplation all that his characters have found important or significant in the history, legend, and myth of their civilization. His medium, which was lacking in "Twilight" and "The Hill," is the dramatic—often melodramatic—story of Sutpen, which epitomizes the history not only of the South but of mankind in modern times. His ultimate purpose seems to be the same as in the early work. The young man in "Twilight" or "The Hill" must

[20] Cleanth Brooks, in *The Yoknapatawpha Country*, pp. 314-15 and 436-41, makes an elaborate effort to show "that Quentin must have learned the secret of Bon's birth on his night visit to Sutpen's Hundred with Miss Rosa," either from Clytie or from Henry Sutpen himself, or possibly from Miss Rosa, who may have learned it from Henry. The text is considerably less explicit. Shreve guesses (p. 274) that Quentin " 'wouldn't have known what anybody was talking about if you hadn't been out there and seen Clytie. Is that right?' " Quentin says, " 'Yes.' " Later (p. 351) Shreve adds, " 'and she didn't tell you in the actual words because even in the terror she kept the secret; nevertheless she told you, or at least all of a sudden you knew—.' " To this Quentin does not reply, and we are never told whether he was ever told by anyone that "in fact" Bon had Negro blood. This "fact" remains pure though plausible conjecture, primarily invented by Shreve, and unconfirmed by any concrete evidence from Quentin or anyone else.

live in a changing world, and perhaps his moment of static contemplation will help him deal with tomorrows. The young men in *Absalom, Absalom!*—Quentin and Shreve, in sympathetic and then empathic relation with Henry and Bon— must do the same. For Quentin the moment is evidently not life-engendering; the explanation based on Bon's putative touch of Negro blood is more damning than saving. But for Shreve, and for at least some readers, this moment points toward the endurance and prevalence of man, whose color is both black and white, and changeable.

The chronology of Sutpen's story, after being outlined in the barest possible way in the skeleton account given on the third page of the text by "the two separate Quentins" (p. 9), is thoroughly, deliberately, and systematically scrambled in the rest of the book as the various narrators plunge in at different points to try to explain what happened and why. The tendency of readers to "unravel" the story by establishing a causally related series of events is continually thwarted; obviously Faulkner was knitting on a different plan. His purpose is suggested by his remark in the *Paris Review* interview that "With me, a story usually begins with a single idea or memory or mental picture. The writing of the story is simply a matter of working up to that moment, to explain why it happened or what it caused to follow."[21] In *Absalom, Absalom!* this "moment" is the point where Quentin encounters the obstacle he is unable to pass. In the Sutpen story it is the murder of Bon. In Quentin's development it is where he fails, balks, refuses to face or accept what has happened, and thereby cuts himself off from the future. In the story as a whole, it is where the three main narrative formulas are transcended, where Shreve pushes on past Quentin's stopping-place and the author works his magic trick of fusing Shreve and Quentin with Henry and Bon, and the present time of the conversation in the Harvard

[21] *Writers at Work*, p. 133. Cf. Henry James' method, particularly in *The Ambassadors*.

dormitory in 1910 with the past time of Henry's ultimatum to Bon, and Bon's to Henry, in Carolina in 1865.

Although Miss Rosa's version of the Sutpen story, as we have seen, does not provide much information, it contributes a great deal to the texture of the book, and especially to the imagery of dynamic stasis. Miss Rosa encounters the crucial moment in a manner almost exactly parallel to Quentin's, when Wash Jones hails her out of her father's house with his news of Bon's murder. Since the *"summer of wistaria"* when, at the age of fourteen, she *"became all polymath love's androgynous advocate"* by virtue of her excited vicarious interest in Judith's developing relation to Bon, she has been waiting eagerly for that relation to be completed and consummated. Now, unable to abandon the momentum of her fervent expectations, she rushes into Sutpen's house, only to be *"stopped dead . . . . motionless in the attitude and action of running,"* first by Clytie, who is herself *"rigid in that furious immobility,"* and then *"in running's midstride again though my body, blind insentient barrow of deluded clay and breath, still advanced"* by the *"cold . . . still"* voice of Judith (pp. 143, 146, 139, 140, 142).

Not content to let the static-dynamic image stand alone, she philosophizes on it in an extravagant but highly illuminating way. She should have realized, she says, and perhaps did realize, that stasis would be all she could hope to find, *"who even at nineteen must have known that living is one constant and perpetual instant when the arras-veil before what-is-to-be hangs docile and even glad to the lightest naked thrust if we had dared . . . to make the rending gash. Or perhaps it is no lack of courage either: not cowardice which will not face that sickness somewhere at the prime foundation of this factual scheme from which the prisoner soul, miasmal-distillant, wroils ever upward sunward, tugs its tenuous prisoner arteries and veins and prisoning in its turn that spark, that*

dream which, as the globy and complete instant of its free-
dom mirrors and repeats (repeats? creates, reduces to a fragile
evanescent iridescent sphere) all of space and time and massy
earth, relicts the seething and anonymous miasmal mass which
in all the years of time has taught itself no boon of death but
only how to recreate, renew; and dies, is gone, vanished:
nothing—but is that true wisdom which can comprehend
that there is a might-have-been which is more true than truth,
from which the dreamer, waking, says not 'Did I but dream?'
but rather says, indicts high heaven's very self with: 'Why did
I wake since waking I shall never sleep again?' " (pp. 142,
143).

Miss Rosa is outrageously strident, in logic and syntax, but
the substance of what she says is central to both the method
and the theme of *Absalom, Absalom!* Her situation and her
analysis of it represent, as well as anything in the book, the
artist's aim, as Faulkner later defined it, of stopping or freez-
ing the motion of life in order to make it communicable in
terms of esthetic value. Her error lies in her effort to live in the
dream of art, and in that error lies the value of her contribution to the art of Faulkner's book. Because she cannot move,
she provides a particularly useful point of view from which the
author can impress the reader with the speed and power of the
life that moves around her.

When Miss Rosa speaks of *"that veil we call virginity"*
(p. 148) and of *"that might-have-been which is the single rock*
we cling to above the maelstrom of unbearable reality"
(pp. 149-50), she is speaking not only for herself but for a
number of other characters who speak less clearly. Sutpen,
with his innocence and his design, is equally barred from the
dynamic reality of life. Mr. Compson is almost as much so in
his effort to freeze the story in the pattern of tragedy. Above
all, Miss Rosa speaks for Quentin when she explains her inability to pass beyond the fact of Bon's murder: *"There are*
some things which happen to us which the intelligence and

the senses refuse just as the stomach sometimes refuses what the palate has accepted but which digestion cannot compass— occurrences which stop us dead as though by some impalpable intervention, like a sheet of glass through which we watch all subsequent events transpire as though in a soundless vacuum, and fade, vanish; are gone, leaving us immobile, impotent, helpless; fixed, until we can die" (pp. 151-52). That is precisely the quality of Quentin's character; and Quentin's character, as the principal medium through which the story comes to us, is the prime obstacle by which the motion of life in the book is artificially arrested. Quentin cannot, or at any rate does not, explain himself, but Miss Rosa's presence, her point of view, and her somewhat frantic meditations explain him, in his artistic function, very well.

One of Miss Rosa's most pathetic illusions is her belief that Sutpen is a tremendously dynamic personage, actually as well as potentially. This belief is the motive of her demonizing, her Gothic shudder in the conviction that such fearful energy must be hellishly superhuman, and her frightening wish that she might share it. The resulting complex is often embodied in imagery drawn from the Persephone myth, as it is in the impression Quentin receives from her in the beginning of Sutpen looking considerably like Dis in the fair field of Enna: "Out of quiet thunderclap he would abrupt (man-horse-demon) upon a scene peaceful and decorous as a schoolprize water color, faint sulphur-reek still in hair clothes and beard . . ." (p. 8). The Persephone parallel is reinforced by Miss Rosa's earliest memories about Ellen, who had married Sutpen about eight years before Miss Rosa came into the world. She tells Quentin that " 'It was as though the sister whom I had never laid eyes on, who before I was born had vanished into the stronghold of an ogre or a djinn, was now to return through a dispensation of one day only, to the world which she had quitted . . . .' " The occasion is a church service which the Coldfields and Sutpens are all to attend; but the advent of Sutpen, with Ellen and their two children, instead of being the peaceful and even gracious encounter that Miss Rosa has imagined in advance, turns out to be the finish of a carriage race. Her first sight of them is " 'a glimpse like the forefront of a tornado, of the carriage and Ellen's high white face within it and the two replicas of his face in miniature flanking her, and on the front seat the face and teeth of the wild negro who was driving, and he, his face exactly like the negro's save for the teeth (this because of his beard, doubtless)—all in a thunder and a fury of wildeyed horses and of galloping and of dust' " (p. 23). To Miss Rosa, motion is diabolical and life is hell. Therefore, when Ellen, just before her death during the war, pleads with Miss Rosa to " ' "Protect her, at least. At least save Judith," ' " Miss Rosa replies, " ' "Protect her? From whom and from what? He has already given them life: he does not need to harm them further. It is from themselves that they need protection" ' " (p. 22).

This statement is true, in the sense that Henry to some extent and Judith in a larger degree do have the dynamic possibilities of life which are blocked in their father by his "innocence" and at which Miss Rosa looks, from the stasis of her frustrating virginity, with envy and despair. When the carriage racing continues after Sutpen has stopped going to church, it is Judith, as Miss Rosa discovers to her horror, " 'who had instigated and authorized that negro to make the team run away. Not Henry, mind; not the boy, which would have been outrageous enough; but Judith, the girl' " (p. 25). The same impression and the same distinction emerge when, after the two children and their Negro half-sister Clytie have been watching a fighting match between Sutpen and one of his slaves, Henry runs to his mother, " 'screaming and vomiting' " (p. 29), but Judith and Clytie remain calmly looking down from the loft of the stable in which the improvised ring has been set up.

Mr. Compson sees this dynamic quality, particularly in

Judith, in a strikingly different way. He describes her adolescence as "that state where, though still visible, young girls appear as though seen through glass and where even the voice cannot reach them; where they exist (this the hoyden who could—and did—outrun and outclimb, and ride and fight both with and beside her brother) in a pearly lambence without shadows and themselves partaking of it; in nebulous suspension held, strange and unpredictable, even their very shapes fluid and delicate and without substance; not in themselves floating and seeking but merely waiting, parasitic and potent and serene, drawing to themselves without effort the post-genitive upon and about which to shape, flow into back, breast; bosom, flank, thigh" (p. 67). The passage is one of Faulkner's earlier efforts to present a direct impression of a young woman moving so harmoniously with the motion of life that no motion can be seen.

The power of motion in Judith becomes more apparent when Mr. Compson describes her response to Sutpen's prohibition of her marriage to Bon. She waits, he says, with trust and love for both of them, and with " 'that true pride . . . which can say to itself without abasement *I love, I will accept no substitute; something has happened between him and my father; if my father was right, I will never see him again, if wrong he will come or send for me; if happy I can be I will, if suffer I must I can'* " (p. 121). She does not suffer, however, as Mr. Compson remarks, from " 'the Coldfield cluttering of morality and rules of right and wrong' " (p. 120), nor is she inhibited by any Sutpen scruples either; she does not even bother to find out what they are. The only thing that can keep her from marrying Bon is his death, as Henry realizes when his own effort to go along with life gives out. He does not try to explain to Judith or argue with her; he knows that words would have no effect.

Judith sets up a tombstone to immortalize Bon, as Sutpen has done for his wife and himself; but she is not content with that. She also makes the more subtle and complex gesture of giving to General Compson's wife the last and perhaps the only letter she has received from Bon, to be kept or destroyed, read or not read. She says, " ' "Because you make so little impression, you see. You get born and you try this and you dont know why only you keep on trying it and you are born at the same time with a lot of other people, all mixed up with them, like trying to, having to, move your arms and legs with strings only the same strings are hitched to all the other arms and legs and the others all trying and they dont know why either except that the strings are all in one another's way like five or six people all trying to make a rug on the same loom only each one wants to weave his own pattern into the rug;[22] and it cant matter, you know that, or the Ones that set up the loom would have arranged things a little better, and yet it must matter because you keep on trying or having to keep on trying and then all of a sudden it's all over and all you have left is a block of stone with scratches on it . . . and after a while they dont even remember the name and what the scratches were trying to tell, and it doesn't matter" ' " (p. 127).[23]

Faulkner remarked in an interview that the personal aim of a writer must be to make a better kind of mark, "that really the writer doesn't want success, that he knows he has a short span of life, that the day will come when he must pass through the wall of oblivion, and he wants to leave a scratch on that wall —Kilroy was here—that somebody a hundred, a thousand years later will see."[24] For this immortality, some quality of life must be communicated, and Judith apparently agrees with Faulkner in thinking that paper may be the best medium. She says of the letter that " ' "at least it would be something just because it would have happened, be remembered even if only from passing from one hand to another, one mind to another,

[22] This passages seems to be derived from the chapters on "The Monkey-Rope" and "The Loom" in *Moby Dick*.

[23] Cf. Shelley's "Ozymandias."

[24]*Faulkner in the University*, p. 61.

and it would be at least a scratch, something, something that might make a mark on something that *was* once for the reason that it can die someday, while the block of stone cant be *is* because it never can become *was* because it cant ever die or perish . . ." ' " (pp. 127-28). Mr. Compson paraphrases this in terms even closer to those of the later interview: " 'to make that scratch, that undying mark on the blank face of the oblivion to which we are all doomed . . .' " (p. 129). The kind of immortality being aimed at cannot be achieved in terms of static endurance, no matter how prolonged; it depends on the living memory of human beings who must die.

Bon's letter does in fact physically endure, to be read by Quentin in 1909. Written from Carolina near the end of the war, it begins by asserting that Bon is alive; it is not, he says, "*a voice from the defeated even, let alone from the dead.*" He knows he is alive because he is hungry, like everyone else alive in the South at the time ("*like saying that we were breathing*"), ragged, and shoeless, and his body has not become reconciled to suffering although his mind can remember nothing else. Half of the letter is a long-winded but not pointless joke about its being written on "*a sheet of notepaper with, as you can see, the best of French watermarks dated seventy years ago, salvaged (stolen if you will) from the gutted mansion of a ruined aristocrat; and written upon in the best of stove polish manufactured not twelve months ago in a New England factory*" (p. 129). The "*conclusion and augury*" which Bon draws from this juxtaposition is that "*We have waited long enough.*" The past, represented by the notepaper, is indeed past, or, as he puts it, "*what WAS is one thing, and now it is not because it is dead, it died in 1861 . . . .*" The war has been a long static moment, its opening burst of gunfire "*arrested, mesmerized raised muzzle by raised muzzle, in the frozen attitude of its own aghast amazement and never repeated,*" and now "*what IS is something else again*" (p. 131), wherefore Bon concludes that "*since because within this sheet*

207

of paper you now hold the best of the old South which is dead,
and the words you read were written upon it with the best . . .
of the new North which has conquered and which therefore,
whether it likes it or not, will have to survive, I now believe
that you and I are, strangely enough, included among those
who are doomed to live" (pp. 131-32). The irony is, however,
that because he has written this letter Bon is doomed to die;
and this is the universal irony of life, which Quentin is unable
to live with, that the past is always dead and that all who live
will die. Judith, unlike Quentin, goes beyond Bon's death and
asserts his immortality, not by keeping his letter but by giving
it away, and she goes on living as best she can.

Her best is relatively good. She helps her father in his effort
to restore the plantation, even going so far as to cooperate in
his seduction of Milly. She offers hospitality to Bon's octoroon
consort, who comes to weep on his grave, and when the octoroon dies she either goes herself or sends Clytie to New Orleans
to bring Bon's quasi-legitimate son, Charles Etienne Saint-
Valery Bon, back to Sutpen's Hundred to live.

But at this point, by Mr. Compson's account, her acceptance
of life breaks down. She feels it her duty to adopt the boy as
her own child, but she is unable to give him the love he needs.
The obstacle, once more, is his slight inheritance of Negro
blood, which prompts Judith and Clytie to isolate him from all
contact with either Negroes or white people. Judith, Mr.
Compson says, is " 'the woman . . . whose every touch of the
capable hands seemed at the moment of touching his body to
lose all warmth and become imbued with cold implacable
antipathy . . . (and your grandfather said, "Suffer little children to come unto Me": and what did He mean by that? how,
if He meant that little children should need to *be* suffered to
approach Him, what sort of earth had He created; that if they
had to *suffer* in order to approach Him, what sort of Heaven
did He have?)' " (pp. 197-98). Charles Etienne reacts violently
and negatively by fighting with both Negroes and white men
and by marrying " 'a coal black and ape-like woman' "

(p. 205), upon whom he begets the last of the Sutpen line, the idiot Jim Bond.

Quentin imagines Judith trying to repair the damage, saying to Charles Etienne, " '*I was wrong. I admit it. I believed that there were things which still mattered just because they had mattered once. But I was wrong. Nothing matters but breath, breathing, to know and to be alive'* " (p. 207). But the best solution she can suggest is that he go away and pass as a white man. He refuses, tactily insisting that he be accepted as a Negro or not at all. The impasse is swept away, somewhat melodramatically, when he contracts yellow fever, Judith nurses him, and they both die, Judith first.

There has been a good deal of argument as to whether Sutpen is or is not intended as a realistic representative of the pre-Civil War Southern aristocracy. The answer lies partly in a distinction between the relatively old established aristocracy, which flourished in spots along the Atlantic Coast, the Gulf Coast, and the Mississippi River, and the more recently established aristocracy of the inland countryside. Faulkner said in a Virginia interview that Uncle Bud McCaslin's comic rescue from Miss Sophonsiba Beauchamp in the story "Was" "had a certain sociological importance in—to show my country as it really was in those days. The elegance of the colonial plantation didn't exist in my country. My country was still frontier. The plantation, the columned porticos, that was Charleston and Natchez. But my country was still frontier. People lived from day to day, with a bluff and crude hardiness, but with a certain simplicity. Which to me is very interesting because the common picture of the South is all magnolias and crinoline and Grecian portals and things like that, which was true only around the fringes of the South. Not in the interior, the back wood."[25]

Sutpen is a backwoodsman by birth and early training; he is

---

[25] *Ibid.*, p. 131; cf. pp. 37-38. This same distinction is analyzed in considerable detail by W.J. Cash in *The Mind of the South*, Book I, Chapter I.

exposed to the old aristocracy of Virginia; he becomes one of the "frontier" aristocrats of north Mississippi. He is fairly typical of the class, and of the first families of Yoknapatawpha, the founders of which are generally self-made men such as old Carothers McCaslin, " 'who saw the opportunity and took it, bought the land, took the land, got the land no matter how' " (*GDM* 256), and Jason Lycurgus Compson, Quentin's ancestor, who, according to the appendix to *The Portable Faulkner*, "rode up the Natchez Trace one day in 1820 with a pair of fine pistols and one meagre saddlebag" and diddled Ikkemotubbe out of a square mile of fine plantation land.[26] Sutpen's antecedents are equally dubious, or more so, but he has enough more material assets so that Faulkner can say in *Requiem for a Nun* that John Sartoris comes to Mississippi "with slaves and gear and money too like Grenier and Sutpen . . ." (p. 44). Sartoris' later career is parallel to Sutpen's in several explicit ways, notably in the violence of its end. Sartoris comes from Carolina, where his family has been established for some time; but William C. Falkner, his ancestor in Faulkner's imagination, and Faulkner's ancestor in reality, came from Tennessee with nothing at all in the way of material goods—and he never acquired a plantation either, although he did build a railroad.

These various circumstances may help to explain why General Compson and his grandson Quentin sympathize with Sutpen, and why the great-grandson of William C. Falkner felt that such a man as Sutpen could be used as a "tool" for expressing the quality of life in a Southern setting. Sutpen's fictional career epitomizes the whole history of aristocracy in north Mississippi as Faulkner uses that history in his work. We should remember, incidentally, that the history went back

[26] *Portable*, p. 740. Cf. *Faulkner in the University*, p. 3: "The first Compson was a bold ruthless man who came into Mississippi as a free forester to grasp where and when he could and wanted to, and established what should have been a princely line, and that princely line decayed."

only about fifty years before the Civil War, hardly a long enough time to establish any social institution very firmly.[27]

The story "Wash," as we have seen, suggests that Faulkner's criticism of aristocracy goes deeper than the "sociological" observation that it was older in some places than in others; this suggestion is carried out in *Absalom, Absalom!* Faulkner seems to accept, as it were in passing, Mark Twain's opinion that the nineteenth-century fad for medievalism, as popularized by Sir Walter Scott, had set "the world in love with dreams and phantoms; with decayed and swinish forms of religion; with decayed and degraded systems of government; with the sillinesses and emptinesses, sham grandeurs, sham gauds, and sham chivalries of a brainless and worthless long-vanished society."[28] Quentin's name suggests that his fixation on aristocratic "ghosts" may be derived from the Sir Walter syndrome. Faulkner also seems to assimilate Mark Twain's feeling, pervasively expressed in *Huckleberry Finn*, that sentimentalism about aristocracy functioned as an ornamental screen to obscure the brutal exploitation on which the system lived. As Goodhue Coldfield reportedly says in *Absalom, Absalom!*, the South "erected its economic edifice not on the rock of stern morality but on the shifting sands of opportunism and moral brigandage" (p. 260). Much of Faulkner's humor, like much of Mark Twain's, plays on the incongruities that are exposed when aristocratic pretensions are snatched aside to reveal brutality and injustice.

The backwoods life before the War had been richly and humorously described by others besides Mark Twain. Faulkner was familiar with accounts of it by George Washington Harris, A.B. Longstreet, and Joseph G. Baldwin, probably

---

[27] Useful discussions of this matter may be found in Walter Sullivan, "The Tragic Design of *Absalom, Absalom!*" *South Atlantic Quarterly*, L (October 1951), 556-60; and Robert D. Jacobs, "Faulkner's Tragedy of Isolation," *Hopkins Review*, VI (Spring-Summer 1953), 182-83.

[28] *Life on the Mississippi, The Writings of Mark Twain* (Hillcrest edn., New York, 1904), IX, 347.

among others. Baldwin, referring to the boom of the 1830s, the period when Faulkner's Yoknapatawpha is emerging, says, "The conditions of society may be imagined:—vulgarity —ignorance—fussy and arrogant pretension—unmitigated rowdyism—bullying insolence, if they did not rule the hour, *seemed* to wield unchecked dominion. . . . Men dropped down into their places as from the clouds. Nobody knew who or what they were, except as they claimed, or as a surface view of their characters indicated." This might have been adopted by Faulkner as his model for the town of Jefferson into which Sutpen "abrupted" in 1833 to establish himself, and Sutpen's method is even more specifically suggested by a later passage in Baldwin: "Swindling Indians by the nation! . . . Stealing their land by the township!"[29] Like Mark Twain, Faulkner uses these facts to ridicule what his acquaintance Arthur Palmer Hudson called "the legend of the old South," that is, "the superstition that a social system founded upon slavery, stratified into castes, dedicated to privilege, and motivated in its public conduct by the pompous absurdities of neo-chivalry, was a perfect society; that the period before the war was a golden age; and that human character reached its perfection in the Old South by and through the system."[30]

Quentin's failure in *Absalom, Absalom!* is partly due to his dismay over the way his ideal vision of what life ought to be in the South is continually undercut by his concrete knowledge of what it is and has been. The irony is similar to that raised by Hightower's memory of the grandfather who gallantly set

[29] Joseph G. Baldwin, *The Flush Times of Alabama and Mississippi* (New York, 1853), pp. 88-89, 238.

[30] Arthur Palmer Hudson, *Specimens of Mississippi Folk-Lore* (Mississippi Folk-Lore Society, 1928), p. vi. Hudson's purpose, as he explained in the introduction to this collection, was to render justice to the rich and racy lower-class culture which, he felt, was more typical of the region than the magnolia mythology that tended to obscure it in the popular mind. Hudson taught English at the University of Mississippi from 1920 to 1930, and he has said that he was "reasonably sure that Mr. Faulkner was acquainted in a general way with the work I was doing in Mississippi folklore" (O'Connor, p. 176, n. 7).

fire to Grant's stores in Jefferson and who was killed stealing chickens from a Confederate roost. Like Hightower, Quentin is immobilized between the glorious vision he would like to believe in and the sordid realities to which his evidence often points. The moral of the whole book emerges from the pervasive counterpoint of static ideal aristocracy against the concrete dynamism of rapid, chaotic, and often violent change. Both Quentin and Sutpen would be better off, actually, if they could abandon the noble but sterile vision and live more consistently than they do by the motto of another fictional Southerner, Johnson J. Hooper's Simon Suggs: "It is good to be shifty in a new country"—and perhaps in an older one, too.

Quentin is never able to escape the rigidly static "morality" which is equated, in the experience of both Sutpen and Miss Rosa, with "virginity," that imperviousness to the concrete experience of motion through time which is the fine bloom of Sutpen's "innocence." It is therefore left to Shreve to put his finger on the still unresolved factor at the end of the story that keeps it from settling into any final stasis. " 'You've got one nigger left. One nigger Sutpen left,' " he says. " 'And so do you know what I think?' " When Quentin has made it clear that he neither knows nor wants to know, Shreve drives his dynamic logic through to an image that thoroughly transcends the time-block that has arrested Quentin, and also the color bar that has, according to the hypothesis advanced by Shreve, occasioned Bon's murder. " 'I think,' " Shreve says, " 'that in time the Jim Bonds are going to conquer the western hemisphere. . . . and so in a few thousand years, I who regard you will also have sprung from the loins of African kings.' " In a final, supreme effort to get Quentin moving, he puts his question in its most exigent form: " 'Now I want you to tell me just one thing more. Why do you hate the South?' "

The question put in this way demands a constructive answer —some such answer as Faulkner suggested in his article on "Mississippi" in *Holiday Magazine,* where he described a semi-fictional person named William Faulkner as "Loving all of it even while he had to hate some of it," especially "the intolerance and injustice"[31]—for there is much in the South, as in other places, to be hated by anyone who loves it enough to dedicate his present and future to living in it, as the real William Faulkner did but as the fictional Quentin Compson cannot do. Quentin's final words, the final words of the book, are therefore a repudiation of the question, the South, and life itself: " 'I dont hate it,' Quentin said, quickly, at once, immediately; 'I dont hate it,' he said. *I dont hate it* he thought, panting in the cold air, the iron New England dark; *I dont. I dont! I dont hate it! I dont hate it!*" (p. 378).

This answer which is not an answer contains, unresolved, the tensions which the book has built up in response to the question in its earlier and simpler forms. In the process of failing to answer, Quentin evokes, more compellingly than any pat formula could do, the quality of the life he cannot live. He dramatizes it by telling the story of Sutpen, which epitomizes the history of the South, in such a way as to show a whole society erected as a static obstacle to the motion of life in the world. The resulting disaster is an almost cosmic objective correlative of Quentin's desperate frustration, and the book in which it is created is one of the greatest of Faulkner's artistic achievements.

[31] *Holiday Magazine*, XV (April 1954), 46, 44.

Six / Work: *The Sound and the Fury*

Henry James said of *The Scarlet Letter*, ". . . it has about it that charm, very hard to express, which we find in an artist's work the first time he has touched his highest mark—a sort of straightness and naturalness of execution, an unconsciousness of his public, and freshness of interest in his theme."[1] *The Sound and the Fury* is the work in which Faulkner first touched his highest mark; and, for all its technical complexity, it has about it much of the same charm.

Like Hawthorne, Faulkner had discovered, rather suddenly it seems, after much experimental effort, how to write as he really wanted to. Discouraged by what he felt to be the failure of his first two published novels, and by his failure for the time being to get the third one published at all, he had decided, he said, to give up the idea of publishing and to write his next book purely for his own satisfaction. "One day I seemed to shut a door between me and all publishers' addresses and book lists. I said to myself, Now I can write. Now I can make myself a vase like that which the old Roman kept at his bedside and wore the rim slowly away with kissing it." In the process of composition, he had had "that emotion definite and physical

[1] Henry James, *Hawthorne* (English Men of Letters edn., New York: Harper & Bros., 1879), p. 107.

and yet nebulous to describe: that ecstasy, that eager and joyous faith and anticipation of surprise which the yet unmarred sheet beneath my hand held inviolate and unfailing, waiting for release."[2]

The pressure of creative energy thus released—again as with Hawthorne—appears to have been intensified by both professional and personal troubles. Hawthorne had recently scrapped what must have been intended as a novel, of which only the fragment "Ethan Brand" survives; it was his second failure in two known tries. Faulkner had tried at least three times,[3] and he reported in the introduction he wrote for the Modern Library edition of *Sanctuary* in 1932 that, "with one novel [*Flags in the Dust*, eventually to be published as *Sartoris*, after being considerably cut, apparently by someone other than Faulkner[4]] completed and consistently refused for two years, I had just written my guts into *The Sound and the Fury* . . . . I believed then that I would never be published again. I had stopped thinking of myself in publishing terms."[5]

Hawthorne, having lost his Custom House job, and then his mother, shortly before he began writing *The Scarlet Letter*, remarked in his introduction on "the period of hardly accomplished revolution, and still seething turmoil, in which the story shaped itself."[6] Maurice Coindreau, in his preface to the French edition of *The Sound and the Fury*, dated 1937, says that that novel was "written during a time when the author was struggling with some personal difficulties," and adds in a

[2] Unpublished typescript in the Alderman Library, University of Virginia; quoted by Millgate, p. 26. Cf. James B. Meriwether, *The Literary Career of William Faulkner*, p. 16.

[3] Four, if Millgate is correct in supposing that an unfinished manuscript called "Elmer" was "originally intended as a novel" (p. 21); five, if the manuscript "Father Abraham" was meant to be the beginning of a novel (Millgate, p. 24).

[4] See Millgate, pp. 25-26, 82-85.

[5] Introduction to *Sanctuary* (Modern Library edn., New York: Random House, 1932), p. vi.

[6] Nathaniel Hawthorne, *The Scarlet Letter* (Centenary edn., Columbus: Ohio State University Press, 1962), p. 43.

footnote that "Deep emotional shocks are a potent factor in the inspiration of William Faulkner," remarking as supporting and more specific evidence that *Light in August* was written after the death of one of Faulkner's children and *Absalom, Absalom!* after that of his brother Dean.[7]

We may never clearly know the relations between Faulkner's private life and his esthetic work; apparently he did not intend that we should. We do know, however, that there must have been a tremendous charge of creative energy to be released, and that in 1928 he was able not only to release it at full pressure but to direct and control it with an equally powerful pressure of artistic discipline. If we cannot fully understand the nature or sources of the energy, we can study the discipline in the work itself.

The Sound and the Fury contained, according to Faulkner's draft introduction, "perhaps the only thing in literature which would ever move me very much: Caddy climbing the pear tree to look in the window at her grandmother's funeral while Quentin and Jason and Benjy and the negroes looked up at the muddy seat of her drawers."[8] Later, in interviews, Faulkner consistently said that his conception of the book had grown from this germ.[9] When someone at Virginia asked about his "impression" of the girl in the tree, Faulkner objected that "impression is the wrong word. It's more an image, a very moving image to me was of the children. 'Course, we

---

[7] Maurice Coindreau, preface to *Le bruit et la Fureur* (Paris: Editions Gallimard, 1949), p. 16. My translation. The original reads "Ecrit alors que l'auteur se débattait dans des difficultés d'ordre intime," and "Les profondes secousses morales sont un facteur puissant dans l'inspiration de William Faulkner." Coindreau does not say what the personal difficulties related to *The Sound and the Fury* were, and no biographer has yet described them.

[8] Millgate, p. 34.

[9] See Coindreau, p. 5; Lavon Rascoe, "An Interview with William Faulkner," *Western Review*, XV (Summer 1951), 300; *Writers at Work*, pp. 130-31; *Faulkner at Nagano*, p. 103; *Faulkner in the University*, p. 1; *Faulkner at West Point*, ed. Joseph L. Fant and Robert Ashley (New York: Random House, 1964), p. 109.

didn't know at that time that one was an idiot, but they were three boys, one was a girl and the girl was the only one that was brave enough to climb that tree to look in the forbidden window to see what was going on. And that's what the book— and it took the rest of the four hundred pages to explain why she was brave enough to climb the tree to look in the window. It was an image, a picture to me, a very moving one, which was symbolized by the muddy bottom of her drawers as her brothers looked up into the apple tree that she had climbed to look in the window. And the symbolism of the muddy bottom of the drawers became the lost Caddy . . . ."[10] Perhaps "explain" is not the right word either, for the story does not explain Caddy's bravery, and Faulkner never, in or out of the story, explained why the "image" fascinated him so. But he did make it clear that the whole book is an effort to focus the looking of the other children—and thereby the reader—at "the muddy bottom of the drawers" of a girl who only later became sufficiently abstracted from the "image" to acquire a name and a fate.

The image associates a girl with a tree, as Faulkner's early work does, but with more ambiguity. Caddy is in one aspect a dryad, and to Benjy she usually smells like trees. But she is not virginal like the poplars of the early poems. She is more the Arician Diana, going to meet her lover Dalton Ames among trees, like Addie and Dewey Dell Bundren, or Lena Grove. Even at the age of seven she climbs a fertile fruit tree, like those in *Soldiers' Pay*, *Sartoris*, and *The Hamlet*; and already her drawers are stained with symbolic mud, making Faulkner's usual association of fecundity with foulness (cf. *Mos* 335; *LIA* 177-78). In another aspect she is like Eve, seeking forbidden knowledge, which happens to be knowledge of death. Perhaps that is why Faulkner remembered the tree as an apple in the interview, which took place in 1957, although he had remembered it as a pear in the draft introduction, writ-

---

[10] *Faulkner in the University*, p. 31.

ten about 1932 or 1933.[11] Perhaps that is also why we are told that "A snake crawled out from under the house" (*S&F* 45) just before Caddy climbs the tree, and why a few minutes later Dilsey says to her, " 'You, Satan. . . . Come down from there' " (p. 54).

Faulkner was generally consistent in the accounts he gave of his procedure in composing the story. In the longest and most detailed one he said, "That began as a short story, it was a story without plot, of some children being sent away from the house during the grandmother's funeral. They were too young to be told what was going on and they saw things only incidentally to the childish games they were playing, which was the lugubrious matter of removing the corpse from the house, etc., and then the idea struck me to see how much more I could have got out of the idea of the blind, self-centeredness of innocence, typified by children, if one of those children had been truly innocent, that is, an idiot. So the idiot was born and then I became interested in the relationship of the idiot to the world that he was in but would never be able to cope with and just where could he get the tenderness, the help, to shield him in his innocence. I mean 'innocence' in the sense that God had stricken him blind at birth, that is, mindless at birth, there was nothing he could ever do about it. And so the character of his sister began to emerge, then the brother, who, that Jason (who to me represented complete evil. He's the most vicious character in my opinion I ever thought of), then he appeared. Then it needs the protagonist, someone to tell the story, so Quentin appeared. By that time I found out I couldn't possibly tell that in a short story. And so I told the idiot's experience of that day, and that was incomprehensible, even I could not have told what was going on then, so I had to write another chapter. Then I decided to let Quentin tell his version of that same day, or that same occasion, so he told it. Then there had to be the counterpoint, which was the other brother, Jason. By that

[11] Millgate, p. 26.

time it was completely confusing. I knew that it was not anywhere near finished and then I had to write another section
from the outside with an outsider, which was the writer, to
tell what had happened on that particular day. And that's how
that book grew. That is, I wrote that same story four times.
None of them were right, but I had anguished so much that I
could not throw any of it away and start over, so I printed it in
the four sections. That was not a deliberate *tour de force* at all,
the book just grew that way. That I was still trying to tell one
story which moved me very much and each time I failed . . . .
And that's the reason I have the most tenderness for that book,
because it failed four times."[12]

Here again is much that Faulkner never explains: why he
chose the innocent child's point of view as his best approach
to the story, why the other narrators were chosen or created
as they were, or why the sections are arranged in a certain way
and not otherwise. But he offers some facts, the central and
most important of which is that the characters gradually
emerged and took individual shape only after the germinal
situation, or "image," had presented itself to his mind. This
order of development is confirmed in the statement quoted by
Coindreau, where Faulkner puts it that he conceived the work
as a short story about the grandmother's funeral, then thought
of using an idiot as narrator, and then fell so much in love with
Caddy that he could not bear to confine her to a short story.[13]

---

[12] *Faulkner at Nagano*, pp. 103-105. Cf. *Writers at Work*, p. 130; Cynthia
Grenier, "The Art of Fiction: An Interview with William Faulkner," *Accent*,
XVI (Summer 1956), 172; *Faulkner in the University*, pp. 1, 32, 84, 139-40;
Faulkner at West Point, pp. 109, 111.

[13] Coindreau, p. 5. The original reads, "Ce roman, à l'origine, ne devait être
qu'une nouvelle, me dit, un jour, William Faulkner. J'avais songé qu'il
serait intéressant d'imaginer les pensées d'un groupe d'enfants, le jour de
l'enterrement de leur grand-mère dont on leur a caché la mort, leur curiosité
devant l'agitation de la maison, leurs efforts pour percer le mystère, les sup-
positions qui leur viennent à l'esprit. Ensuite, pour corser cette étude, j'ai
conçu l'idée d'un être qui serait plus qu'un enfant, un être qui, pour résoudre
le problème, n'aurait même pas à son service un cerveau normalement consti-
tué, autrement dit un idiot. C'est ainsi que Benjy est né. Puis, il m'est arrivé
ce qui arrive à bien des romanciers, je me suis épris d'un de mes personnages,

The sum of all these statements, in spite of some inconsistencies and probable inaccuracies, is that Faulkner began with a symbolic situation, which had strong mythological undertones, and that he invented a complex of characters and events by means of which to develop its artistic possibilities. He seems not to have thought about a theme until later.

Whenever someone asked him what his favorite was among his own works, Faulkner always named *The Sound and the Fury*. But he always said, not that it was his best, or even that he liked it best, but rather that, as he put it in one of the interviews quoted above, it was the brain child that gave him the most trouble, or it was his most splendid, or gallant, or magnificent failure.[14] Partly, no doubt, this is modesty; but partly it must represent the other side of what Faulkner said about writing his guts into this book. The exaltation and the unconsciousness of possible publishers and readers that he felt during its composition is not inconsistent with his feeling afterward that the result on paper fell short of the creative incandescence which he had been trying to capture and immobilize. The very effort to immobilize is a betrayal of the divine energy. So, for Faulkner, the greater the failure, the more magnificent the success—and the more intensely mixed the author's feelings.[15]

Another assertion Faulkner consistently repeated is that in *The Sound and the Fury*, as in other works of his middle period, he was doing the writer's duty as he described it in the Nobel Prize Address.[16] One critic—and only one that I know

---

Caddy. Je l'ai tant aimée que je n'ai pu me décider à ne la faire vivre que l'espace d'un conte. Elle méritait plus que cela. Et mon roman s'est achevé, je ne dirais pas malgré moi, mais presque."

[14] See *Faulkner at Nagano*, pp. 9, 103, 106, 162; *Writers at Work*, p. 130; Grenier, p. 172; *Faulkner in the University*, pp. 61, 77; *Faulkner at West Point*, p. 49.

[15] Walter J. Slatoff, it seems to me, reads this paradox backward in his *Quest for Failure*. Faulkner's quest was for success—of a kind that made failure inevitable.

[16] For the most explicit statement, see *Faulkner in the University*, pp. 4-5.

of—was perceptive enough to understand what he was doing, and bold enough to say so at the time. Evelyn Scott, a fellow poet and novelist, in a pamphlet-sized essay published by Jonathan Cape and Harrison Smith (the publishers of *The Sound and the Fury*) in 1929, made a declaration which strikes me as being so essentially right and true that I would like to quote it at length.

"The question has been put by a contemporary critic, a genuine philosopher reviewing the arts [probably Joseph Wood Krutch, in *The Modern Temper*, published earlier in 1929], as to whether there exists for this age of disillusion with religion, dedication to the objective program of scientific inventiveness and general rejection of the teleology which placed man emotionally at the center of his universe, the spirit of which great tragedy is the expression. *The Sound and the Fury* seems to me to offer a reply. Indeed I feel that however sophistical the argument of theology, man remains, in his heart, in that important position. What he seeks now is a fresh justification for the presumption of his emotions; and his present tragedy is in a realization of the futility, up to date, of his search for another, intellectually appropriate embodiment of the god that lives on, however contradicted by 'reason.'

"William Faulkner, the author of this tragedy, which has all the spacious proportions of Greek art, may not consider his book in the least expressive of the general dilemma to which I refer, but that quality in his writings which the emotionally timid will call 'morbid,' seems to me reflected from the impression, made on a sensitive and normally egoistic nature, of what is in the air. Too proud to solve the human problem evasively through any of the sleight-of-hand of puerile surface optimism, he embraces, to represent life, figures that do indeed symbolize a kind of despair; but not the despair that depresses or frustrates. His pessimism as to fact, and his acceptance of all the morally inimical possibilities of human nature, is unwavering. The result is, nonetheless, the reassertion of humanity in defeat that is, in the subjective sense, a triumph. This is no Pyrrhic victory made in debate with those powers of intelligence that may be used to destroy. It is the conquest of nature by art. Or rather, the refutation, by means of a work of art, of the belittling of the materialists; and the work itself is in that category of facts which popular scientific thinking has made an ultimate. Here is beauty sprung from the perfect *realization* of what a more limiting morality would describe as ugliness. Here is a humanity stripped of most of what was claimed for it by the Victorians, and the spectacle is moving as no sugar-coated drama ever could be. The result for the reader, if he is like myself, is an exaltation of faith in mankind. It is faith without, as yet, an argument; but it is the same faith which has always lived in the most ultimate expression of the human spirit."[17]

It is a grim faith, as I have remarked before, and the expression of it in *The Sound and the Fury* is by no means plain or simple. But it is there, as Scott says, and it can be all the more strongly felt because, instead of being explicitly stated, it is made a pervasive aspect of the whole structure and texture of the story.

On the structure of *The Sound and the Fury* Faulkner's comments have been evasive. When someone asked him at Virginia if he had made "any conscious attempts in *The Sound and the Fury* to use Christian references," he said, "No. I was just trying to tell a story of Caddy . . . ." The questioner insisted, "But Benjy, for example, is thirty-three years old, the traditional age of Christ at death"; and Faulkner then said, "Yes. That was a ready-made axe to use, but it was just one of several tools."[18] A few days later he was asked, "What sym-

---

[17] Evelyn Scott, *On William Faulkner's "The Sound and the Fury"* (New York: Jonathan Cape and Harrison Smith, 1929), pp. 6-7. The circumstances of publication suggest a presumption that Faulkner may have collaborated in some way, but no biographer has yet commented on the possibility.

[18] *Faulkner in the University*, p. 17.

bolic meaning did you give to the dates of *The Sound and the Fury?*" He said, "Now there's a matter of hunting around in the carpenter's shop to find a tool that will make a better chicken-house. And probably—I'm sure it was quite instinctive that I picked out Easter, that I wasn't writing any symbolism of the Passion Week at all. I just—that was a tool that was good for the particular corner I was going to turn in my chicken-house and so I used it."[19]

Remembering his explicit use of the phrase "that Passion Week of the heart" as Fairchild's definition of genius in *Mosquitoes* (p. 339), we can confidently assume that Faulkner knew what he was doing when he placed his story of Caddy in the temporal setting of the Easter weekend. Doubtless, as he said, the Passion story was only one of several tools used to organize the book. Doubtless also he wanted us to know that the book was not written to inculcate the traditional moral or theological values of Christianity. But it seems quite clear that he did use externally provided structural patterns, and that the story—or legend, or myth—of the Crucifixion and Resurrection of Christ was one of them.

Carvel Collins was the first critic effectively to notice this fact[20] and to point out some of the parallels. Each of the Compson brothers, Benjy, Quentin, and Jason, is like Christ in certain ways, and the experience of each day—Quentin's Thursday, Jason's Good Friday, Benjy's Holy Saturday, and the author's Easter Sunday—has something in common with that of Christ on the corresponding day of His Passion. Collins' general conclusion is that "the Compson sons are in parallel with Christ but, significantly, by inversion. . . . God's Son passed through the events of the Passion and rose as a redeemer; the Compson sons pass through parallel events but go down in failure." The reason for the failure, Collins says,

[19] *Ibid.*, p. 68.

[20] Robert M. Adams had suggested it in his article "Poetry in the Novel: or, Faulkner Esemplastic," *Virginia Quarterly Review*, XXIX (Spring 1953), 426-27, but he had not developed it systematically.

is that "love, which Christ preached as an eleventh command-ment, is lacking or frustrated or distorted in their family."[21] This is cogent from a moral or psychological point of view, but I suspect that there may be an even more compelling artis-tic or technical reason for the inversion.

Each of the Compson brothers, in his own peculiar way, is a static obstacle to the motion of life. Each remains static to the end, in order to provide as much counterpoint as pos-sible to the dynamic forces of life which are personified in Caddy and her daughter Quentin, and in the total organiza-tion of the story. Each of the brothers, like most of Faulkner's other static figures, is in some sense crucified because of his in-ability to move with the moving world. Each helps to show the motion of life, as Horace Benbow, Joe Christmas, and others do, by standing still against it and being overwhelmed by its power. To them, life signifies nothing because they cannot participate in it. Without them, Faulkner's tale about life would signify nothing because he would have no dramatic, contrapuntal way of demonstrating the motion.

Collins had previously suggested that Freud's description of human personality in terms of the id, the ego, and the super-ego acted as an externally provided structural device. In this hypothetical plan, Benjy is parallel to the id, Quentin to the ego, and Jason to the superego. It would seem equally obvious that Caddy is parallel to the libido. The Freudian pattern operates, according to Collins, in such a way as to show "the effect which the failures of the Compson parents have on the Compson sons, whether the three sons are regarded on a realis-tic level as individuals or on a symbolic level as parts of the personality of one symbolic child. All three of the sons (or all three parts of the symbolic composite son, if you will permit) are injured by lack of love."[22] Collins preferred the concept of

---

[21] Collins, "The Pairing of *The Sound and the Fury* and *As I Lay Dying*" (1957), p. 118.

[22] Collins, "The Interior Monologues . . . ," p. 53. The whole argument occupies pp. 35-56.

"the symbolic composite son," or, as he put it in his later article, the hypothesis that "a hidden and abstract level" of the story "merges" the brothers "for certain purposes into one personality." He was not prepared to say "Whether Mr. Faulkner did or did not consciously put this second system [the Freudian pattern] into the novel . . . . But one would like to think so, for to merge the three sons into one in this way helps not only to pull together the parallel with Christ but to elucidate further the theme of the effects of lack of love."[23]

This formula strikes me as being extremely helpful. I would modify it only by suggesting that the brothers are not merged by the Freudian pattern, but that it represents a potential wholeness toward which they all need to grow. Because they stubbornly fail or refuse to merge, each one remains a static fragment, and whatever capacity for love and life they, in combination with Caddy-as-libido, might have developed together is inhibited, frustrated, and wasted. The parallel with Christ is therefore necessarily inverse. The wholeness and redeeming power of Christ is contrasted to the impotence of the Freudian fragments, and the counterpoint serves to generate a powerful image of stopped motion.

Christ is most powerfully present in the Easter sermon of Reverend Shegog, and in the person of the preacher himself, who is almost visibly converted before the eyes of the congregation. At first he looks "like a small, aged monkey" (p. 365) and sounds "like a white man. His voice was level and cold. It sounded too big to have come from him and they listened at first through curiosity, as they would have to a monkey talking." But he performs with a "virtuosity" that arouses kinesthetic sensations: ". . . he ran and poised and swooped upon the cold inflectionless wire of his voice, so that at last, when with a sort of swooping glide he came to rest again beside the reading desk with one arm resting upon it at shoulder height and his monkey body as reft of all motion as a mummy or an

23 Collins, "The Pairing . . . ," p. 119.

emptied vessel, the congregation sighed as if it waked from a collective dream and moved a little in its seats" (p. 366).

Then suddenly the mummy comes to life in a fashion that implies far more than mechanical motion, and the vessel is filled with an inspired and moving eloquence. " 'Brethren,' " says the preacher, in the first directly quoted words of the sermon, " 'Brethren and sisteren . . . . I got the recollection and the blood of the Lamb!' " These words involve him and the congregation in a transcendent act of communion: as he speaks on, "He was like a worn small rock whelmed by the successive waves of his voice. With his body he seemed to feed the voice that, succubus like, had fleshed its teeth in him. And the congregation seemed to watch with its own eyes while the voice consumed him, until he was nothing and they were nothing and there was not even a voice but instead their hearts were speaking to one another in chanting measures beyond the need for words, so that when he came to rest against the reading desk, his monkey face lifted and his whole attitude that of a serene, tortured crucifix that transcended its shabbiness and insignificance and made it of no moment, a long moaning expulsion of breath rose from them, and a woman's single soprano: 'Yes, Jesus!' " (pp. 367-68). When he says " 'the recollection,' " he means, in some sense, the body of Christ, which Christ enjoined the disciples to eat "in remembrance of me";[24] but, instead of eating, Reverend Shegog is eaten, the Word consuming his body until he stands as an avatar of Christ, to Whom the congregation's fervent response is made.[25]

The climax of the sermon, which is the only part of it given substantially in the preacher's own words, is perhaps the finest set piece and the most audaciously successful tour de force in all of Faulkner. It does not literally retell the story of the Pas-

[24] *Luke* 22:19.
[25] I owe the basic idea here to a paper presented by Morris Eaves in a Faulkner seminar at Tulane University in May 1967.

sion; perhaps that has already been done in the earlier part of
the sermon, or perhaps the preacher assumes, as the author
certainly does, that his audience knows it by heart. What we
are given instead is a poetically rhetorical development of the
emotional pattern of the Passion story, a sequence of feelings
associated with the life, death, and resurrection of Christ. The
quoted part of the sermon therefore has the literary form of an
elegy, such as Milton's "Lycidas" or Whitman's "When Lilacs
Last in the Dooryard Bloom'd." The force of Reverend Shegog's rhetoric, which is very powerful, arouses the elegiac emotions of sorrow, despair, and rejoicing in the congregation and
the reader of the book. This rhetoric succeeds partly because
it uses poetic rhythms, as well as poetic images, to build emotional intensity, and partly because the preacher's own emotional sympathy with both Christ and the congregation enables
him to telescope time, so that he and his audience, in and out
of the book, are witnesses to the Passion as if it were happening now.

  " 'Listen, breddren!' " he says. " 'I sees de day. Ma'y settin
in de do' wid Jesus on her lap, de little Jesus. Like dem chillen
dar, de little Jesus. I hears de angels singin de peaceful songs
en de glory; I sees de closin eyes; sees Mary jump up, sees de
sojer face: We gwine to kill! We gwine to kill! We gwine to
kill yo little Jesus! I hears de weepin en de lamentation of de
po mammy widout de salvation en de word of God!' "
(p. 369). Like the speakers of the earlier elegies, Reverend
Shegog enforces the feeling of death to its ultimate intensity
in the despair that each man must feel when he fully realizes
that all men die. " 'I sees hit, breddren! I sees hit! Sees de blas-
tin, blindin sight! I sees Calvary, wid de sacred trees, sees de
thief en de murderer en de least of dese; I hears de boasting en
de braggin: Ef you be Jesus, lif up yo tree en walk! I hears de
wailin of women en de evenin lamentations; I hears de weepin
en de cryin en de turnt-away face of God: dey done kilt Jesus;
dey done kilt my Son! . . . O blind sinner! Breddren, I tells

you; sistuhn, I says to you, when de Lawd did turn His mighty face, say, Aint gwine overload heaven! I can see de widowed God shet His do'; I sees de whelmin flood roll between; I sees de darkness en de death everlastin upon de generations.' "

Then, with a rebound as sudden as that in "Lycidas," he makes the typical elegiac turn from universal despair to universal comfort and joy. " 'Den lo! Breddren! Yes, breddren! Whut I see! Whut I see, O sinner? I sees de resurrection en de light; sees de meek Jesus sayin Dey kilt Me dat ye shall live again; I died dat dem whut sees en believes shall never die. Breddren, O breddren! I sees de doom crack en hears de golden horns shoutin down de glory, en de arisen dead whut got de blood en de ricklickshun of de Lamb!' " (p. 370).

The sermon, like a typical elegy, asserts the power of life in the face of death and despair. Christ, here as elsewhere in Faulkner's work, represents the triumph of life, or motion, over all obstacles. But the artist, as Faulkner insisted, must show this power by imposing an artificial stasis, by way of counterpoint, and that is what *The Sound and the Fury* does, particularly in its conclusion. At the very end, Benjy and Jason are brought together, and both are displayed as inverted Christ figures, their inversion consisting essentially in the fact that they are, each in his own peculiar way, incorrigibly static. Luster's attempted innovation in turning the surrey left at the monument is protested by Benjy and suppressed by Jason, and the Compson world relapses into its changeless and hopeless routine: "The broken flower drooped over Ben's fist and his eyes were empty and blue and serene again as cornice and façade flowed smoothly once more from left to right; post and tree, window and doorway, and signboard, each in its ordered place" (p. 401). Benjy is no savior; he is like the image borrowed from Bishop Andrewes in Eliot's "Gerontion" of Christ unborn: "The word within a word, unable to speak a word . . . ." Jason is at least equally paradoxical. He has the magic initials, his day is Good Friday, and he takes as forward a part as any in the doings of Easter Sunday. But his gospel is of hate rather than love, greed rather than charity, death rather than life.

Another externally provided structural pattern cited by Collins is the "Out, out, brief candle" speech in the fifth act of *Macbeth*. Collins finds references in Benjy's section to the "tale / Told by an idiot" and the "brief candle," in Quentin's to the "walking shadow," and in Jason's to the "poor player . . . ."[26] Faulkner's own reported comments, however, suggest that in using this parallel he may have had thematic rather than structural considerations in mind. At Virginia he was asked whether the speech was "applicable to Benjy as is generally thought, or perhaps to Jason?" He said, "The title, of course, came from the first section, which was Benjy. I thought the story was told in Benjy's section, and the title came there. So it—in that sense it does apply to Benjy rather than to anybody else, though the more I had to work on the book, the more elastic the title became, until it covered the whole family."[27] An account published twenty years earlier is somewhat more precise and perhaps more accurate. According to Maurice Coindreau, in his preface to the French edition, Faulkner said to him that the book " 'had no title until the day when the well known words *The Sound and the Fury* rose up out of my subconscious. And I adopted them, without reflecting at the time that the rest of the Shakespeare passage would apply as well, if not better, to my somber story of madness and hate."[28] The *Macbeth* parallels are present, certainly, but they do not strike

[26] Collins, "The Interior Monologues . . . ," pp. 32-35.

[27] *Faulkner in the University*, p. 87.

[28] Coindreau, pp. 5-6; my translation. The original reads, " 'Il n'avait pas de titre jusqu'au jour où, de mon subconscient, surgirent les mots connus *The Sound and the Fury*. Et je les adoptai, sans réfléchir alors que le reste de la citation shakespearienne s'appliquait aussi bien, sinon mieux, à ma sombre histoire de folie et de haine.' " I must say that neither Coindreau's French nor my rendering of it back into English sounds very much like Faulkner's usual manner of speaking.

me as being nearly so important structurally as the other two
patterns that Collins found.

The influence of T.S. Eliot is pervasive in *The Sound and
the Fury*,[29] and especially visible in Quentin's section. Quentin
is like Prufrock in his impotence and in his anticipation of
drowning, and he is like the speaker of "Gerontion" in his use
of the shadow image in connection with impotence and
death. The setting of the first part of "A Game of Chess" in
The Waste Land, with the lady's chair, mirror, fire, and
"hair / Spread out in fiery points" is paralleled in a cluster of
scenes remembered by Benjy. Mrs. Compson's chair is in the
library, where the mirror used to be, and where a fireplace is
still in use. Benjy remembers his mother and Caddy in that
room, and in his mother's bedroom, which also had a mirror
and a fire. "*Her hair was on the pillow*," he recalls. "*The fire
didn't reach it, but it shone on her hand, where her rings were
jumping*" (p. 75). He says of Caddy, "Her hair was like fire,
and little points of fire were in her eyes" (p. 88), and of Caddy's daughter Quentin, "The fire was in her eyes and on her
mouth. Her mouth was red" (p. 82). Eliot's use of Shakespeare
quotations in the same section of the poem, "Those are pearls
that were his eyes" and—if it is a quotation—from the "Out,
out" speech the word "to-morrow," is paralleled by Faulkner's
title, by Quentin's speculation that perhaps "the eyes will come
floating up" (p. 144), and by Quentin's reference to "*the beast
with two backs* . . . ." (p. 184). The general feeling of Quentin's section and, in a way, of the whole book is in harmony
with the injunction in the second part of "A Game of Chess":
"Hurry up please its time . . . ." It is even possible that
Quentin's "Oh Oh Oh Oh" in the remembered scene with
Natalie (p. 168) recalls Eliot's ironic "O O O O that Shake-
speherian Rag—"

---

29 See my "Apprenticeship," pp. 116-17.

In themselves, these parallels are not very important, but they point to something that is. Faulkner, as we have observed, learned at the time he wrote *The Sound and the Fury* to use the "mythical method" advocated by Eliot in "Ulysses, Order and Myth." In *The Sound and the Fury*, he not only used the method but some of the same myths that Eliot had used in *The Waste Land* and that Fitzgerald had adapted in *The Great Gatsby* and Hemingway in *The Sun Also Rises*, notably the legend of the Holy Grail according to Jessie L. Weston in *From Ritual to Romance* and the related myths and rituals reported in Sir James Frazer's *The Golden Bough*. As Eliot had done, Faulkner further embroidered the legend with allusions and images borrowed from a considerable variety of other literary sources. In doing all this, he also, consciously or not, used the structural pattern of *The Waste Land* itself, which is a kind of elegy for Western civilization, as one of his major "tools" for the fabrication of his masterpiece.

The main contrapuntal opposition in *The Sound and the Fury*, as in *The Waste Land*, sets a fertile female principle of life over against a male principle which is sterile and therefore essentially static, or dead. Caddy, in her close association with trees, flowers, and water, is a fertility symbol like the hyacinth girl in *The Waste Land*. The hyacinth girl's male companion is evidently sterile because of sexual impotence:

> I could not
> Speak, and my eyes failed, I was neither
> Living nor dead, and I knew nothing . . . .

Caddy is betrayed by the sterility of the two brothers she loves, Benjy the idiot and Quentin the impotent, and the one she cannot love, the embodiment of Freudian socio-sexual repression, Jason.

Of the three, Quentin is the most like Eliot's spokesmen, both in his intelligence and in his futility. Faulkner, however, has made a significantly different use of setting. Quentin's

April is even crueller than that described by Eliot because his north Mississippi homeland, however waste it may be spiritually, is burgeoning with promise of the Southern summer, which Quentin remembers, in contrast with June in New England, for "A kind of still and violent fecundity that satisfied ever bread-hunger like" (p. 140). In *The Waste Land*, "the cricket" gives "no relief" because it is associated with dryness and the shadow that represents fear of death; in Yoknapatawpha, Quentin associates crickets with honeysuckle and with his fear of life as he remembers going toward the branch where Caddy lay with "the water flowing about her hips" (p. 186) before seeking her lover among the trees. Quentin is lapped to the ears in a humid warmth of fertility which he can neither share nor bear. In *The Sound and the Fury* it is not the land that is waste, but the fragmented human spirit, which dies in the midst of an abundance it cannot assimilate. Instead of the pathetic fallacy that Eliot uses, Faulkner sets up a much more comprehensive and powerful pathetic counterpoint: the fertility of nature, and particularly Caddy, as life, against the sterility of the Compson brothers, particularly Quentin, as death in life or as death pure and simple. Perhaps, from this point of view, Caddy resembles not only the Arician Diana but the Egyptian Isis, whose lover, Osiris, was also her brother. Osiris was torn into fragments which had to be reassembled before fertility could be restored. Symbolically, if Caddy could combine her three brothers into one complete, positively Christ-like man, and then commit the incest that Quentin talks about but cannot consummate, a rebirth of life as motion might result.

Several features of *The Sound and the Fury* indicate that Faulkner probably went directly to Eliot's sources in *From Ritual to Romance* and *The Golden Bough*, and used them to make some points of his own.[30] For example, Eliot does not

---

[30] For a general statement on this influence, see my "Apprenticeship," pp. 151-52.

refer literally to castration, but Weston does, and Faulkner's
Benjy is castrated. In Weston, but not in Eliot, the ritual of
self-castration is prominently mentioned; in *The Sound and
the Fury* Quentin enviously recalls Versh's story of the man
who "mutilated himself," and Quentin goes a step farther by
saying "But that's not it. It's not not having them. It's never to
have had them then I could say O That That's Chinese I dont
know Chinese." His father has told him that "it's because you
are a virgin"; and Quentin's trouble is in fact that same crip-
pling "virginity" or "innocence" that Sutpen suffers in
Absalom, Absalom! If anything, Quentin suffers more than
Sutpen, because of his more severe sexual deficiency. If we assume that Faulkner adopted Weston's account of the primitive
origins of the Grail legend and identified the Grail generally
with the principle of fertility, then Quentin is a hopelessly unqualified seeker. Like the young Perceval, he is unable to ask
the right question, and therefore incapable of restoring anyone to fertility. As Mr. Compson tells him, "Purity is . . . contrary to nature" (p. 143). And to life.

Just after entertaining these thoughts and memories, Quentin hides his pair of flatirons under the end of a bridge and
observes a big old trout which some boys tell him cannot be
caught. Weston points out that in the Grail legend, the fertility cults, and the Christian tradition, imagery associated with
fish and fishing has to do with physical and spiritual fertility. The catching and eating of fish is therefore an important
symbolic act in the legends and in rituals designed to suggest
or facilitate rebirth, a fact which Faulkner seems to have had
well in mind when he wrote *As I Lay Dying*. But Quentin
apparently wants no rebirth—"when He says Rise the eyes will
come floating up . . . . And after awhile the flat irons would
come floating up"—except perhaps "*If it could just be a hell beyond that: the clean flame the two of us* [himself and Caddy]
more than dead" (p. 144). He ends his conversation with the
boys by advising them not to catch the trout. He is no fisher,

of either fish or men; no Grail king, no Christ, no savior.[31]

Quentin is like Horace Benbow and Gavin Stevens in being a sentimental and absurdly unsuccessful knight errant, particularly when it comes to rescuing maidens in distress. The problem, as usual, is that the maidens' distress is not what he supposes, and that he is totally unqualified to relieve it.[32] The obvious model for this behavior is Don Quixote, who was one of Faulkner's favorite characters. The fact that Caddy's fiancé, Herbert Head, calls Quentin a "half-baked Galahad of a brother" (p. 136) suggests another possible source. Weston says that Sir Galahad is "the product of deliberate literary invention, and has no existence outside the frame of the later cyclic redactions" of the Grail story, where the real meaning of the quest, as a symbolic pagan fertility ritual, has been lost or suppressed.[33] Perhaps Faulkner looked, a trifle sardonically, on *The Sound and the Fury* as a still later (post-Tennyson) cyclic redaction, describing a situation in which the real meaning of the quest is impossible for a "half-baked Galahad" such as Quentin even to conceive.

When Carvel Collins paired *The Sound and the Fury* with *As I Lay Dying*, he did not explicitly suggest that the Persephone myth was a pattern used in *The Sound and the Fury*, but only that "the all-loving Demeter" used in *As I Lay Dying* was a "Greek counterpart" to Christ as His story was used in *The Sound and the Fury*.[34] It seems to me, however, that

[31] This interpretation does not agree with a suggestion made by Faulkner in an interview (*Faulkner in the University*, p. 18) where he said of Quentin that "when he wants the old fish to live, it may represent his unconscious desire for endurance, both for himself and for his people." It seems to me that Faulkner, as he sometimes did, must have forgotten the context.

[32] Faulkner remarked in another interview (*Faulkner in the University*, p. 141), in answer to a question about both Quentin and Gavin, "It is the knight that goes out to defend somebody who don't want to be defended and don't need it. But it's a very fine quality in human nature. I hope it will always endure. It is comical and a little sad."

[33] Weston, p. 178; cf. p. 18.

[34] Collins, "The Pairing . . . ," p. 120.

Caddy is as much a Persephone analogue as Dewey Dell
Bundren is, that Mrs. Compson presents some significant,
though mostly inverted, parallels with Demeter, and that Miss
Quentin can be regarded as Kore, the resurrected spirit of
the corn, or of fertility. Caddy is explicitly associated with the
myth by a reference to the swineherd Eubuleus;[35] and in a
closely preceding passage Quentin figures Dalton Ames as
Pluto by remembering that *"with one hand he could lift her
to his shoulder and run with her"* (p. 184). Various scattered
references to pigs, five or six in Benjy's section and two in
Quentin's, reinforce this reference, especially when Quentin
splashes himself and Caddy with *"mud"* (pp. 169-70), liberally
laced with manure, in the hogwallow after kissing Natalie—
the only occasion he recalls when he showed any sign of sexual
potency.

Quentin's comparison of Ames's shirts with asbestos (pp. 113,
130) also suggests his association of Ames with Pluto, and
Herbert Head, who carries Caddy off later in an automobile,
resembles Pluto as god of wealth. Quentin himself expresses
the wish to carry Caddy to hell: "Nobody else there but her
and me. If we could just have done something so dreadful that
they would have fled hell except us" (p. 97). Later Miss Quentin says to Jason, " 'I'm bad and I'm going to hell' " (p. 235);
Jason says, "far as I'm concerned, let her go to hell as fast as
she pleases . . ." (p. 297). In this sequence the role of Pluto is
played by the show man in the red tie, about whom Jason uses
the words "hell" and "damn" several times, most conspicuously
when he says, "I'll make him think that damn red tie is the
latch string to hell, if he thinks he can run the woods with my
niece" (p. 301). Jason, unsuccessfully pursuing them to Mottson, makes an even more absurd Demeter than Mrs. Compson.

Like the Christ pattern, the Grail pattern, and the pattern
of elegy, the Persephone story as it appears in *The Sound and
the Fury* has many of its values inverted. Caddy is finally

[35] See Frazer, pp. 469-70, my "Apprenticeship," pp. 151-52, and *S&F* 184.

banished from the Compson world rather than abducted into any other; and Miss Quentin is hardly a satisfactory reimbodiment. The reason for the inversions is that Faulkner is telling his own story, which is different from the myth, at the same time that he is using the myth to give his own story temporal and cultural dimensions it would otherwise lack. The use of several myths at once is good for his purpose partly because they are not even parallel to one another. No matter how we try to put them together, they do not fit. Therefore no one of them, or combination of them, can be made to serve as a simple key or explanation to account for what Faulkner is doing. They contribute structural patterns to Faulkner's work, but they do not govern in it. Rather, because they refuse to boil down into anything single or simple, they serve to keep all values in suspension for that static moment of illumination into which Faulkner tries to compress all of time, or experience, or history, or life.

It may be significant that the days of the four sections are not presented in chronological order. The Saturday of the Easter weekend of 1928 comes first, and it is followed by Thursday, June 2, 1910, then by Good Friday and Easter Sunday of 1928. Perhaps Faulkner had an epic pattern in mind, beginning *in medias res*, looping back in time, and then returning to the conclusion. If so, he greatly complicated the pattern by having his first two narrators, Benjy and Quentin, jump back and forth in time, usually without any explicit notice to the reader, in a bewildering fashion. All is not chaos, however. Benjy's section has the longest time span and the greatest volume of explicit reference to past events. Quentin's, although it terminates its version of the story eighteen years earlier, also covers a fairly long span, and time is about as confused in Quentin's handling as it is in Benjy's. Jason's section is much more clear, and much more concerned with events of its day, though not without reference to preceding ones. The author's section deals almost exclusively with Easter Sunday. The effect is of a temporal focus, wide and blurred in the beginning, growing progressively narrower and clearer as the story moves on. As Perrin Lowrey has observed, with an appropriate apology for oversimplification, the four sections, in the general weight of their emphasis, are sufficiently progressive so that "the novel, though apparently chaotic, is actually roughly chronological."[36]

Even Benjy's section is not altogether chaotic. The careful analysis of it by George R. Stewart and Joseph M. Backus distinguishes thirteen different time sequences, which are more or less coherent series of events. Analysis of Stewart and Backus's tables indicates that, except for the references to "Mr. Compson's Death," each of these sequences is presented, within itself, in a generally chronological order. The temporal confusion arises from the fact that the sequences overlap, so that the chronology within them is continually interrupted by the jumping back and forth among them. They proceed, in a sense, simultaneously; events of Saturday, April 7, 1928, are mingled with at least twelve other series of events dating from various times between 1898 and 1912.[37]

[36] Perrin Lowrey, "Concepts of Time in *The Sound and the Fury*," *English Institute Essays, 1952*, p. 63.

[37] See George R. Stewart and Joseph M. Backus, " 'Each in Its Ordered Place': Structure and Narrative in 'Benjy's Section' of *The Sound and the Fury*," *American Literature*, XXIX (January 1958), 440-56. The tables of analysis are on pp. 443 and 444. Stewart and Backus identify 103 "units," or temporally homogeneous bits of narrative, referring variously to the thirteen "levels" or fictional time sequences. The "level" of the narrative present has thirty-two "units," all of which are presented in chronological order. The "level" dealing with "Damuddy's Death" has eighteen, all in chronological order except the brief introductory "unit." The "level" of "The Name-Changing" has twenty, of which three are not in order. "Mr. Compson's Death," the only "level" severely scrambled in itself, has seven "units," three in chronological order and four in reverse order. In the remaining nine "levels," none of which has more than five "units," there are five "units" out of order, and each is the only one in its "level." There are also three "unassigned lines" which Stewart and Backus were not able to place in the time scheme at all. Out of the 103 assigned "units," only thirteen—an average of one per "level"—are out of chronological order within their "levels."

The effect is that Benjy's remembered life is compressed into what amounts to a single moment of static recollection or contemplation. But the feeling of chaotic stasis induced by the temporal jumbling is contrapuntally juxtaposed to an equally emphatic sense of time passing, which is continually enforced by the chronology. The reader probably should not, as he runs, try to "straighten out" the chronology, but rather to feel both the powerful underground movement and the equally powerful frustration of it. The simultaneous presence of both tendencies in this section is what makes Benjy, for Faulkner's purpose, such an effective literary device: an essentially timeless mind which contains thirty years of time.

The temporal aspect of *The Sound and the Fury* is intimately related to its moral aspect. When Faulkner was asked, "What is the trouble with the Compsons?" he said, "They are still living in the attitudes of 1859 or '60."[38] The statement is a suggestive oversimplification. *The Sound and the Fury* conveys a strong sense of history, even though its text makes little explicit reference to historical events. There is a continual play on ideas, feelings, and attitudes associated in various ways with a traditional image or concept of aristocracy which is emotionally attractive but which was rendered obsolete by the Civil War.

This feeling is partly embodied in humorous irony. "Blood," says Jason, deriding the Compson heritage, "governors and generals. It's a damn good thing we never had any kings and presidents; we'd all be down there at Jackson chasing butterflies" (p. 286). Jason resembles in some ways the folk protagonist defined by Daniel Hoffman as "The self-determinative hero," whose "powers prove the self spiritually indomitable and adaptable to the wildest vicissitudes of fortune and nature. . . . His character is aggressive, competitive, shrewd. He seeks mastery over nature. With respect to society, he seeks to dem-

[38] *Faulkner in the University*, p. 18.

onstrate superiority over other individuals but not ordinarily
does he recognize society as an organic structure, in which
power can be exercised for extra-personal ends." As Jason
passes a number of country churches on his way to Mottson
in pursuit of Miss Quentin and the man in the red tie,
"it seemed to him that each of them was a picket-post where
the rear guards of Circumstance peeped fleetingly back at him.
'And damn You, too,' he said, 'See if You can stop me,' thinking of himself . . . dragging Omnipotence down from His
throne, if necessary; of the embattled legions of both hell and
heaven through which he tore his way and put his hands at
last on his fleeing niece" (p. 382).

Hoffman remarks that heroes of this type do not experience
genuine rebirths,[39] and Faulkner emphasizes this defect, along
with others, in his presentation of Jason, whose efforts to dominate nature and society, particularly by speculating in cotton,
are systematically unsuccessful. Old Job's characterization of
him as " 'a man whut so smart he cant even keep up wid hisself' " (pp. 311-12) is devastatingly correct. He is finally stopped
on Sunday by the unimpressive circumstance of a frail little
old man with a hatchet. His absurd crucifixion results in no
rebirth and no vision in his mind of any organic society in
which he could be a productive member. The best he can do
is to trade on the family prestige which he professes to hold
in contempt, and try desperately to protect his own " 'position in this town' " (p. 234) by keeping Miss Quentin off the
streets. His most effective way of making aristocratic pretensions ridiculous is by being himself the last of an aristocratic
line.

The ridicule is heightened by Jason's relation to his mother
and by her behavior toward him and toward her other children, her husband, and her brother, the children's uncle Maury
Bascomb. Mrs. Compson is one of Faulkner's most howlingly
funny characters, at the same time that she is horribly true to

[39] Hoffman, p. 81. See also pp. 356-57.

a certain type of American, and more specifically Southern, female gentility. As an aristocrat, she is evidently something of a parvenue, feeling that the Bascombs are socially inferior to the Compsons and asserting therefore that they are intrinsically better—an assertion that is not supported by her own behavior or Uncle Maury's, or that of Jason, who she insists "is more Bascomb than Compson . . ." (p. 127). When Caddy becomes pregnant, Mrs. Compson arranges her marriage to Herbert Head, but the marriage breaks up, and Mrs. Compson banishes her daughter from the family, all in aid of preserving the appearances of respectability. Mr. Compson's remark to Quentin that "your Mother is thinking of morality whether it be sin or not has not occurred to her" (p. 126) is an accurate if cynical assessment. Like Narcissa Benbow in *Sanctuary*, Mrs. Compson cares nothing at all about what is done, but only about how it looks to the neighbors, and she insists—too much, as her fashion is—that her own status is inviolable. When Miss Quentin runs off, and Mrs. Compson jumps to the perhaps wishful conclusion that there has been another suicide in the family, her cry is " 'It cant be simply to flout and hurt me. Whoever God is, He would not permit that. I'm a lady' " (p. 374). The phrase "Whoever God is," in the mouth of Mrs. Compson, is surely one of the most delicious ironies ever perpetrated.

Mr. Compson embodies a much more attractive illustration of the aristocratic ideal, but he is completely ineffective; and in both respects, as we have seen, Quentin is a true heir. Spoade recognizes him after his encounter with Gerald Bland as " 'the champion of dames,' " adding, " 'Bud, you excite not only admiration, but horror' " (p. 207). The fight with Bland—if it can properly be called a fight—is overlaid in the narrative by Quentin's earlier, equally humiliating failure to drive Dalton Ames out of town. Faulkner added a contrapuntal comment in the Appendix to *The Portable Faulkner* by placing a thumbnail sketch of Andrew Jackson before those of the

Compsons and stating as Jackson's most cherished belief "the principle that honor must be defended whether it was or not because defended it was whether or not" (p. 738)—a formula Faulkner liked so well that he used it again, almost word for word, in *Requiem for a Nun* (p. 107). This "principle" may succeed, up to a point, if it has a man like Jackson or Sir Lancelot to back it, but with Sir Galahad Quentin Compson it becomes funny, pathetic, and even, as Spoade observes, horrible.

The horror is felt by Quentin himself, most keenly when his inadequacy as a knight-errant is expressed in terms of sexual impotence. He tells his father that he was afraid to ask Caddy to commit incest with him because she might have consented; he refuses the gun Ames offers him; and he is unable to use his knife on Caddy, although she encourages him "to push it harder" (p. 189). Guns and knives, according to the Freudian doctrine popularly known in the 1920s, were standard phallic symbols. Quentin's desire for complete sexlessness for himself is matched by his opposition to Caddy's sexual activity. *"Why must you do like nigger women do in the pasture the ditches the dark woods hot hidden furious"* (pp. 113-14), he protests. The smell of honeysuckle, which he once liked, becomes associated in his memory with sex, and from then on it and other flower odors overpower him with nausea.

The complex of association comes full circle when he remembers his father's saying, "Because women so delicate so mysterious . . . . Delicate equilibrium of periodical filth between two moons balanced. Moons he said full and yellow as harvest moons her hips thighs. Outside outside of them always but. Yellow. Feet soles with walking like. Then know that some man that all those mysterious and imperious concealed. With all that inside of them shapes an outward suavity waiting for a touch to. Liquid putrefaction like drowned things floating like pale rubber flabbily filled getting the odour of honeysuckle all mixed up" (p. 159). The sexual nausea described here undermines Quentin's morale and his social effectiveness, perverting his notions of honor and making him ridiculous as a defender of chastity. He is driven to suicide by the close relation of sex to life and by the fact that mature sex behavior is a normal result of growing up. His exalted but naïve ideal of aristocratic purity, which rules out normal mature sex behavior, prevents him from acting like a real aristocrat because the theory requires aristocracy to be in effect impotent.

It is Quentin, more than any other Compson, who is "still living in the attitudes of 1859 or '60"; and Quentin's section of the book is, in itself, more obscure than any other, partly because it operates the most radical distortion of time. Memories erupt into Quentin's mind in so fragmentary a form and with so little regard for sequence that, if we had not already gained some acquaintance in Benjy's section with most of the matters they refer to, some of them would remain completely cryptic. What is important, however, is not the confusion of the reader, but the suggestion that Quentin is literally unable to live in present time, or in the past either, since his memories never go back to a time when sexual activity of some ominously developing kind (the muddy stain on Caddy's drawers) was not involved. Quentin resembles Prince Hamlet in a number of ways, but never more than in the degree to which he finds his time out of joint, and himself unable to put it right. Quentin's section is the most intense of the four in its technical containment of the energy of change, because Quentin's opposition to the course of time is the most intensely passionate.

Quentin serves another useful function as a narrator because his obsession with aristocratic attitudes enables him to be a sensitive reporter of other people's behavior in relation to the hierarchies of social value. The extremes of status in his Harvard environment are represented by his roommate, Shreve MacKenzie,[40] who has no social pretensions, and Spoade, whose

---

[40] So called in *The Sound and the Fury*. In *Absalom, Absalom!* his last name is McCannon.

social pretensions are so well accredited that Mrs. Bland "never had been able to forgive him for having five names, including that of a present English ducal house" (p. 113). Quentin envies Spoade for his cavalier treatment of social conventions and of time. When the other students run to be on time for chapel, "Spoade was in the middle of them like a terrapin in a street full of scuttering dead leaves . . . moving at his customary un-hurried walk. . . . It was his club's boast that he never ran for chapel and had never got there on time and had never been absent in four years and had never made either chapel or first lecture with a shirt on his back and socks on his feet" (pp. 96-97). Quentin calls him, with a touch of Southwestern humor, "the world's champion sitter-a-round, no holds barred and gouging discretionary" (p. 113). When Quentin has been beaten by Bland, Spoade says that " 'He ought to go back so they'll know he fights like a gentleman . . . . Gets licked like one, I mean' " (p. 207). But Shreve, who has previously re-marked, " 'God, I'm glad I'm not a gentleman' " (p. 125), thinks otherwise, and Spoade is too much of a gentleman to insist. Shreve, for his part, is too much of a democrat to worry about social hierarchies. " 'Let them go to hell,' " he says to Spoade. " 'We're going to town' " (p. 207). If Quentin could successfully emulate either Spoade's confidence or Shreve's flexibility, he might be able to survive.

The prize exhibit in the Cambridge gallery consists of Mrs. Bland and Gerald, who have a great deal of ambition and money, but who have to run as fast as they can to stay where they are, partly because they are not at all sure where that is. Mrs. Bland is impelled to attack Shreve, calling him "that fat Canadian youth" (p. 131) and trying to have him displaced as Quentin's roommate. Shreve defends himself with humor, calling Mrs. Bland " 'Semiramis' " (p. 125) and characteriz-ing her as " 'cruel fate in eight yards of apricot silk and more metal pound for pound than a galley slave and the sole owner and proprietor of the unchallenged peripatetic john of the late

Confederacy'" (p. 131). The "peripatetic john" is Gerald, who rows and boxes and sits "in his attitudes of princely boredom" while his mother tells "about Gerald's horses and Gerald's niggers and Gerald's women" (p. 112). At a time when he is watching Gerald's racing shell grow distant on the river, Quentin remembers "Dalton Ames," thinking, "It just missed gentility" (p. 113). But he also admits to some genuine admiration, associating Bland with the trout "hanging like a fat arrow stemming into the current" (p. 144) and the "gull motionless in midair, like on an invisible wire" (p. 110), which he associates in turn with time defined by Mr. Compson as "the symbol of your frustration . . ." (p. 129). Quentin may be thinking, half consciously, that if he could cancel the motion of time by moving against its current he might be able to endure. He concedes, at any rate, that Gerald "would be sort of grand too, pulling in lonely state across the noon, rowing himself right out of noon, up the long bright air like an apotheosis, mounting into a drowsing infinity where only he and the gull, the one terrifically motionless, the other in a steady and measured pull and recover that partook of inertia itself, the world punily beneath their shadows on the sun." Quentin, however, is unable either to hold himself motionless in the midst of "all things rushing" (p. 149) or to rise above the motion. His shadow waits for him, as he superstitiously feels, in the water where he intends to stop all motion by drowning himself.

The reference to this superstition is introduced by the phrase "Niggers say" (p. 111), and Quentin thinks about Negroes often. Sometimes his remarks on them are general, as when he says he has realized since coming to live in the North "that a nigger is not a person so much as a form of behaviour; a sort of obverse reflection of the white people he lives among" (p. 106). Sometimes he realizes that this reflection may embody a specific criticism. He remembers Benjy looking into a mirror and Dilsey saying, in reference to his change of name, that "it was because Mother was too proud for him." Quentin remarks, "They come into white people's lives like that in sudden sharp black trickles that isolate white facts for an instant in unarguable truth like under a microscope"; but he fails to see anything beyond such static moments, and his remark trails off: "the rest of the time just voices that laugh when you see nothing to laugh at, tears when no reason for tears" (p. 211). He misses something again when the Negro called the Deacon, an expert exploiter of young Southerners at Harvard, says of Southerners in general, " 'You're right. They're fine folks. But you cant live with them' " (p. 123). Quentin pays no attention to the statement, although it is at least as true for him as it is for any Negro.

This failure of understanding is due at least partly to an effort Quentin is making to see Negroes in the image of an aristocracy which would be even better than that represented by Spoade, because it would be more static and therefore more reassuring. He has a vision of it in the person of an old Negro on a mule at a Virginia railroad crossing, who responds ritually to the challenge " 'Christmas gift!' " The fixed pattern of the ritual and the fixed relation which its observance implies between Negroes and white people in the South takes Quentin home spiritually more quickly than the train can take him physically. "Then the train began to move. I leaned out the window, into the cold air, looking back. He stood there beside the gaunt rabbit of a mule, the two of them shabby and motionless and unimpatient. The train swung around the curve, the engine puffing with short, heavy blasts, and they passed smoothly from sight that way, with that quality about them of shabby and timeless patience, of static serenity: that blending of childlike and ready incompetence and paradoxical reliability that tends and protects them it loves out of all reason and robs them steadily and evades responsibility and obligations by means too barefaced to be called subterfuge even and is taken in theft or evasion with only that frank and spontaneous admiration for the victor which a gentleman feels for anyone who beats him in a fair contest, and withal a fond and un-flagging tolerance for white folks' vagaries like that of a grand-parent for unpredictable and troublesome children, which I had forgotten" (pp. 107-108).

If we compare this collection of condescending clichés with the total concrete impression of Negroes that the reader builds up out of Benjy's descriptions, which precede it, and Jason's and the author's, which follow it, we see how inadequate it is. Quentin's understanding of Negroes is not really much better than Jason's; the only significant difference is that Quentin thinks he likes them. Both regard Negroes as being static, only because they themselves are static. The Negroes in the book generally, and old Job and Dilsey in particular, are moving fairly harmoniously with the current of life, whereas the rest-less and sporadically violent activities of Quentin and Jason only look like motion because they cut across and oppose the motion of life. The comment on Dilsey in the appendix to *The Portable Faulkner*, "They endured" (p. 756), states the same moral that Shreve tries to make Quentin understand at the end of *Absalom, Absalom!* As the Compsons and the white Sutpens and the other aristocrats who will not or cannot change are crushed in the movement of change, the Negroes inherit more and more of the earth to which they are so much more vitally related.

We may never quite know why Faulkner was so deeply stirred by the image of the muddy drawers in the tree, or what made him fall in love with the little girl who wore them, or how he came to write of her as he did. But we do not really need to. The story came out of his private into our public do-main primarily because he organized it by means of the myth-ical method, using patterns that appeal to all civilized minds, in order to achieve his artistic aim of stopping motion so that it can be seen. All of the technical resources used—the struc-ture, the imagery, the style, the characters, the setting, and even the mysteriously originated basic situation or image—contribute to the fulfillment of that aim. The whole book is an extended concentration on the "frozen moment" of dynamic stasis which the basic image embodied in Faulkner's initial, relatively formless intuition. All the power of motion suggested by the resurrection of Christ, the return of Persephone, the Freudian pattern of personality development, the actual and the legendary history of the South, the quest for fertility in the Grail legend and the ancient cults, the elegiac sequence of emotions, and even the blind "sound and fury" of Macbeth's despairing speech is focused from every direction on that vibrant moment of static awareness. The result is not only Faulkner's masterpiece but, in my opinion, one of the great books of the world.

Index

Index

Index

Index

Index

Index

Index

motion, 3-9, 11-16, 18, 19, 21, 24-27, 29, 30, 32-36, 38, 41, 42, 46-49, 50, 52-54, 56, 62, 70-72, 74-75, 78, 82, 83, 84, 86-99, 104-13, 116-29, 131-34, 136, 138-40, 142, 147, 149-57, 161, 163-65, 167-71, 175, 179, 180, 187, 190, 192-94, 201-205, 213-14, 225-27, 229, 233, 239, 243, 245-48. *See also* myth

Mottson, 236, 240

"Mule in the Yard," 108

Murray, Gilbert, 9

myth, 9-11, 23, 43, 52, 58-59, 62, 64-69, 71-78, 82, 85, 86, 94, 96, 100, 102, 103, 105, 115, 121, 135-37, 147, 162, 170n39, 173, 175, 181, 183, 184, 186, 188, 199, 203, 212, 221, 224, 230-32, 234-37, 247-48

"Myth and Symbol in Criticism of Faulkner's 'The Bear,' " 148

Natalie, 231, 236

Natchez Trace, 158, 210

New England, 207, 214, 233

New Orleans, 12, 30, 31, 41, 45, 95, 128, 196, 197, 198, 208

New Orleans Sketches, 12, 21, 31-34, 39, 42, 45, 47, 128

New Republic, 16

New Valois, 95

Nile, 101

Nirvana, 89, 90, 91

Nobel Prize address, 13, 34, 119, 181, 221

North, the, 178, 208, 245

Novels of William Faulkner, 137n12

Nuit etoilée, La, 124n16

O'Connor, William Van, 137n12, 212n30

"Ode on a Grecian Urn," 12

O'Donnell, George Marion, 135

Odyssey, the, 59, 61

Old Frenchman place, 60, 65, 69

Old General (Marshal), the, 162-69

"Old Man," 8

"Old People, The," 141, 145, 146

Olympus, 86, 118, 119

On William Faulkner's "The Sound and the Fury," 223

O'Neill, Eugene, 28, 29, 43, 167

"Open Boat, The," 113n13

Ord-Atkinson Aircraft Corporation, 97

Osiris, 233

"Other Countries, Other Wenches," 12n8

"Out of Nazareth," 12, 33, 34, 39, 42, 45

"Ozymandias," 206n23

"The Pairing of *The Sound and the Fury* and *As I Lay Dying*," 59n5, 72n21, 74n22, 225n21, 226n23, 235n34

Pan, 18, 19, 20, 77

"Pantaloon in Black," 145

Parchman, Mississippi, 160

Paris Review, 3, 49, 72, 200

Peabody, Dr. Lucius Quintus, 80, 82

Perceval, 69, 234

Percy, W. A., 28

Perluck, Herbert A., 137n12

Persephone, 9, 59, 60, 61, 68, 69, 72, 73, 74, 75, 77, 86, 105, 154, 170n39, 173, 203, 235, 236, 248

Peter, 77

Pharaoh, 144

Pickett, George Edward, 178

Pilate, Pontius, 167

Playboy of the Western World, The, 29

Pluto, 60, 68, 73, 118, 236

Poe, Edgar Allan, 10, 119, 185

"Poetry in the Novel: or, Faulkner Esemplastic," 224n20

Popeye, 6, 13, 60, 61, 63, 64, 65, 69, 70, 83, 153

Portable Faulkner, The, 14, 172n1, 210, 241, 247

"Portrait of a Lady," 11

Pound, Ezra, 20

Powers, Margaret, 35, 38, 39, 42

"Priest, The," 39, 128

Priest, Lucius, 14, 169

Priest, Lucius Quintus Carothers, 169, 170

"Procrustean Revision in Faulkner's *Go Down, Moses*," 141n19

Index

Index

Snopes, Mink, 9, 119, 120, 126, 127, 159, 160
Snopes, Montgomery Ward (Monty), 159
Snopes, Orestes (Res), 158
Snopes, Wallstreet Panic (Wall), 122, 159
Snopeses, 56, 121, 139, 158, 159
Soldiers' Pay, 22, 34-40, 42, 45, 46, 49, 53, 56, 125, 166, 170, 218
Sound and the Fury, The, 4, 6, 8, 16, 22, 26, 27, 31, 37, 39, 40, 46, 57, 58, 59, 65, 70, 71, 78, 115, 147n24, 172, 173, 174, 215-48
sources, 9-11, 20, 29, 30, 39, 59, 60-69, 75-77, 85, 86, 89, 101, 147, 148, 181, 211, 230-32, 235, 236
South, the, 10, 52, 56, 87, 135, 136, 144, 148, 149, 151, 173, 174, 175, 178, 179, 181n13, 183, 184, 187, 189, 199, 207, 209, 210, 211, 212, 213, 214, 233, 241, 246, 248
Specimens of Mississippi Folk-Lore, 212n30
Spoade, 241, 242, 243, 244, 246
Spratling, William, 33, 42
"Square Beatific, The," 137n12
Stein, Jean, 3
Steinbauer, Jenny, 44, 46
Stevens, Gavin, 121, 153, 156, 158, 159, 160, 235
Stevens, Gowan, 68, 69
Stevens, Wallace, 182
Stewart, George R., 238
Stuart, Jeb, 51
Stone, Phil, 21, 30, 43n17
Suggs, Simon, 213
Sullivan, Walter, 211n27
Sultan, Stanley, 137n12
Sun Also Rises, The, 11, 58, 232
"Sunrise out of the Waste Land," 59n4
Sutpen, Ellen Coldfield, 198, 203, 204
Sutpen, Henry, 179, 180, 182, 186, 187, 190, 191, 192, 194, 195, 196, 197, 198, 199, 200, 201, 204, 205
Sutpen, Judith, 180, 182, 187, 190, 192, 195, 197, 198, 201, 204, 205, 206, 208, 209

Sutpen, Thomas, 173-79, 181-93, 197-205, 208-10, 212-14, 234
"Sutpen and the South: A Study of *Absalom, Absalom!*," 173n5
Sutpens, 185, 187, 191, 203, 205, 209, 213, 247
Sutpen's Hundred, 184, 199n20, 208
Sweeney, 185
"Sweeney among the Nightingales," 101, 185
Swiggart, Peter, 185n19
Swinburne, Algernon Charles, 10, 39
symbolism, 25, 26, 27, 42, 46, 48, 52, 72, 74, 80, 82, 85, 91, 100, 110, 115, 146, 158, 177, 180, 193, 221, 224, 225, 226, 233, 234
Symbolists, 10
Synge, J. M., 29

Tales of the Grotesque and Arabesque, 185n18
Talliaferro, Ernest, 41, 42, 44, 46
Tangled Fire of William Faulkner, The, 137n12
Tate, Allen, 135
Taylor, Houghton W., 84, 85
Tennie, 140, 141, 142, 150
Tennyson, Alfred, Lord, 69, 146, 235
Terrell (Tomey's Turl), 140, 141, 142, 143, 144, 149, 150
Test Pilot, 96
"That Evening Sun," 47n19
Theodore, 47n18
These 13, 47n19
Thisbe, 186
Thompson, Lawrance, 58n2
Thoreau, Henry David, 10, 18
Tillich, Paul, 93
time, 6-8, 11, 16-19, 23-27, 30, 36, 40, 43, 44, 47-53, 55, 56, 58, 71, 72, 74, 75, 78-81, 86, 92, 94, 97-100, 104, 107, 109-11, 115-17, 121, 122, 132, 134, 136, 137, 139, 140, 143, 146, 147, 149, 150, 157, 175, 179, 180, 186-87, 190-96, 199-202, 207, 208, 212-14, 228, 239, 243-46, 248
"Time in Faulkner: *The Sound and the Fury*," 132n5
Times-Picayune, 31, 32, 33, 34

258

Index

Index